116

Graphis Inc. is committed to presenting exceptional work in international Design, Advertising, Illustration & Photography.

INSP IRE

Published by **Graphis** I CEO&Creative Director: B. Martin Pedersen I Publishers: B. Martin Pedersen, Danielle B. Baker I Editor: Anna Carnick
Designer: Yon Joo Choi I Production Manager: Eno Park I Editorial Assistants: Ariel Davis, Melanie Madden I Production Associate: Catrine
Bodum I Support Staff: Rita Jones, Christine Mauritzen, Carla Miller I Interns: So-Young Kang, Deirdre O'Connor, Hyewon Park, Dami You

Remarks: We extend our heartfelt thanks to contributors throughout the world who have made it possible to publish a wide and international spectrum of the best work in this field. Entry instructions for all Graphis Books may be requested from: Graphis Inc., 307 Fifth Avenue, Tenth Floor, New York, New York 10016, or visit our web site at www.graphis.com.

Anmerkungen: Unser Dank gilt den Einsendern aus aller Welt, die es uns ermöglicht haben, ein breites, internationales Spektrum der besten Arbeiten zu veröffentlichen. Teilnahmebedingungen für die Graphis-Bücher sind erhältlich bei: Graphis, Inc., 307 Fifth Avenue, Tenth Floor, New York, New York 10016. Besuchen Sie uns im World Wide Web. www.graphis.com.

Remerciements: Nous remercions les participants du monde entier qui ont rendu possible la publication de cet ouvrage offrant un panorama complet des meilleurs travaux. Les modalités d'inscription peuvent être obtenues auprès de: Graphis, Inc., 307 Fifth Avenue, Tenth Floor, New York, New York 10016. Rendez-nous visite sur notre site web: www.graphis.com.

Contents

InMemoriam 6
Commentary 8
Annual Reports 28
Books 32
Branding 52
Brochures 66
Calendars 80

Catalogues 85
DVDs 94
Editorial 95
Environmental 110
Exhibits 120
Illustration 124
Interactive 128

Invitation 136
Letterhead 140
Logos 144
Menus 154
MusicCDs 156
Outdoor 156
Packaging 160

PaperCompanies 180
Posters 182
Products 200
Promotions 206
ShoppingBags 222
Signage 223
Stamps 224

T-Shirts 227
Transportation 230
Typography 232
Credits 235
Index 246

pages 2, 8: Landor Associates I *page 4:*
Craig Cutler I *page 6:* Peter Kraemer

InMemoriam

Edmund C. Arnold, *Newspaper Designer, 1913~2007*

Bill Belew, *Costume Designer, 1931~2008*

Laurel Burch, *Designer, 1945~2007*

Liz Claiborne, *Fashion Designer, 1929~2007*

John Dalton, *Architectural Designer, 1927~2007*

Philip B. Dusenberry, *Advertising Executive, 1936~2007*

Raymond Epstein, *Chairman of Epstein, 1918~2007*

Gianfranco Ferré, *Fashion Designer, 1944~2007*

Richard Guyatt, *Professor/Designer, 1914~2007*

George Kovacs, *Designer, 1926~2007*

Roy Kuhlman, *Graphic Designer, 1923~2007*

Charles Laforest Goslin, *Graphic Designer/Professor, 1932~2007*

James Lee, *Copywriter, 1970~2007*

Sol LeWitt, *Artist/Graphic Designer, 1928~2007*

Martti Mykkänen, *Graphic Designer, 1926~2008*

Silas H. Rhodes, *Co-founder, SVA/Creative Director, 1915~2007*

Steven Robinson, *Fashion Designer, Dior, 1968~2007*

George Sadek, *Graphic Design Educator, 1928~2007*

Viktor Schreckengost, *Industrial Designer, 1906~2008*

Ettore Sottsass, *Product Designer/Architect, 1917~2007*

Philip Thompson, *Graphic Designer, 1928~2007*

Benno Wissing, *Designer, 1923~2008*

Martin J. Weber, *Graphic Artist, 1905~2007*

Hans Wegner, *Furniture Designer, 1914~2007*

Sandy Wilson, *Architectural Designer, 1922~2007*

LeRoy Winbush, *Graphic Designer, 1915~2007*

"6 Blocks" photograph by Craig Cutler.
For more of Mr. Cutler's work, see the latest *Graphis Photography Annual*.

ACH EVE

This year, we shine the spotlight on three very different individuals with one common thread. Designers Ahn Sang-Soo, Harry Pearce and Stefan Sagmeister use Design to connect on a very personal level with a worldwide audience. Motivated in turn by environmental, economic and political instability, human rights atrocities, and personal life lessons, these men call attention to issues and ideas that affect us all. Their work makes us stop, hopefully think, and possibly even act. We are proud to honor them here.

FOR STEPHAN 1.11 2007

"Obsessions create good designs and bad lives."

Stefan Sagmeister, *Designer*

Signed portrait by Henry Leutwyler

Stefan Sagmeister's latest project, Things I have learned in my life so far, *is based on a list of life lessons jotted down in the Designer's diary while on sabbatical in 2000. These very personal lessons have been represented typographically using a variety of mediums — everything from hangers to body paint, furniture to food, lightboxes to giant, white, inflatable monkeys — and have become both a book and an exhibit at New York's Deitch gallery. The success of Sagmeister's venture comes as no surprise to his fans and peers; he has trained us to expect the best. His trailblazing role in the Design community is well-established; from his self-mutilation for an AIGA lecture poster, to his collaborations with Lou Reed, to his branding work for True Majority, he has consistently wowed us. In this particular case, however, it's the marriage of broadly resonant, personal statements and innovative design execution that make his latest project so intriguing. And what's more fun than watching someone who knows all the rules break them? We caught him while on tour promoting his latest project.*

Your new book features a collection of typographical representations that spell out life lessons in an astonishing variety of mediums. What new lessons have you learned from and since the project?

There are a couple of new ones on my list, but I have not learned them from doing this project. They are:
– Don't work with assholes.
– Obsessions create good designs and bad lives.

Did you ever imagine, as you were listing these lessons in your diary, that they'd find a niche in the public sphere?

No, not at all. They were jotted down quickly as a summing-up list for myself. The idea of publication did not enter my mind at all. Which is a good thing, too, since that idea has skewed the content of my diary ever so slightly ever since.

Why do you believe this project has struck such a chord with people?

At the core many of us, no matter how and where we live, are somehow similar and concerned about similar things. By and large I can assume that most things that are important to me resonate with other people too. Or, as a contributor to our site, *ThingsIhaveLearnedInMyLife.com*, put it: "If what you do does not resonate with you, it does not matter to anyone else."

Daniel Nettle writes in his introductory essay for the book, "Reflection is a deeply personal activity that takes different forms for different individuals." How does this quote apply to the year off that inspired the series?

I had more time on my hands to write in my diary (I have kept one since I was 13 or 14). I had jotted that list down quickly just to see for myself what I do think I know by now. At the same time, I was contemplating becoming a filmmaker, which then seemed appealing to me. I also thought this would be a ten-year process. It occurred to me that it might be more fruitful to see if I have something to say in the language I already know how to speak — Graphic Design — rather then throwing that language out and concentrating on learning a new one (Film).

Where did you go during your time off? In retrospect, what was the most important aspect of your sabbatical?

I traveled but generally stayed in New York. The most important outcome of the sabbatical was that I found the joy of being a Designer again.

Where do you plan to go on your next break?

I want to design the next experimental year differently, so I said: Not New York, and not another city, which meant a landscape, not in the US or Europe (know too well), and not Africa or South America (don't know well enough), which meant Asia. The most beautiful landscapes I know in Asia are in Sri Lanka and Indonesia, and considering Sri Lanka still has a low-level civil war going on, Indonesia it became. I am going there next week to make sure.

Is this the most personally satisfying Design project you've done? And which typographical installation was the most fun to execute?

Yes, I'd say that this is the most satisfying one. From a pure-fun point of view, the filming of "Keeping a Diary supports personal development" in Singapore was a whole lot of fun. We shot in the August heat in Singapore and were in a good mood all the way till October.

Any highlights (or lowlights) to speak of?

A highlight was signing the show about the book up at Deitch Projects in New York and witnessing audiences' moods being lifted by the show. Most people in that gallery had smiles on their faces (the intense smell of bananas helped).

How has your design style evolved over the years?

From trying hard not to have a style (unsuccessfully) to allowing one.

Your work often contains a definite shock factor. Is stirring up controversy part of the fun of Design, or do you consider it an obligation?

As I get older, stirring up controversy is much less of a factor. Shock, like humour or any kind of surprise, can be an effective communication tool if it is put in the right context and for the right purpose.

You spend a considerable amount of time on personal work, and you seem to go out of your way to pursue projects that you are passionate about. Do you think that staying true to yourself is crucial to success as a Designer (or otherwise)?

There is an incredible amount of inauthentic work in the public sphere, and I am bored by it (I suspect many other people are too). As a person, I can feel if someone is authentic, be that in a personal contact or in a piece of communication designed by a Designer.

In pursuing personally motivated projects, what challenges have you run across?

Financing them.

Knowing your propensity to list, we couldn't help but ask: Considering your career thus far, what are your five favorite Sagmeister design projects to date?

This, of course, changes; newer jobs tend to be closer to my heart than older projects. Right now:
1. This series, *Things I have learned in my life so far.*
2. The True Majority work.
3. The David Byrne CD plus book.
4. The Casa da Musica identity.
5. The Zumtobel annual report.

What about beauty? What makes your top five list of beautiful sights?

1. After wandering the narrow streets of the old city in Jerusalem, to get outside on the plaza and see the Dome of the Rock Mosque.
2. Watching the sunrise at Ankor Wat, Cambodia.
3. Just last week, visiting Steven Holl's extension to the Nelson-Atkins Museum of Art in Kansas City at night.
4. Rio de Janeiro, seen from above, next to the statue of Christ the Redeemer.
5. The cathedral in Cologne, Germany.

Five examples of outstanding Design?

1. Art Spiegelmann, Maus.
2. Jonathan Barnbrook's design for Damien Hirst's book *I Want to Spend the Rest of My Life Everywhere, with Everyone, One to One, Always, Forever, Now.*
3. Joerg Zintzmeyer, Swiss bank notes
4. Rick Valincenti: Herman Miller trade show video.
5. Andrey Logvin, Russia, Trinity poster.

What has been your greatest professional learning experience?

When I was in Hong Kong, I learned in two short years everything about all the things I don't want to do in my life.

Now you teach as well. What is the most important lesson you can pass on to your students?

It is possible to do the kind of work you want to do.

Finally, who has been your greatest professional mentor, and why?

Tibor Kalman. 15 years ago, as a student in NYC, I called him every week for half a year and got to know the M&Co receptionist really well. When he finally agreed to see me, it turned out I had a sketch in my

portfolio rather similar in concept and execution to an idea M&Co was just working on. He rushed to show me the prototype out of fear I'd say later he stole it out of my portfolio. I was so flattered.

When I finally started working there five years later, I discovered it was, more than anything else, his incredible salesmanship that set his studio apart from all the others. There were probably a number of people around who were as smart as Tibor (and there were certainly a lot who were better at designing), but nobody else could sell these concepts without any changes, get those ideas with almost no alterations out into the hands of the public.

Nobody else was as passionate. As a boss he had no qualms about upsetting his clients or his employees. I remember his reaction to a logo I had worked on for weeks and was very proud of: "Stefan, this is TERRIBLE, just terrible, I am so disappointed." His big heart was shining through nevertheless. He had the guts to risk everything. I witnessed a very large project where he and M&Co had collaborated with a famous Architect and had spent a year's worth of work. He was willing to walk away on the question of who would present to the client.

Tibor had an uncanny knack for giving advice, for dispersing morsels of wisdom, packaged in rough language later known as "Tiborisms." "The most difficult thing when running a design company is not to grow," he told me when I opened my own little studio. "Just don't go and spend the money they pay you or you are going to be the whore of the ad agencies for the rest of your life" was his parting sentence when I moved to Hong Kong to open up a design studio for Leo Burnett.

These insights were also the reason why M&Co got so much press; journalists could just call him and he would supply the entire structure for a story and some fantastic quotes, to boot. He was always happy and ready to jump from one field to another: corporate design, products, city planning, music videos, documentary movies, children's books, and magazine editing were all treated under the mantra, "You should do everything twice; the first time you don't know what you're doing, the second time you do, and the third time it's boring."

He did good work containing good ideas for good people.

Interview by Anna Carnick
With Melanie Madden, Contributing Editor

About Stefan Sagmeister:
Stefan Sagmeister formed the New York-based Sagmeister Inc. (*www.sagmeister.com*) in 1993 and has since designed for clients as diverse as the Rolling Stones, HBO, and the Guggenheim Museum. Having been nominated five times for the Grammy he finally won one for the Talking Heads boxed set.

He has also earned practically every important international Design award. In the beginning of 2008, Abrams published his comprehensive book titled *Things I have learned in my life so far*. Solo shows on Sagmeister Inc.'s work have been mounted in Zurich, Vienna, New York, Berlin, Tokyo, Osaka, Prague, Cologne, Seoul and Miami.

He teaches in the graduate department of the School of Visual Arts in New York and lectures extensively on all continents. A native of Austria, he received his MFA from the University of Applied Arts in Vienna and, as a Fulbright Scholar, a master's degree from Pratt Institute in New York.

(page 10) Stefan Sagmeister Portrait by Henry Leutwyler.
(pages 12-15) Things I have learned in my life so far by Stefan Sagmeister; Art Director/Artist/Author/Writer: Stefan Sagmeister; Designer: Matthias Ernstberger; Editor: Deborah Aaronson; Illustrators: Yuki Muramatsu, Stephan Walter; Photographer: Henry Leutwyler; Print Producer: Anet Sirna-Brude; Typographers: Matthias Ernstberger, Stefan Sagmeister; Essays by Steven Heller, Daniel Nettle, and Nancy Spector; Published by Harry N. Abrams, Inc. (www.hnabooks.com)

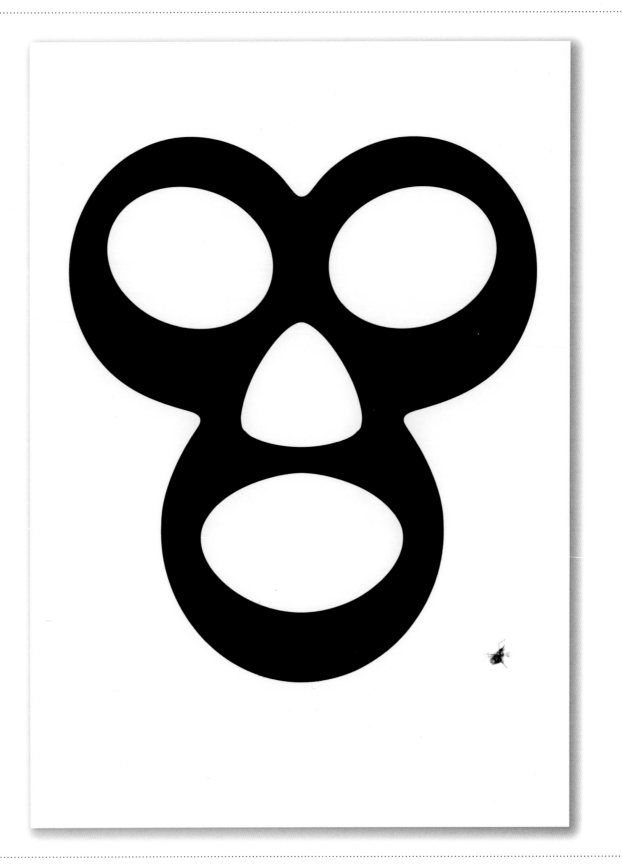

"Stefan has redefined the basic description of what it means to be a Graphic Designer in our time.
Because so much of his work is self initiated,
he operates outside the usual conventions of most professional practice.
By any standard, his work continually disrupts our expectations and
makes us think deeply about everything he shows us."

Milton Glaser, *Designer*

"Stefan is able to meld Art and Graphic Design so perfectly as to make you
question where one ends and another begins.
He not only made me look but made me think!"

Henry Leutwyler, *Photographer*

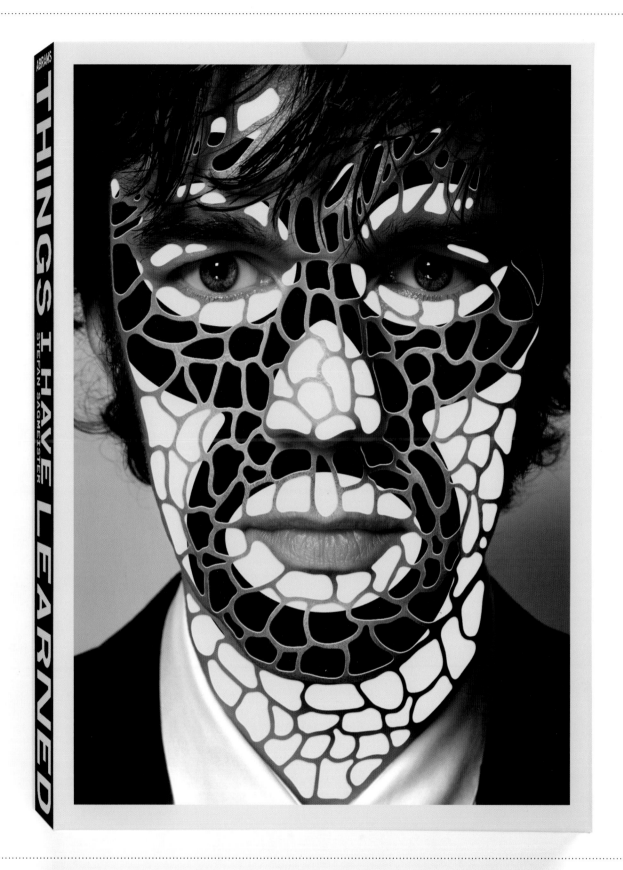

"It gives me the biggest thrill to find the hidden message 'Stefan loves Anni.'
This message has appeared in different publications, always tricky to find! Sometimes friends ask,
'Did you see that?' I'm like, 'See what?' This secret message has kept my heart warm at all times...
Stefan, Anni loves you back."

Anni Kuan, *Fashion Designer*

"Working with Stefan has and always will be the high point of my Graphic Design adventures.
He is a staggeringly talented wonder and quite the artist himself.
He has designed logos for me — album covers, lyric books — each and every project a pleasure
not only for his talent and generous spirit, but because he is also great fun. I love him."

Lou Reed, *Artist & Musician*

Ahn.Sang.Soo: Life.Peace

This year, Korean Designer Ahn Sang-Soo's work will be celebrated in retrospective exhibits around the globe. Looking back on his career, the acclaimed Typographer says the most important thing he's learned is that we're all ultimately connected, each of us a small, but integral piece of the larger puzzle. Below, he considers his contributions to the Hangul typeface and describes in detail his life.peace logo — published here for the first time — which displays the interconnectedness of the heavens, the natural environment, animals of land and sea, and the human race.

This year your life's work is being presented in a handful of retrospective exhibits. Looking back, what are the big lessons you've learned over the course of your career?

I think there is a huge net in this world, one that connects all of us. I work inside this net, and it encourages and inspires me. My work goes through the net and out into the larger world. Eventually, it comes back to me. The net was too subtle to be sensed when I was young, but now the net is huge, like the universe. I am only a tiny part in it.

When you look back on your career, what makes you most proud?

Development of Hangul typefaces. Hangul is the Korean Alphabet created 600 years ago as an alternative to Chinese.

How has the Hangul aesthetic influenced your own design philosophy?

Hangul was originally designed to combine Korean sound, culture and nature. It represents everything Korean. It represents the harmony of human beings and the universe. The Hangul philosophy is different, simple and humanistic. It is creative, easy Typography designed for a broad audience. I believe this approach can be applied to all designs, and it has become my own personal Design motto.

What are you working on now?

a.book.of.gutenberg.galaxy.project.. called "between.sejong.and.gutenberg."

Let's talk about your life.peace logo. Tell us a little about the Life-Peace Fellowship (LPF) in Korea.

LPF is a union of people who wish to make the world a better and more peaceful place. They dedicate themselves to the realization of this peace through study, pilgrimages, conferences, lectures, cultural events, and regional meetings held each year in the summer and winter. Their philosophy is this: To make the world peaceful, I must first be peaceful.

What inspired you to create the life.peace logo?

As we all know, our ecological crises threaten all of us. Simultaneously, political and economic issues threaten peace as well. The Korean Peninsula has been especially vulnerable for about 100 years. We have an unhappy history in this regard. Also, rapid industrialization has resulted in terrible side effects. So naturally, in Korea, there have been many discussions about life and peace. I became interested in this movement and wished to participate in it.

Three years ago, on 12/31/04, at midnight, I created the life.peace logo. I designed the logo at the request of an old friend, Buddhist monk Rev. Dobeop, who was involved in the Life-Peace movement. I showed him the logo while sitting in a small room on Jiri Mountain. He liked it a lot.

You've since identified your logo as a universally applicable, copyright-free symbol. Did you initially design it with the hope of broader use?

at.first.rev.dobeop.asked.me.to.design.it.. as.soon.as.i.designed.. i.was.just.happy.. i.designed.her.. she.will.grow.. i.should.care.for.her.during.baby.time.. after.that.she.will.grow.independently.

I actually explained the idea of this logo to my foreign friends. They were excited about it and wanted to use the logo for their campaigns. So I let them. As a copyright-free logo, anyone can use it for a life.peace-motivated campaign.

Please explain your logo's symbolism.

The lower part is the human being.

The right part represents beings with four legs.
The left part represents beings that live in the water and sky.
The top part symbolizes the grass and trees.
All these lives are connected. We are one body.
If the four-legged beings are sick, we are all sick.
If the beings in water cannot live, we cannot survive.
If they are happy, we are happy.
If we harm them, that means we harm our own bodies.
We live with them.
We live by relying on them.
If they don't live, we cannot live.
We are not here to conquer them.
We are but one of nature's many beings.
We are one body.
To live with respectful minds to all beings,
That is life.peace.

What makes this logo stand out from other "green" logos?

When I see some commercial Western green logos, I do get their meanings immediately. But for me, they are not as interesting or attractive. The life.peace logo is different. Once you understand the meaning of this logo, you become more interested in it, even addicted to it.

It is very symbolic. It represents the hope of people who wish for world peace. This logo can be a talisman — one that people draw on paper, imbue with their hopes and wishes, and place anywhere in the home to symbolize their hope. The talisman makes people happy and brings them comfort. Also, this logo is not just for nature; it relates to all beings existing in this world and the universe. I wanted to talk about the peace and harmony of all beings and nature, how each part relates.

How did your background in Asian culture and Typography influence the life.peace logo?

A long time ago, people first used the pictogram for communication. A pictogram or pictograph is a symbol representing a concept, object, activity, place or event by illustration. The basic building blocks of the Chinese language are pictograms. The Korean language, which evolved from Chinese, thus has a definitive link to the pictogram.

Before the Korean alphabet was created, Koreans used Chinese for communication, but we pronounced the characters differently. With this in mind, I figured that the life.peace logo could ultimately be a language character. I used the concept of the Chinese ideograph to develop and name the logo. Thus, the meaning of this logo is "oulim" (harmony), and it is pronounced "salm" (life) in Korean.

Oulim "salm." Harmony "life."

What are your favorite campaigns or posters that utilize this logo?

One poster is about the tsunami. I mixed the logo and image for this poster. The second poster was created for an exhibition by Galerie Anatome, Paris, in 2006. The Galerie Anatome planned this exhibition with Galerie VU', pairing together 80 Designers and 80 Photographers. I worked with Photographer Anne Rearick and created this poster. I love this photo. I don't know where it was taken, but I love this girl's smile. She looks so happy and peaceful, like she does not know anything bad in this world. This poster makes me smile.

Interview by Yon Joo Choi, Melanie Madden and Anna Carnick

We approached three internationally respected Designers — Melchior Imboden, Niklaus Troxler and Finn Nygaard — to get their thoughts on Ahn Sang-Soo. We only asked for a line or two, but they just couldn't help themselves. They gushed. Below, read what they had to say about their friend...

Melchior Imboden, *Graphic Designer, Photographer, and AGI President (Switzerland)*

"The first time I met Ahn was at an international Poster Design biennial in Brno, Czech Republic, around ten years ago. We have met time and again at various Design congresses, competitions, exhibitions and AGI meetings all around the world, and have become very close friends over the years. Whenever I meet him, his profound interest in people, regardless of their profession or cultural background, never ceases to amaze me. His encounters with people are captured on film and recorded in his sketchbook, noted in the form of signs and pictogram-like drawings, in something like his personal form of stenography. He also asks people to sketch in his book, thus initiating dialogues.

Another distinctive feature is his camera, which he uses to make portraits of people, all of whom have to hold their hand in front of one of their eyes: a signature of his portraits. He publishes these portraits on the Internet, and we're curious to see what will follow.

His passion for the human being, his research, profession and travel is reflected in his tremendously complex work in developing the transition of the traditional Hangul, the Korean alphabet, into a functional medium, just one of his many achievements in his work as a Typographer, Photographer, Poster, Book and Exhibition Designer.

Because of his exceptional achievements, he is invited as a jury member, guest speaker, guest professor and workshop leader all over the world. For this reason, it comes as no surprise that you are more likely to meet him anywhere in the world than in Seoul!"

Niklaus Troxler, *Designer*

"I have known Ahn Sang-Soo for about six years. In 2002, he organized an incredible Typography exhibition in Seoul. He invited all the most important Typography Designers around the world to participate.

When I met him shortly after this event, I found a very impressive person with a wide, open mind. He is an important bridge builder between the East and West. He is very interested in Graphic Design in all shades. His personal work is very impressive in both Design and Composition. He communicates with his Korean letters so that we can *feel* his messages. Even when we cannot read his texts, we believe we understand them — it's incredible. That's because he works with Design matters, with all the tools Designers can understand: composition, abstraction, structure, movement... Also, for as long as I've known him, he has constantly taken photographs of everybody. You have to cover one eye!

This is special! The one-eyed Photographer. You can find hundreds of one-eye photographs on his blog (*ssahn.com*)!"

Finn Nygaard, *Designer*

Ahn Sang-Soo. "silence · precision · energy · silence · silence · ink · esthetics · good friend · silence · silence · square · dot · silence · eye · hand · silence · poster · silence · brush · colour · typography · silence · activity · silence · silence · see you · silence"

This is my feeling about Ahn Sang-Soo.

About Ahn Sang-Soo:

A leading figure in Korean Typographic Design, Ahn Sang-Soo has invented a number of eye-catching typefaces that break out of Hangul's traditional square frame. Ahn obtained his BFA and MFA in 1981 from Hongik University in Seoul. He received his Ph.D in 1996 from Hanyang University in Seoul and Honorary Doctor of Design in 2001 from Kingston University, London. From 1981 to 1985, he was Art Director for *Madang* and *Meot* magazines. Subsequently he began Ahn Graphics Design firm. Then, in 1991 he began his professorship in Typography at Hongik University, his alma mater. He has also been the Editor and Art Director of the underground art-culture magazine *Report/Report* since 1988.

Internationally, Ahn was Vice President (1997-2001) of Icograda, and the Chairman of both Icograda Millennuim Oullim Congress 2000 and TypoJanchi 2001. He is the recipient of the 1998 grand prize of Zgraf8, and the 2007 Gutenberg Award, and has been honored by the Korean Language Academy for his contribution to the advancement of Hangul. Major projects include a new design system for the Korean Buddhist Chogye Order (2004), the official symbol design for the 50th anniversary of Korean Liberation (1995), and the Life-Peace movement symbol (2004). Check out his blog at *ssahn.com*.

About Life-Peace Fellowship:

Life-Peace Fellowship promotes world peace and harmony amongst all creatures. Its members believe the only way to move beyond our current social, ecological and economical crises is to respect the necessarily symbiotic and cooperative relationship amongst all living things. This begins with inner peace: to make the world peaceful, I must become peaceful. The two pillars of the movement are self-reflection and social participation. Now five years old, LPF has ten local branches and 5000-plus members nationally. For more information, please visit *lifepeace.org*.

(page 17) Ahn Sang-Soo Portrait by Michael Levi; (page 19) 80+80 Poster by Ahn Sang-Soo, Photography by Anne Rearick; (page 20) Tsunami Poster by Ahn Sang-Soo; (page 21) Poster for Gutenberg Award Exhibition, Leipzig, Germany.

"I've learned so much from Ahn's attitude towards others, and from his sincere approach to work. I dream that one day, our life.peace logo will be more famous than even the Samsung logo!"

Hwang Dae-kwon, *Vice Chairman, Life-Peace Foundation Steering Committee*

"His profound interest in people, regardless of their profession or cultural background, never ceases to amaze me."

Melchior Imboden, *Designer, Photographer, and AGI President (Switzerland)*

"He is an important bridge builder between the East and West."

Niklaus Troxler, *Designer*

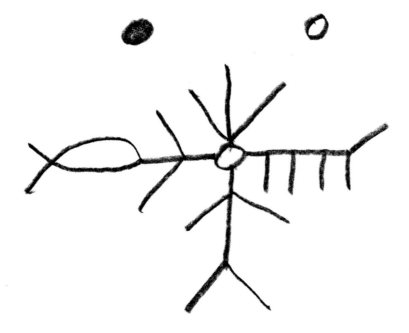

생명평화

life.peace

To Bear WITNESS: The Harry Pearce Interview

Pentagram London Partner Harry Pearce has spent over two decades producing award-winning graphics for a range of clients. 14 years ago, he teamed up with WITNESS, a charity founded by musician Peter Gabriel that uses video and online media to bring awareness to human rights violations worldwide. He has since created all of WITNESS' design material, including the potent Burma poster carried by activists in televised street protests from Bangkok to New York City. Recently, we sat down with Pearce to discuss his pro-bono ventures with WITNESS, his commitment to the cause of human rights, and his thoughts on Design as a vehicle for social and political change.

What drew you to WITNESS as an organization?
In the early days of my first design partnership, Lippa Pearce, we made a commitment to providing pro-bono work for charities. While we had little money, we hoped we could make a positive contribution to causes through Design. We saw a situation where big money often got the best design work, and causes without the same kind of financial resources couldn't justify investing in the kind of design that would really help raise their profile. In a slightly tongue-in-cheek way, we saw ourselves as Robin Hood characters, using the money we made from working for our commercial clients to support worthy but impoverished projects. I was particularly inspired by Peter Gabriel, the founder of WITNESS. Peter's idea of "Little brother turning the cameras back on Big Brother" was so powerful, as the historical significance of the amateur footage of the Rodney King beating in Los Angeles in 1992 had shown, that I very quickly became engrossed in the organization's work. At the time, I was working with the Lawyers Committee for Human Rights (now known as Human Rights First) in New York through Peter's recommendation, so it was a natural transition to become involved in WITNESS, their partner organization.

What were your motivations from a Design standpoint?
The material that WITNESS generates is profoundly moving and powerful. I desperately wanted all their graphic communications to accurately capture the significance of their work. I had visions of a WITNESS film landing on someone's desk, poorly presented, and failing to get noticed.

In your collaborations with WITNESS, what work are you most proud of?
The *Infantry* poster has probably had the greatest impact. It's been exhibited worldwide and has become iconic. The idea behind it is so simple: in war the most vulnerable in any battle are the infantry, the ground soldiers. In society our infants fill that position. If you combine both, as with a child soldier, it's a shocking proposition. But, for me, the day-to-day continual support for WITNESS is what really counts. I think it's this ability to continue to contribute to a project I'm so passionate about that makes me the most proud.

One of the most extraordinary moments of my career occurred recently as I was watching news footage of the protests that took place in support of the Burma uprising. Across the world, I saw images of my *Burma* poster being taken onto the streets as a symbol of protest. To have a piece of Graphic Design spontaneously used like this is the most meaningful thing that has ever happened to a piece of my work. It's profoundly moving that people should protest with it in this way.

When designing the Burma *poster for WITNESS, how did you define the problem, and what was your approach? Specifically, how does your poster speak to the situation in Burma?*
Each year WITNESS champions one major initiative amongst its many human rights projects. In 2006, it was decided that WITNESS would highlight the plight of communities in eastern Burma, where over 3000 villages have been burnt and the people forcibly removed or driven into the surrounding jungles. Over the last ten years, over one million civilians have fled the brutal attacks of the military regime.

In late August 2007 protests began in Burma, the biggest challenge to the junta's power in nearly 20 years. A popular uprising led by Burma's Buddhist monks ensued, which to the world's horror was remorselessly suppressed. When I began to design a poster to promote this campaign, I was supplied with a selection of photography from the devastated areas. Despite the power and importance of this photography, I felt that what was needed to help WITNESS differentiate itself was a single iconic image to give a sense of place and visually articulate the situation. The final solution, in which I literally set fire to the word "Burma," suggested that much more than the villages were at stake.

Why a poster? Does this medium have particular qualities that make it more accessible or effective than other art forms?
I think it's important that the poster isn't viewed in isolation. The *Burma* poster was my contribution to a much larger effort that involved political campaigning and creative works from a wide range of art forms, including film, animation, music and speeches. The convenient thing about the *Burma* poster was that it provided an instant visual hook that helped unite all of the elements of our activities to form a coherent whole. In many ways, my decision to create a typographic statement, rather than use photography, helped to make the poster a symbol for the campaign. I believe the poster medium has the power to establish an iconic image in a direct and singular way.

Are you currently working on anything else for WITNESS?
WITNESS is a full-time commitment. As well as working on a constant stream of design work in the studio, I also sit on the WITNESS "advisory board." I am about to spend several days in New York with the WITNESS team to create the design vision for the forthcoming year. The main focus of our energies will be concentrated on developing a new project called The Hub, a multilingual online portal dedicated to human rights media and action. Launched just a few months ago by the wonderful Gillian Caldwell (WITNESS' recently departed Executive Director) and Peter Gabriel, The Hub provides the opportunity for individuals, organisations, networks and groups around the world to bring their human rights stories and campaigns to global attention — rather like a YouTube for human rights. To my mind, it's one of the most important global human rights initiatives in recent history.

What makes a design successful?
One that answers all the questions posed of it, simultaneously elevating its culture.

Do you believe that Graphic Design can affect social or political change? And if so, how?
This needs to be a book! Being a Graphic Designer comes with a great responsibility. Graphic Design has a profound effect on almost every aspect of our lives, not least in the social-political arena. Although we're rarely aware, it is through visual language that we interpret so much of our world. From the tiniest typographic nuance to the loudest poster on the street, we are visually bombarded.

It is beyond question that Graphic Design has a huge influence on social and political conditions. Design is a visual articulation of an inner will, an active and reactive force, both for good and bad. The question that really matters is in whose hands it resides.

Can you point to any issues where Design has had a measurable impact on the social or political climate?
The Polish Œsolidarity logo, under which some 10 million people united in the Strike for Freedom, clearly helped contribute to the fall of communism. It had such a profound effect on me. I'm sure many people around the world didn't understand all the issues it involved but felt the emotion. That image became a metaphor for freedom. Such a rough, visceral mark, but so perfect for its moment in time.

What is the most challenging aspect of designing for a political cause?
The biggest challenge, in my eyes, is to create work that is relevant and lives up to the quality and importance of its subject matter.

Where do you get your inspiration?
I rely on my intuition to guide me, and always seek to make something as emotional as possible. For me, inspiration lies in between every line; we just need eyes to see it.

What is your favorite design project?
I always look for and try to create work that moves people. Sometimes great Design is not a conscious act. I constantly photograph typographic anomalies all around the world. Wherever I go I have a camera. The number of images now runs into thousands — rubbish to most people, inspiration to me.

45 years of military dictatorship, 3000 villages emptied,
1 million people driven from their homes.
This is eastern Burma... Act now

Burma Issues is unique in that we focus on marginalized communities as the target group to build a peace based on justice for everyone. Our approach is based on community organisation and empowerment concepts. It takes four forms: grassroots organising, activist development, information for action and international peace campaigns.

www.burmaissues.org

WITNESS uses the power of video to expose human rights abuses. By partnering with local organizations around the globe, WITNESS empowers human rights defenders to use video to catalyze grassroots activism, political engagement and lasting change.

www.witness.org

SEE IT
FILM IT
CHANGE IT

Your favorite poster of all time?
I admire so many posters that this is impossible to answer. However, I will say a great favorite of mine is *Bloodbath*, designed by Yossi Lemel in 2002, which comments on the long period of intense violence between Israelis and Palestinians. Its power comes from an everyday image, which, with the slightest alteration, has turned into a visual poleax. The cold, clinical feeling of the white tiles simultaneously evokes bathroom and morgue. The image needs no explanation. It stays with you long after you've turned away. There is no evidence of any of the violence that this image suggests. Its resonance is increased by its restraint. You create the headline because there's none to read. The human rights arena is full of shocking imagery easily plundered and readily used. Yet the stillness of this stark, simple image invades minds saturated with visual violence — a brilliant subversive shock.

Finally, who sets the standard of excellence in Design today?
Without doubt I'd put Stefan in that spot. He continually surprises with his work, and I know he never lets himself off the hook. Much beautiful work is coming out of Japan; I think we all should be looking East with great regard.

Interview by Ellen Fure and Melanie Madden
With Anna Carnick, Contributing Editor

About Harry Pearce:
Harry Pearce studied Graphic Design at Canterbury College of Art and moved to London in 1982. In 1990, after eight years in the industry working for clients such as Porsche, Holsten, BAA and Royal Mail, he co-founded Lippa Pearce Design, one of the UK's most respected design agencies. He joined Pentagram's London office as a partner in 2006. Harry's work touches many disciplines, from spatial design and identity to print, packaging and posters. He has worked with a diverse range of public and private sector clients, including The Co-operative, Halfords, Phaidon Press, Kangol, the London Science Museum, Shakespeare's Globe, the British Film Institute, the National Railway Museum and Boots the chemist, a client with whom he has had a 23-year relationship. He is dedicated to supporting human rights and has produced pro-bono work for charities such as Christian Aid and the Lawyers Committee for

Human Rights. Over the last 14 years he has developed a unique relationship with WITNESS, a New York-based charity founded by songwriter and activist Peter Gabriel. Harry's partnership with WITNESS has produced some of his most acclaimed pieces of work, including the award-winning *Infantry* and *Burma* posters. He is also a member of the charity's advisory board. Harry has won numerous national and international design awards, including two D&AD Silver awards. His work has been included in every edition of the D&AD annual since the inception of Lippa Pearce, and he been has featured in many touring exhibitions. In addition, his work is included in the permanent collection of the Bibliothèque nationale de France in Paris. A frequent speaker and contributor to design discourse, Harry has given a number of lectures at international conferences such as Kyoorius Design Yatra in India, Emzin in Ljubljana, as well as for colleges, museums and design organisations such as the British Museum, D&AD and the Typographic Circle in the UK. Harry attended a royal celebration of British design at Buckingham Palace in 2004. In 2005 he was elected a member of the Alliance Graphique Internationale (AGI) and had his work exhibited as part of the prestigious organisation's 50th anniversary celebrations.

About WITNESS:
WITNESS was founded in 1992 by Musician and Activist Peter Gabriel and the Reebok Human Rights Foundation as a project of the Lawyers Committee for Human Rights (now Human Rights First). Today, it is an independent non-profit organization with offices in Brooklyn, New York, and human rights partners based around the world. WITNESS uses video and online technologies to open the eyes of the world to human rights violations. Its mission is to empower people to transform personal stories of abuse into powerful tools for justice, promoting public engagement and policy change.

For more information on Harry Pearce, please visit *www.pentagram.com*. To learn more about WITNESS, check out *www.WITNESS.org*.

(page 22) Portrait of Harry Pearce by Richard Foster; (page 23) Burma Poster by Harry Pearce; Size AO; Litho print; Photographed by Richard Foster; (page 24) Bloodbath, designed by Yossi Lemel; (page 25) Infantry Poster by Harry Pearce, Andy Mosley; Size AO; Screen Print; Photographed by Panos Pictures.

"Working with Harry is a mixture of good Karma and great design."
Peter Gabriel, *Musician and Activist*

"I have known and worked with Harry for over 22 years. Throughout those years I have admired him for his dedication to his craft; he is the best Designer I know. He can work on the most complex of projects, solving them effortlessly with style, intelligence and wit.
He also loves working with the smallest of clients, bringing as much understanding, passion and attention to their problems as his large clients. He sees the world in ways that other people miss.
His dedication to social issues such as human rights shows how big his heart is.
He is brilliant because he cares and knows the difference he can make.
He is also aware of his responsibility within our profession and his position within its history.
He also has the wickedest sense of humour of anyone I know. He is my best friend and I love him!"

Domenic Lippa, *Partner, Pentagram Design*

INFANTRY

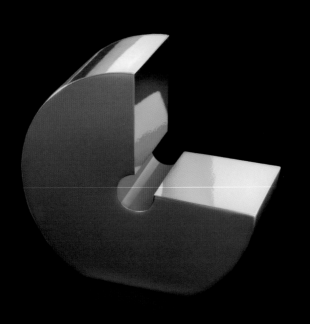

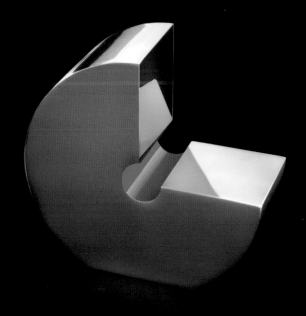

GraphisGold&PlatinumAwardWinners

Award photographs by Henry Leutwyler

Building of the Dominant Brand Leader

Alexandria Real Estate Equities, Inc.
2006 Annual Report:
Building of the Dominant
Brand Leader

ng of minant Leader

Alexandria Real Estate Equities, Inc.
2006 Annual Report:
Performance of the Dominant
Brand Leader

ALEXANDRIA

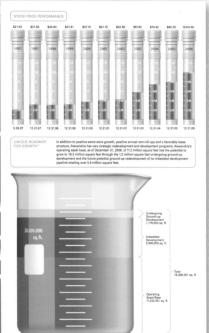

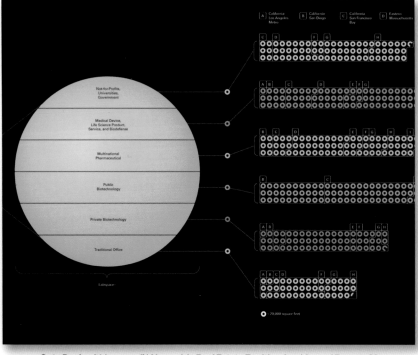

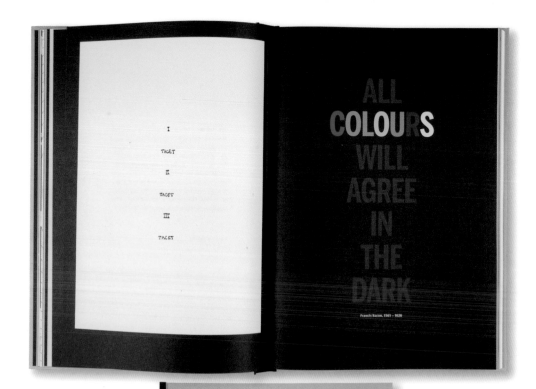

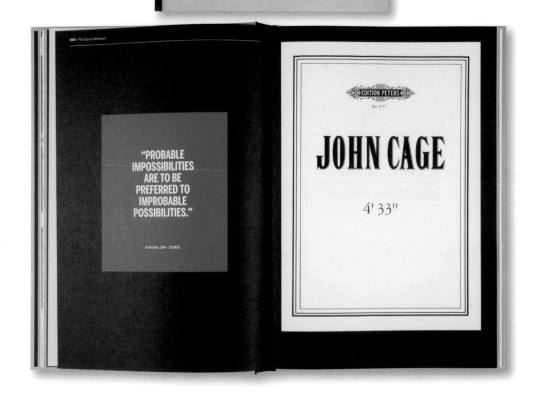

ARE WE THERE YET?

The sights and sounds of a busy shopping street; gridlocked traffic, a mill of people, tourists and window shoppers ambling along.

Darting in amongst all this, a determined pedestrian. This woman knows what she wants and she knows where to find it.

She's near her destination. Ahead, the department store. She makes for the entrance, leans against the glass door and steps across the threshold.

Once in, momentum carries her forward.

A few metres in: she stops to take stock. You wouldn't know it from her demeanour, but her senses are working overtime. Her eyes are adjusting to the difference in light; she's listening, taking in smells, sensing the temperature – getting to grips with this new environment.

She is standing in the shop, but she isn't really there yet.

She never saw the logo when she got to the door; she was looking for the handle. The items she wanted were right next to her, but she completely missed them. And she blanked the assistant who offered her help.

It'll be a few more seconds until the shopper arrives. In the meantime, she's in the transition zone.

Transition zone is a term coined by Paco Underhill to describe the inactive retail space at the front of every shop. Customers use this area to adjust from the outside to the inside.

Jo Twist (left) also known as (aka) Doctor Schnook.

This photo, taken by a military observer from the deck of an aircraft carrier, depicts an F/A-18 passing through a condensation cloud. Visible for just a fraction of a second, condensation clouds form in transonic conditions when extreme disparities in airflow create shock waves which lead to rapid changes in pressure and temperature. They are not, as commonly believed, the visual manifestation of the sound barrier.

Doctor Schnook (left) aka Jo Twist

ALTER EGO

For those of us who have visited a virtual world such as Second Life, the chance to create an avatar – an animated persona – is surely one of its most fascinating features. It seems the urge to transform our physical appearance – and everything this implies – is almost universal.

The word 'avatar', Sanskrit in origin, means 'the manifestation of a god in human form'. Certainly, creating one does give you the god-like power to transcend the restrictions of your appearance and identity, and you would expect this freedom to result in the birth of some very strange 'gods' indeed.

Surprisingly, however, Second Life is not entirely populated by beings with animal heads, little clothing and scaly purple skin. Most avatars look 'normal' (if you ignore the fact that nearly all have impossibly slender, superhero physiques).

A recently published book *Alter Ego: Avatars and their Creators** juxtaposes pictures of individuals and their avatars, revealing how people play with identity online. Sometimes, the appeal is pure escapism: a stressed-out mother can morph into a scantily-clad vamp; a lonely teenager can live like a rock star. The book shows that, rather than reinventing themselves completely, many individuals use their avatar to express aspects of their personality.

The boundaries between existing and new social spaces – between real and virtual reality – are becoming increasingly blurred as, inch by inch, technology overcomes the 'biological platform'. "What will it be like when technology allows us to touch and feel inside the virtual world?" asks entrepreneur Ailin Qin, also known as Anshe Chung.

* By Robbie Cooper and Julian Dibbell. Published by Chris Boot, 2007.

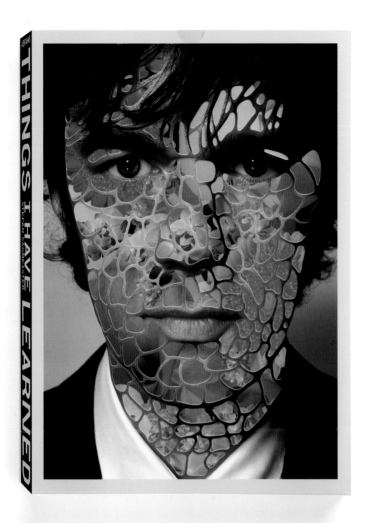

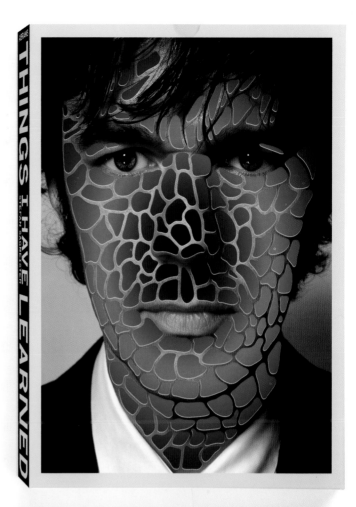

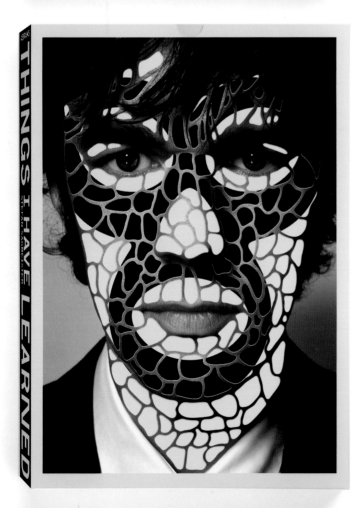

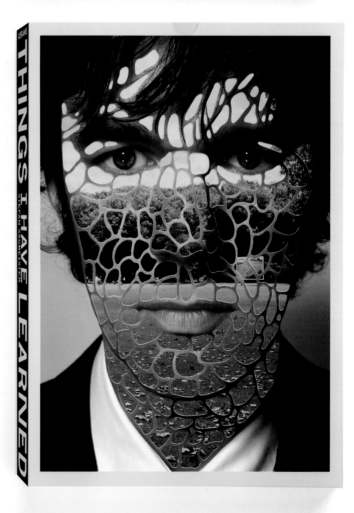

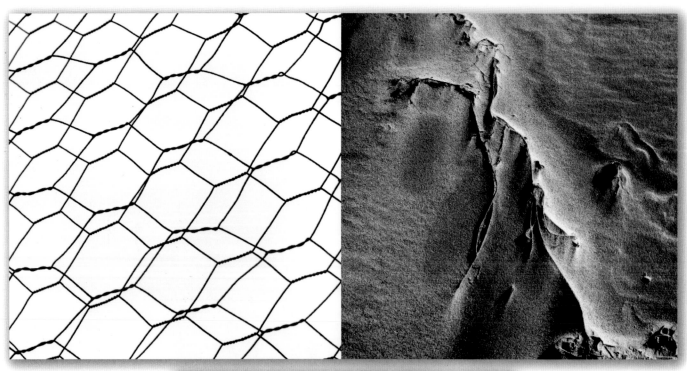

THE FURNITURE OF POUL KJÆRHOLM: CATALOGUE RAISONNÉ

the ring's sloping sides. The cushion also had leather tabs, as on PK 80, that could be laced under the O-rings to attach it securely. When the cushions were removed, the stools could be stacked in a spiral for compact storage, and the O-rings acted as bumpers to prevent the steel bases from scratching the painted plywood.

While Kjærholm's choice of materials appears to have been inevitable, the use of leather was not. One of the initial sketches illustrated a variety of materials, including spiraling cord, stretched filaments that may have been halyard line, as well as the eventual solution of a welted and buttoned cushion covered in leather. A few samples were made with canvas seats and painted bases prior to the final decisions on materials and finishes. PK 33 has been in continuous production since 1959. The same year, Kjærholm created a larger version for Tårnby town hall, where he furnished the public areas. Six stools were made with a diameter of 60 cm and a height of 40 cm. During the Kold Christensen era, the cushions were produced with the typical palette of leathers and also offered in red Niger leather in 1966–68. Since 1982, Fritz Hansen has produced PK 33 in the original dimensions with a frame of matt, chrome-plated spring steel.

116

PAUL POIRET

POIRET

DENISE POIRET: MUSE OR MANNEQUIN?

Caroline Evans

Gerschel & Baumann (American, active 1915–18)
Denise Poiret at the Plaza Hotel, New York, 1913

In 1905, Denise Boulet, the nineteen-year-old daughter of a provincial textile retailer from Elbeuf in Normandy, married Paul Poiret, six years her senior. She bore him five children and remained married to him for twenty-three years. When they divorced in 1928, Poiret told the governess, "Make sure to tell Madame to take anything she wishes." She took all sorts of mementos including her own extensive wardrobe, the children's outgrown clothes, and some of her husband's the gold lamé fancy-dress costume he had worn at the "Thousand and Second Night" party in 1911, his colored waistcoats, and his 1920s dressing gown in eighteenth-century style.

Poiret died in 1944 at sixty-five, but his wife lived to a great age. At seventy-nine, she opened her trunks to Palmer White, author of *Poiret* (1973). Out came "the original coats and gowns Poiret had created for her. Out, too, came packets of letters, personal diaries, photos and newspaper clippings." Her hoard was all the more precious because very little was left after Poiret closed his atelier in 1929. A notorious spendthrift, Poiret threw it all away in the end—arguably his marriage as much as his business, since the two were intertwined. But where he spent, Denise Poiret saved; like a prudent housewife, she kept the family heirlooms intact. Her treasure trove suggests that her role in the Maison Paul Poiret was more than either muse or mannequin, and, when the marriage ended she became her husband's posthumous (and unwitting) curator and collection manager.

In 2005, the family archive went on sale. Suddenly, in a Paris auction house, Denise Poiret's ghost was raised in the objects that carried a trace of her physical presence across the decades—the dresses with silk linings that had once registered the imprint of her body like a mold; the photographs that, at the click of a shutter, fixed forever a moment in her life. There is little other evidence to determine her precise role in the Maison Paul Poiret, and in many ways she remains a mystery. The photographs and dresses provide a unique link because they are indexical objects that connect directly to that time, that body, and those places. They are the hieroglyphs through which to read her.

Henri Manuel (French, 1874–1947)
Denise Poiret, 1919

Poiret started designing for her during their engagement. Pygmalion-like, he claimed that he alone saw her early potential. Be that as it may, the photographs of their subsequent life together reveal that his wife, too, was a stylist, in the way she put her clothes together, in her grace in front of the camera, and her ease in the salons and formal gardens of her home. In the eighteenth-century hôtel on the avenue d'Antin, where they lived from 1909 to 1924, the Poirets achieved a synthesis of work and life. Their apartments abutted the couture house, and their aesthetic extended into their daily lives, an early example of what today is called "lifestyle marketing." Denise Poiret was artistic director of the Maison Paul Poiret, and, like Marie Worth, wife of the nineteenth-century couturier Charles Frederick Worth, her husband's best advertisement. Paul Poiret used her slim figure as the prototype body shape for his sheath gowns that hung from the shoulder, starting with the Empire-line silhouette that he developed from about 1906. In 1913, he told *Vogue*, with typical hyperbole, "My wife is the inspiration for all my creations, she is the expression of all my ideals."

We can only speculate how active a role Denise Poiret played in the construction of her image. She was featured as the favorite of Poiret the Sultan, locked in a golden cage with her ladies, in his orientalist phantasmagoria at the "Thousand and Second Night" party. Poiret's autobiography describes how, when all 300 guests had arrived, he approached the cage "followed by all my women" and released her. "She flew out like a bird, and I precipitated myself in pursuit of her, cracking my useless whip. She was lost in the crowd. Did we know, on that evening, that we were rehearsing the drama of our lives?"

Denise Poiret accompanied her husband on his first formal mannequin tour of Europe in October and November 1911. The couple drove across Europe for weeks in a beige Renault Torpedo. The nine mannequins wore navy-and-beige plaid uniforms, while their modeling clothes went ahead by train. Denise and Paul traveled in matching beige overcoats, color coordinated to the car and the chauffeur's livery: literally, a matching couple.

In 1913, they sailed for the United States on a promotional tour with one hundred dresses, each meticulously inventoried by her in an accounts ledger. As her personal wardrobe these escaped import duty, something that had plagued the 1911 tour, when the Polish customs had demanded duty

Opposite: Georges Lepape (French, 1887–1971)
Pochoir from *Les choses de Paul Poiret*, 1911

'Bois de Boulogne' Dinner Dress worn by Denise Poiret, 1919

Among Poiret's many collaborations with artists, the most enduring was with Raoul Dufy. The artist's boldly graphic approach reflected Poiret's personal preference for the kinds of simplified forms with intense coloring produced by his decorative arts company, Atelier Martine. The naive and artisanal effects sought by the designer, which at Atelier Martine were based on designs that were done by young female students, were in the case of Dufy related largely to his use of woodblock printing.

After working with Poiret on a number of textile designs that achieved quick success, Dufy was hired away by the luxury silk manufacturer Bianchini-Férier. While there was a brief rift following this decampment, Poiret eventually incorporated Dufy prints in what were to become some of his most signature creations. In this dress, the "conversational" print by the artist depicts a series of alfresco vignettes, recalling scenes from the Bois de Boulogne, against a lush millefleur background. Dufy's earliest prints appear to be based on the tradition of eighteenth- and early-nineteenth-century toiles de Jouy. Here, however, with the rich colors and congested patterning in which figure and ground elements have been given equal emphasis, the textile seems closer to Persian miniatures and Moghul lacquer ware.

Poiret has treated the printed silk as if he were constructing a tabard, by having a planar bodice with front and back skirt panels open at the sides. Because black silk tulle forms the sleeves of the dress, and an underskirt of silk tulle and silk broadcloth is visible below the dropped waist, the ensemble conveys the effect of a full black tulle and silk underdress with an apron or pinafore-like overpiece. All of these details, the tapestry-like print, the faux-tabard construction, and the low waistline, contribute to the ensemble's vaguely medieval appearance.

Introduction: Poiret's Modernism and the Logic of Fashion
Nancy J. Troy

Paul Poiret dominated the world of fashion in the early twentieth century. Not only did he introduce a radically simplified female silhouette, but he also pioneered the sale of women's clothes together with lifestyle accessories such as perfume and decorative objects for the home. His meteoric rise to prominence as a couturier in the years just before the outbreak of World War I depended not simply on the distinctive character of his clothing and other designs but also, and perhaps more crucially, on his ability to project an aura of originality in the face of mass production. In the 1920s, when that balancing act could no longer be sustained, Poiret's star status went into a gradual but inexorable decline.

Alongside his striking innovations in costume style and construction, Poiret developed a sharply honed marketing strategy that called for promoting his dresses and other fashionable products as works of art, while presenting himself as an inspired artist and patron of the arts. Although he embraced modernism in the range of contemporary artists whose work he supported, his attitude was marked by elitist individualism tinged with nostalgia for a vanishing era of authenticity and integrity, a time when artists could effortlessly sustain a myth of purity and independence from the constraints of commodity culture. Paradoxically, Poiret's modernity and his notoriety were achieved through his inspired deployment of art discourse, which distanced him from the vulgar crowd and appealed to a wealthy, discreet clientele; at the same time, however, by marshaling the visual and performing arts, architecture, interior decoration, and graphic design, he attracted constant attention from the press, became visible to a vast public audience, and created a seemingly unquenchable demand for his dresses.

Just as his deployment of the arts as promotional vehicles to advance his signature style enabled Poiret to position his clothes (and himself along with them) at the pinnacle of fashion, so, too, the popularity he achieved by this means assured the vulnerability of his dresses to copying and pastiche. The very strategies he used to portray his clothes as unique, even avant-garde creations—indeed, as works of modern art—encouraged the production of a profusion of copies destined for mass consumption. The resulting widespread availability of his designs amounted to a popularization that simultaneously validated his singular preeminence in fashion and destroyed his aspirations to status as an artist among the cultural elite.

Given the nature of haute couture as an artisan-based enterprise, Poiret's business was capable of creating only a limited quantity of high-quality, work-intensive products; once demand exceeded that limit, standardized methods of quantity production, to which his couture house was ill-adapted, were inevitably set into motion. When manufacturers better equipped to satisfy a mass market began to exploit the enormous consumer demand Poiret's own designs elicited, he found himself in an impossible bind. Faced with uncontrolled and often illegal copying of his own unique models, he tried to restrain such mass production in order to protect his elite business; at the same time, he was compelled to enter the mass market not only to support his high-end trade but also to protect his financial interest in the exploitation of his designs. Both of these options were likely to be losing propositions because, in the first instance, it was impossible to prevent illegal or unauthorized copying; and, in the second, once he offered less expensive garments to a mass market, exclusive, high-end clients would refuse to pay the top prices required for him to break even on his made-to-order merchandise. This conundrum highlights the inherently contradictory nature of what might be described as the logic of fashion—the insurmountable problem faced by the couturier when unique creations saturated with artistic aura are subjected to the conditions of mass production for widespread consumption in an industrialized economy.

Poiret's desire to resolve this predicament, which is characteristic of modernist art as well as fashion, led him in 1916–17 to adopt a different but no less contradictory marketing strategy, offering his own reduced-price copies of his dresses, models that in 1916 he would advertise in *Vogue*, oxymoronically, as "genuine reproductions." In doing so, Poiret effectively erased the distinction between originality and reproduction, much as Marcel Duchamp did in choosing his readymades during these same years. Where Duchamp embraced the commodity as part of his effort to expose the precarious status of high art in a rapidly changing economic and social environment, Poiret tried to make mass-produced clothing palatable in the couture context by introducing clothes that were described in the *Vogue* advertisement

Coat, 1923

A complicated piecing of two different but related textiles emphasizes the straight lines of this coat. Poiret's signature rose is woven into two broad, faintly ombré running lengths bracketed by narrow unmatched stripes. The actual design of this textile is evidenced only by the incorporation of the outer boundaries of the pattern to form the garment's sleeves. Another fabric, of confronting scalloped stripes, is inserted at either side of the coat. The narrow band cuffs are in the same plain, loosely woven wool that comprises the lining. The yarn of the lining is identical in color to the ivory ground of the floral and striped patterned textiles that make up the body of the coat. The design reveals none of the virtuosity of its construction, with the coat's apparent simplicity obscuring its technical complexity.

a brief account of a life lived
so far...

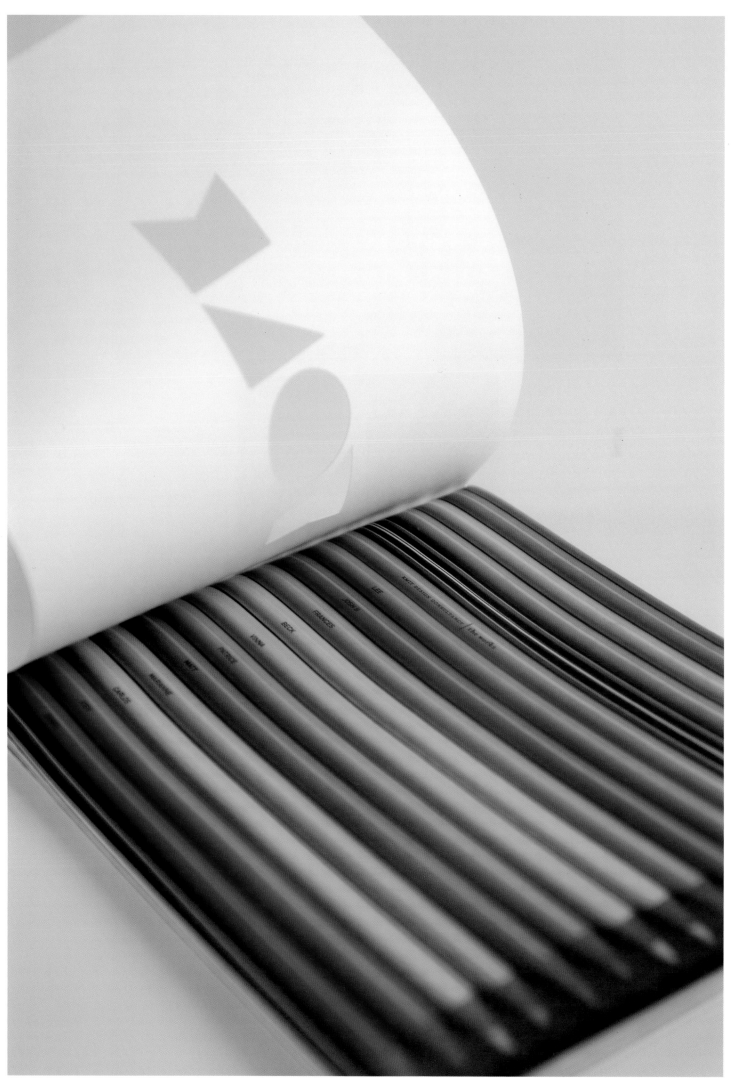

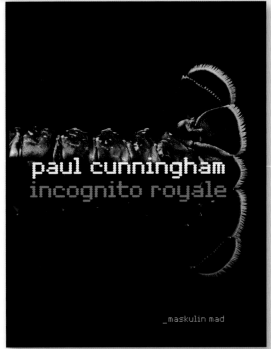

paul cunningham
incognito royale

_maskulin mad

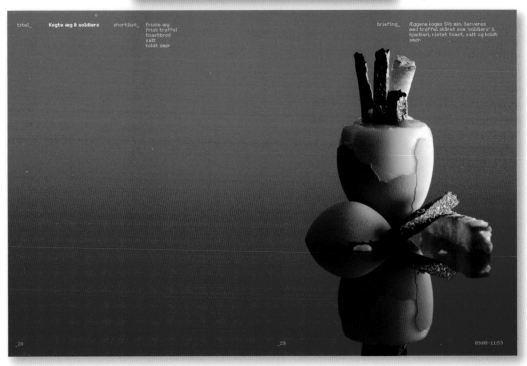

titel_ **Hummer Thermidor**   shortlist_   4 friske hummere à ca. 300 g pr. stk.
80 g smør
80 g mel
4 dl varm mælk
80 g revet gruyère
2 æggeblommer
½ tsk paprika
citronsaft
friske brødkrummer

briefing_   Hummerne koges i 2½ min. i godt
saltet vand. Kødet pilles fra haler
og kløer og holdes varmt. Skallerne
gemmes. Smørret smeltes, melet
vendes i. Varm mælk tilsættes lidt
ad gangen under konstant omrøring.
Gryden tages af varmen. Ost og
æggeblommer tilsættes. Smages til med
paprika, citronsaft og lidt havsalt.
Hummerkødet skæres i store stykker
og blandes i den varme sauce. Det hele
anrettes i hummerskallerne, drysses
med brødkrummer og gratineres under
grillen i ovnen eller i en salamander.
¶

_174   _175   24:00 - : -

titel_ **Coca Cola-float**   shortlist_   Høje slanke glas fyldes halvt med iskold
Coca Cola og toppes med vaniljeis.

briefing_   Perfekt junk food-dessert.
¶

_112   _113   18:00-23:59

intro_   _maskulin mad

_10   _11   fotograf_andreas wiking

Searching for the New Normal

By Rexanne Williams

My personal journal as my greatest fear is realized — the death of my child.

YOUR INNER

CEO

UNLEASH THE
EXECUTIVE
WITHIN

ALLAN COX

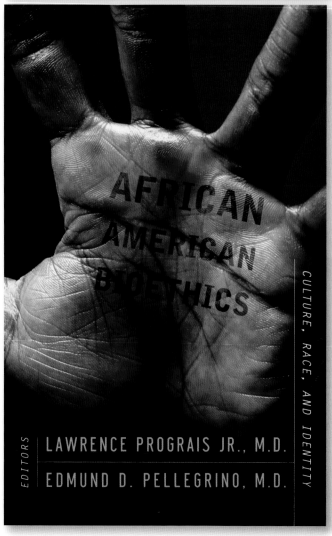

AFRICAN AMERICAN BIOETHICS

CULTURE, RACE, AND IDENTITY

EDITORS

LAWRENCE PROGRAIS JR., M.D.

EDMUND D. PELLEGRINO, M.D.

Reed Hill (top left) | Rexanne Williams
The DesignWorks Group (top right) | Career Press
The DesignWorks Group (bottom) | Georgetown University Press | Books**42**

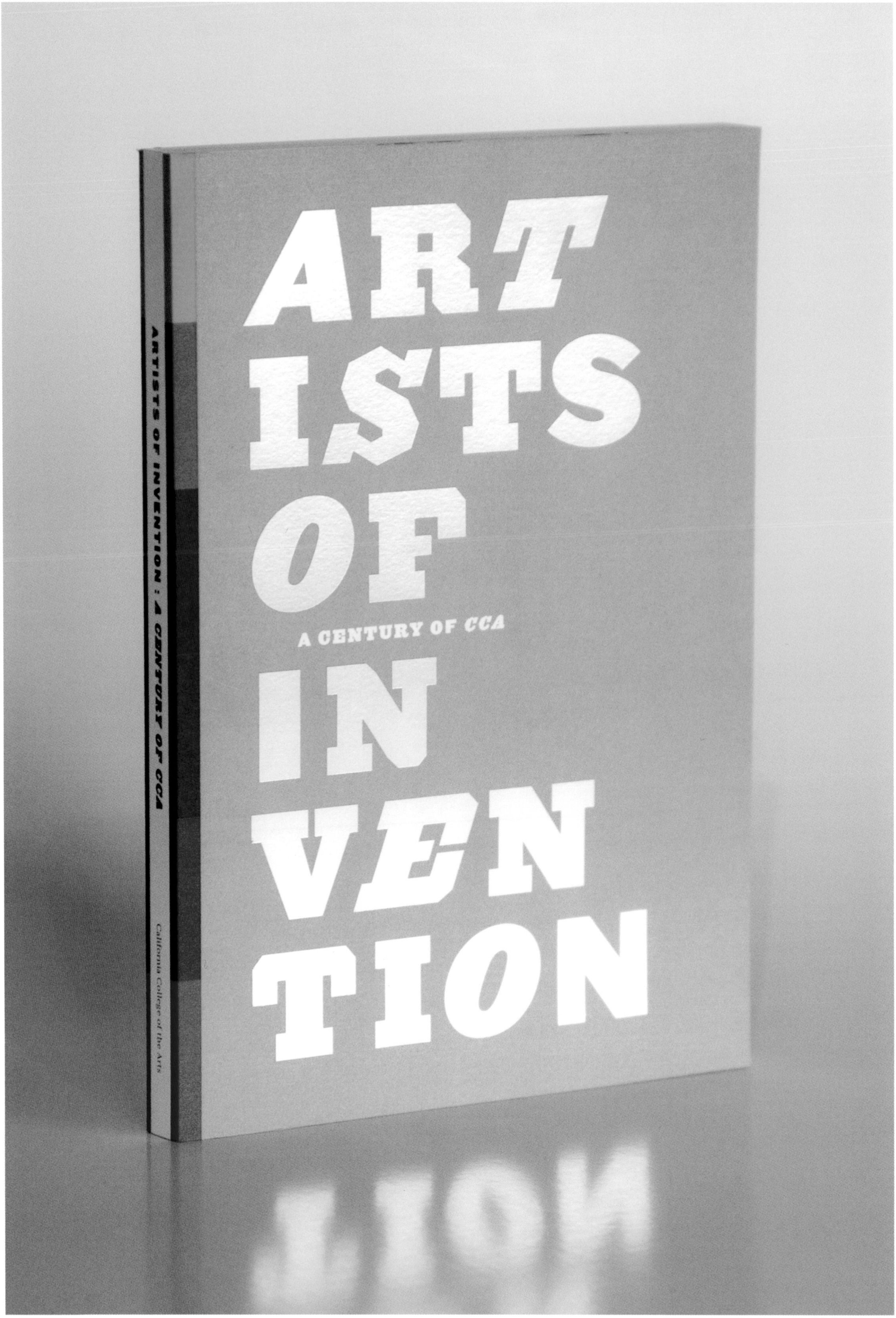

ART
ISTS
OF
A CENTURY OF *CCA*
IN
VEN
TION

ARTISTS OF INVENTION : A CENTURY OF CCA

California College of the Arts

VOLUME

John Wardle Architects

Thames & Hudson

Surf Coast Beach House

Anglesea, Victoria
2000–03

Victoria's coastal regions are losing the simple holiday shack. Development over the past decades fuelled by increasing demand has seen the rude shacks replaced by a suburban architectural language that more closely mirrors affluence and the demands for comfort and amenity. This house is located above the sand dunes at Anglesea, where many holiday shacks were lost in the Ash Wednesday fires of 1983. In the economy of its planning, its materials and its setting it retains the memory of the type.

Planning of the house form reflects a returning theme in the work of the practice, expressing a preference to extrude space along the longitudinal axis. This house is organized over two levels, with the lower level containing the functions that are best served by discrete spaces, the bedrooms and service areas, and the upper level are planned as the main bedroom and living spaces can openly interlace.

This arrangement of open living on the first floor can be recognized as typical of beach houses, which strive to maximize the view to the sea and coastal landscape. The long axis is the upper level is the dynamic axis, while the shore is present. The presence of this orientation is reinforced by the detailing of the axial over-scaled rooflines at the western end, in contrast to the flat detailing along the southern face. The cyclist slides against the flat side wall and is squeezed out of the end.

Colours have only been applied to the surfaces that must twist away from the parallel, highlighting these planning deviations. All parallel and perpendicular surfaces are white. The elements are arranged to an itinerary a play of separation and exposure of the views to the land and seascape beyond.

Theatre of Occupation
Max Creasy

Page 2–3   Where I End And You Begin (The Sky Is Falling In)   4.29   Radiohead   Hail To The Thief
Page 4–5   2+2=5 (The Lukewarm)   3.16   Radiohead   Hail To The Thief
Page 6–7   Sail To The Moon (Brush The Cobwebs Of The Sky)   4.18   Radiohead   Hail To The Thief
Page 8–9   There There (The Bonny King Of Nowhere)   5.23   Radiohead   Hail To The Thief

Page 14–15   Sit Down, Stand Up (Snakes & Ladders)   4.19   Radiohead   Hail To The Thief

Theatre of Construction
Max Creasy

Page 299–300   Staff Portrait
Page 303–304   Construction at Melbourne Grammar School
Page 305–306   Construction at Melbourne Grammar School
Page 307–308   Construction at Melbourne Grammar School
Page 309–310   Construction at Melbourne Grammar School
Page 313–314   Construction at Melbourne Grammar School

16–17

ESSAY ON SOME WORKS OF JOHN WARDLE ARCHITECTS

: LEON VAN SCHAIK

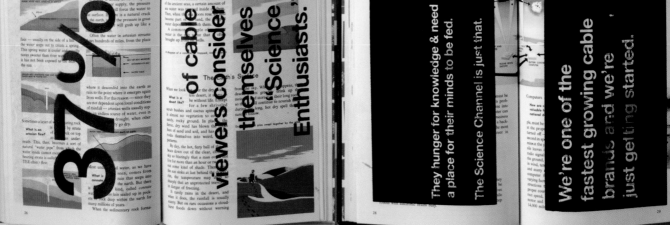

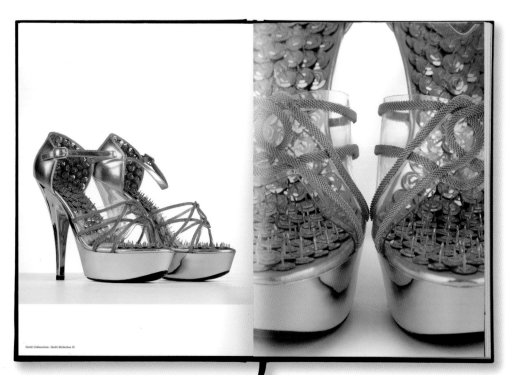

Gold Collection: Gold Stilettos II

Untitled bed, 2004

Feast
Gozba

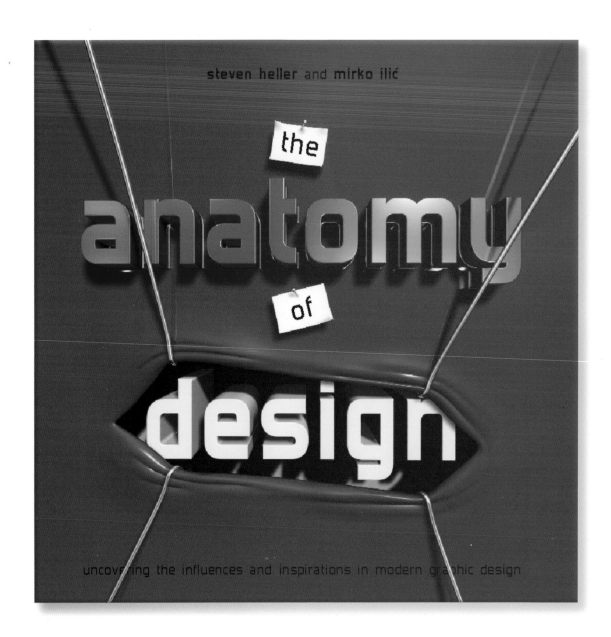

steven heller and mirko ilić

the

anatomy

of

design

uncovering the influences and inspirations in modern graphic design

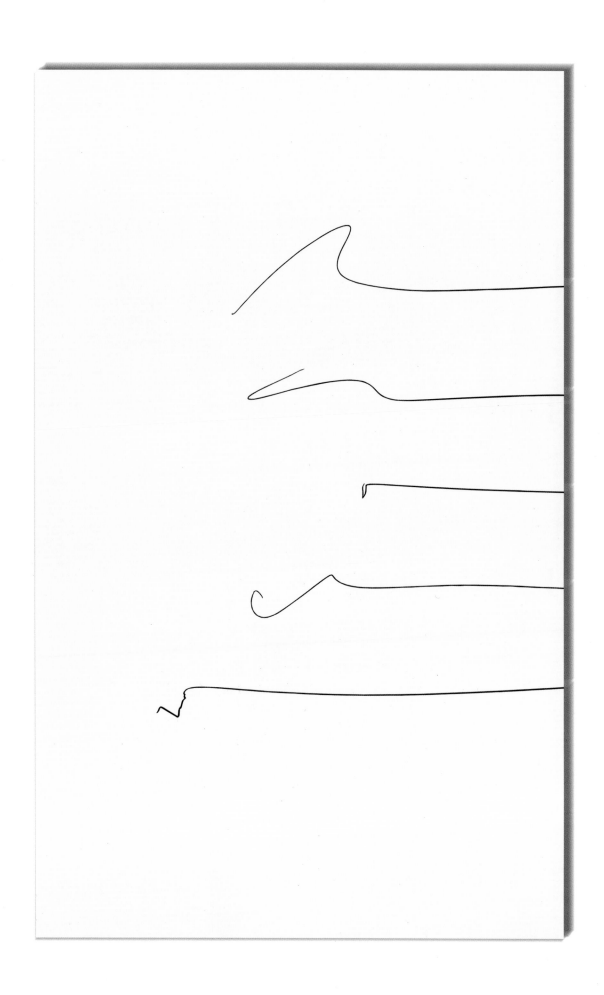

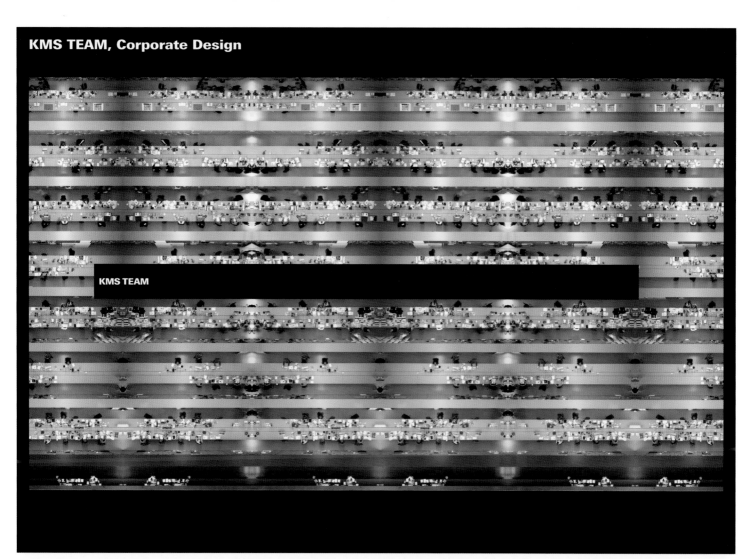

KMS TEAM

KMS TEAM, Corporate Design
Idee

Ganzheitlich denken

Regie führen

Reduktion und Authentizität

Wahrnehmung steuern

In die Tiefe gehen

Idee

Netzwerke bilden

Begegnung

KMS TEAM, Corporate Design
Orientierung

KMS TEAM, Corporate Design
Personalisierte Aufkleber, Paketband

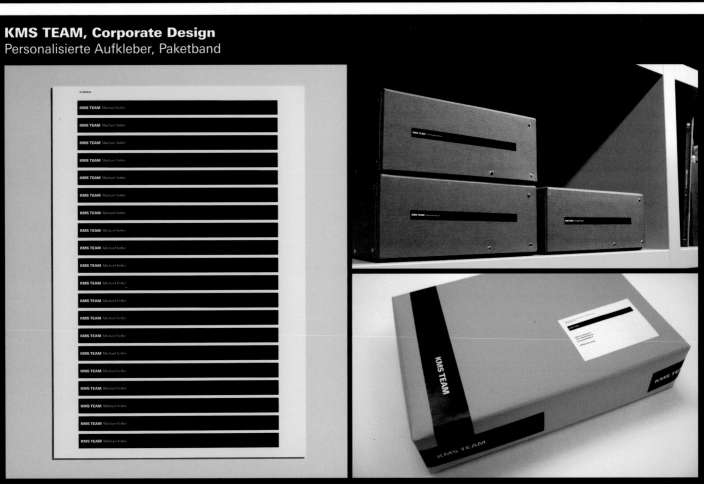

KMS TEAM, Corporate Design
Internetauftritt

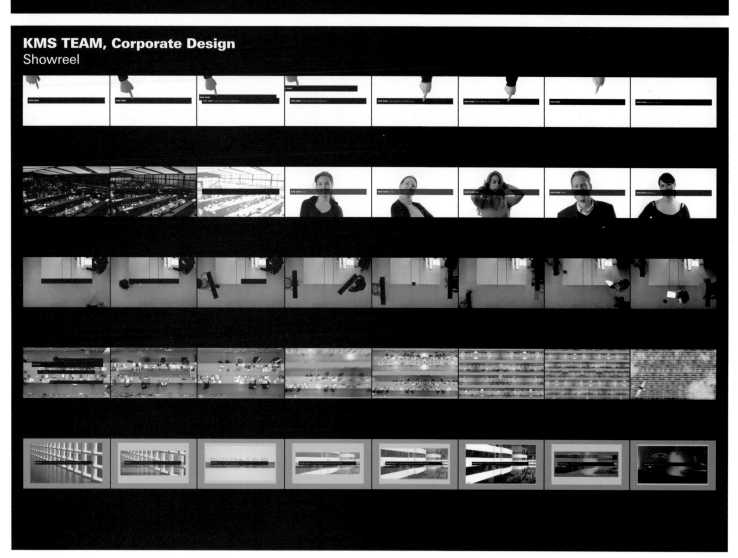

KMS TEAM, Corporate Design
Showreel

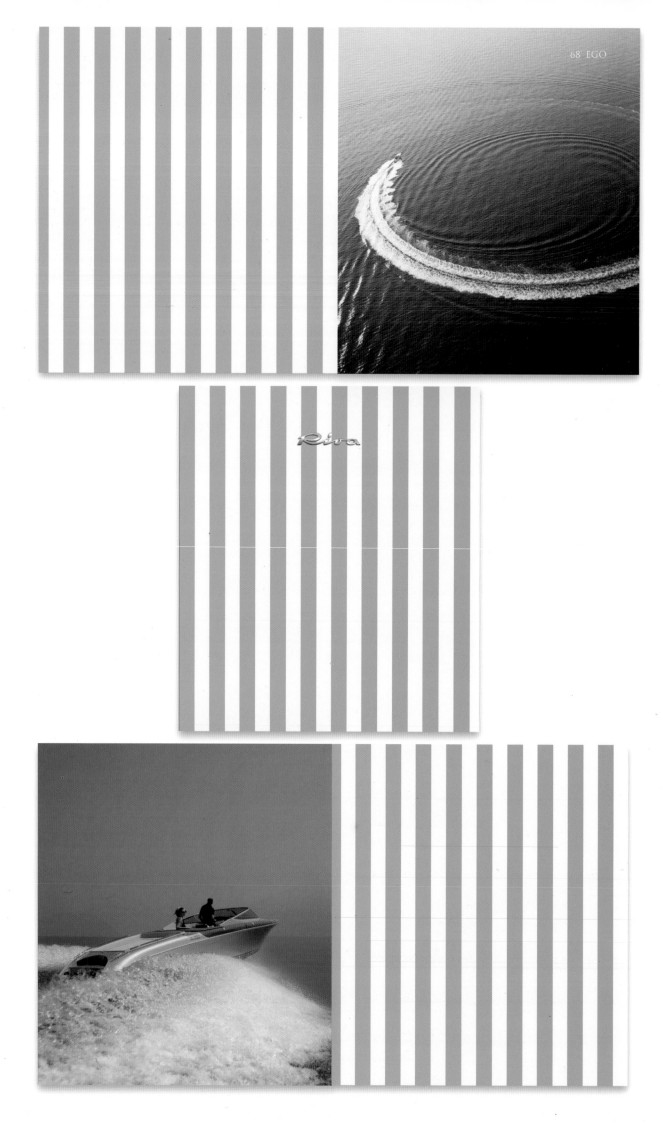

68' EGO

Riva

RIVA SPA - VIA PREDORE 30 - 24067 SARNICO (BG) - WWW.RIVA-YACHT.COM - A FERRETTIGROUP COMPANY
TW2
Riva
SHUTTLE - SUNRIVA - AQUARIVA - RIVARAMA -RIVALE - 63' VERTIGO - 68' EGO - 75' VENERE - 85' OPERA SUPER - 115' ATHENA

BEG¹N

INSP|RE

ACH EVE

A new generation of graduates. consectetuer adipiscing elit. Aenean aliquet, tortor at ali quet mattis, risus eros tempus lacus, vitae varius nulla nibh vel velit. Sed mauris erat, fermentum rhoncus quis, aliquet a, nunc. Morbi pellentesque. Sed faucibus magna ac dui. Duis congue dui. Duis neque pede, euismod vitae, dictum ac, sollicitudin et, diam. Pellentesque habitant morbi tristique senectus et netus.

F¹RST GRADUATE

Tiffany Foster **D&AD**   T+44 (0)20 7840 1138

Michael Hockney D&AD   T+44 (0)20 7840 1112

Leonie Paris D&AD   T+44 (0)20 7840 1122

2008 Honda ACCORD

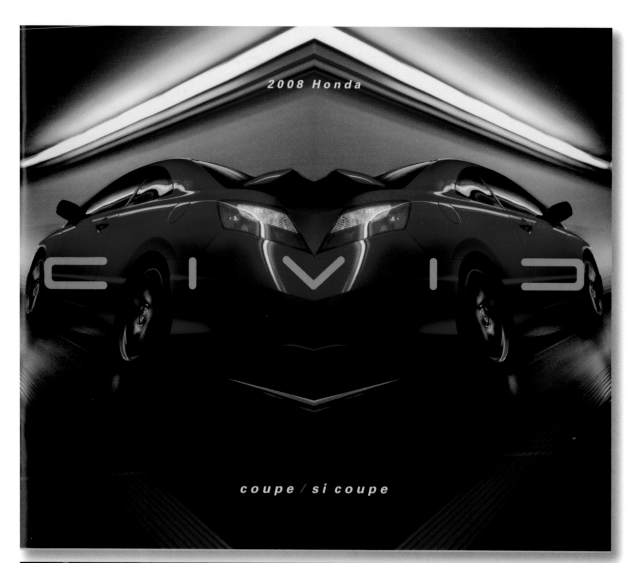

2008 Honda

CIVIC

coupe / si coupe

2008 Honda

CIVIC

sedan / hybrid / si sedan

Eames® Lounge Chair and Ottoman (1956)
Designers: Charles and Ray Eames. With cold vapor for the "warm, receptive, look of a well-used first baseman's mitt," the Eames® back is one of the most significant chairs of the 20th century. This original is as authentic. Fully licensed product of Herman Miller, Inc. Eames is a licensed trademark of Herman Miller, Inc. Ottoman for sit-at-ready and Walnut, priced $3,045–$4,025, as shown. Personalize. Learn more, leather 891.424.94125

For *the* person on your list, give the gift of *the* chair. When approaching the design of a lounge chair, Charles and Ray Eames asked themselves, "Can we make it better?" The result is their iconic Eames® Lounge and Ottoman, which debuted on the *Today* show in 1956. Five decades later, it's still relevant to how we live. Give the gift of Eames.

Design Within Reach
Gifts
Holiday 2007

For every person there is a gift, and not just a gift for one season, but one for all time. The secret these items share is smart design. Each one is unique in how it solves a problem or makes something more comfortable or easier to use. In that way, they're not just objects, but more like tools. Celebrate this season of giving by sharing tools for living.

DESIGN
WITHIN
REACH

5 in Uno Set of Glasses (1970)
Designers: Joe Colombo. Let your table with extra glass having five sizes set of five jewel-like lead crystal glasses that nest together or separate to serve water and liqueur. Never a different glass or more? The glasses, in use, left to right: spirit, wine/water or aperitif/dessert water and liqueur/brandy. Dishwasher safe. Glasses in five sizes. 91.11937 $220/set

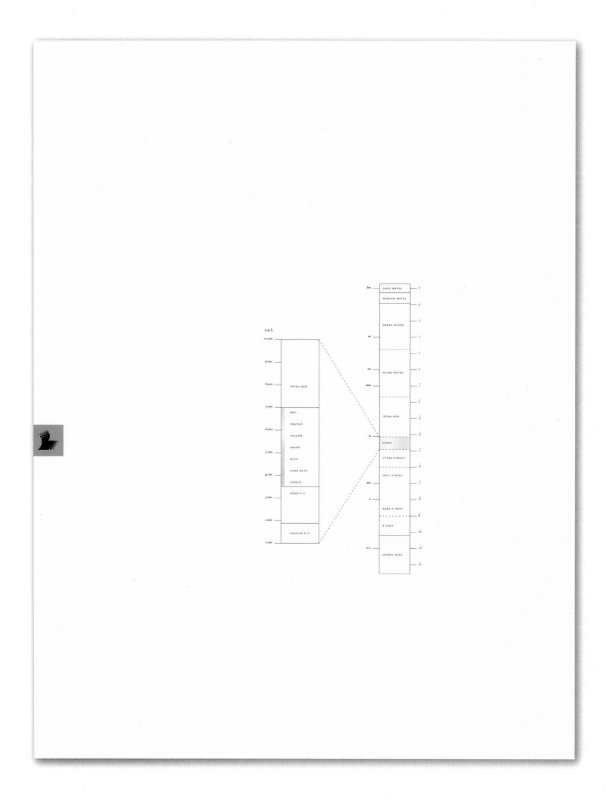

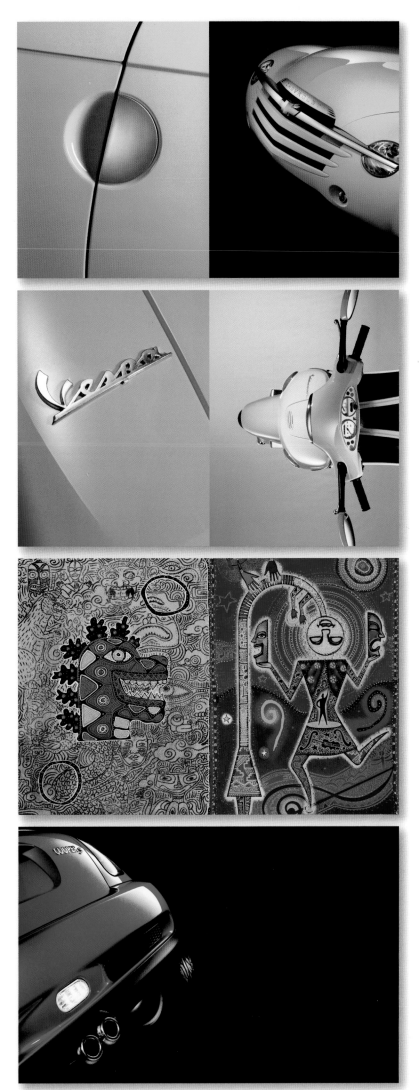

Robert Louey Design (this spread) | Lithographix, Inc. | Brochures **71**

Samsung's ongoing dedication to understanding human desires together with the potentials of digital technology in fulfilling peoples' wants and wishes is what became the concept—and ultimately the realization—of Ultra. We made Ultra tangible by people, and in turn, Ultra became the new dimension of mobile innovations.

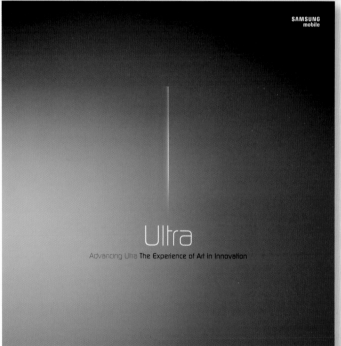

mobile

Ultra

Advancing Ultra **The Experience of Art in Innovation**

The **Ultra** Edition **10.9**

Crown Jewel

The coronation of streamlined and slim:
Shiny reflective LCD screen dazzles while
3.2 mega-pixel camera with auto focus and
other features impress.

SGH-U600

- GSM / GPRS / EDGE
- 850/900/1800/1900 MHz
- 103.2 x 49.3 x 10.9 mm
- 3.2 Megapixel Camera with Auto Focus
- 262144 TFT Screen (2.2", 240 x 320)
- Yahoo Ready Yahoo Search, IM, E-mail
- Smart Search / Smart Editor / Smart Messaging
- VOD / uVideo / uTrack
- Multi-Format Music & Video Support
- Bluetooth Stereo Music Profile (A2DP)
- External Memory: microSD
- External Card Recognition
- Music Library
- Document Viewer

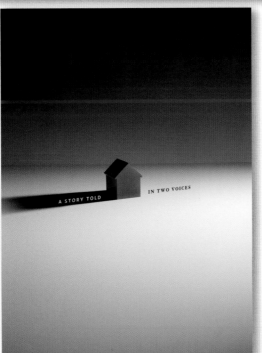

A STORY TOLD   IN TWO VOICES

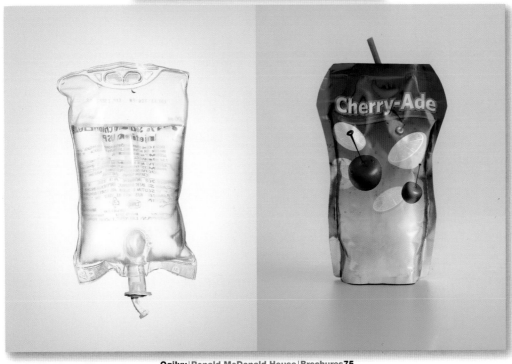

Hear the passion

PREMIER

Welcome to the brave new sound of Pioneer Premier, and welcome to the revolution in how much music is heard. Go where no sound has gone before and experience a world of pure, sublime audio. Evolve and discover a new world of sound.

Don't just hear the music; be it.

PRS Series

Pioneer inspires clarity. Listen to your music as it was intended to be heard with powerful, crystal clear sound. Pioneer's Premier Reference Series (PRS) sound is so precise and detailed, every song can virtually transform into an emotional, live performance right in your drivers' seat. The PRS Series offers the best, optimal sound purity and always maintains more open, smooth and multidimensional sound.

A Series

Pioneer's A Series speakers enrich your music by producing clear, open sound. Experience sublime sound and a powerful performance that surpasses the competition and allows your music to come alive! Extra power handling, reliability and exceptional sound performance made affordable.

sadi

VISIONS

SAMSUNG ART & DESIGN INSTITUTE NEWSLETTER
FALL | WINTER   2006

⑬

Februar

4	11	18	25	mo
5	12	19	26	di
6	13	20	27	mi
7	14	21	28	do
1	8	15	22	29	fr
2	9	16	23		sa
3	10	17	24		so

Juni

mo	2	9	16	23	30
di	3	10	17	24	
mi	4	11	18	25	
do	5	12	19	26	
fr	6	13	20	27	
sa	7	14	21	28	
so	1	8	15	22	29

August

4	11	18	25	mo
5	12	19	26	di
6	13	20	27	mi
7	14	21	28	do
1	8	15	22	29	fr
2	9	16	23	30	sa
3	10	17	24	31	so

Oktober

	6	13	20	27	mo
	7	14	21	28	di
1	8	15	22	29	mi
2	9	16	23	30	do
3	10	17	24	31	fr
4	11	18	25		sa
5	12	19	26		so

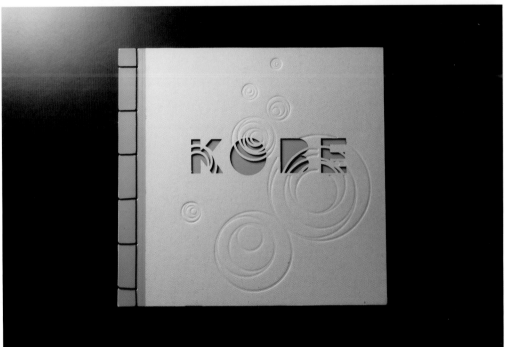

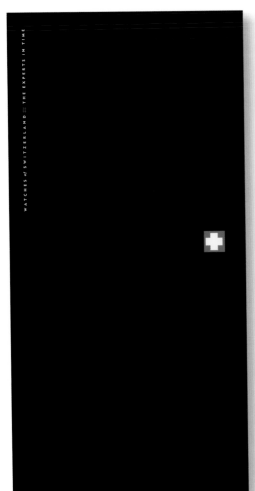

Left: Grand Carrera
Automatic chronograph movement
with unique 'rotating disk' system,
stainless steel case and bracelet,
100m water resistant.
ø 42mm AUD $6,950

TAGHeuer
SWISS AVANT GARDE SINCE 1860

Link
Automatic chronograph movement,
stainless steel case and bracelet,
fixed bezel with tachymetre,
200m water resistant.
ø 42mm AUD $3,950

Carrera Ladies
Automatic movement with date,
stainless steel case and bracelet,
set with 67 diamonds on the dial
and case. Mother of pearl finish
on the dial, 50m water resistant.
ø 27mm AUD $4850

Aquaracer
Calibre 'S' Quartz mechanical
movement, with time, chronograph and
regatta functions, stainless steel case
and bracelet, 200m water resistant.
ø 42mm AUD $3,950

Link
Quartz movement with chronograph
function, stainless steel case and
bracelet, set with 56 diamonds on the
dial and case. Mother of pearl finish
on the dial. 200m water resistant.
ø 33 mm AUD $5,950

she soon discovered that savoir faire was everywhere.

2008/9

● Art Center College of Design

Painting, photography, sculpture, experimental film and video, and installation art—these are all fields that fall into the category of Fine · Art Media. At Art Center, this major is taught by a faculty of artists who exhibit their own work, as well as by visiting artists who conduct workshops. Fine Art Media students can study a broad-based fine art program, or choose between two special tracks, Fine Art Imaging and Photography, and Fine Art Painting/ Illustration. Art Center fosters a fine art environment that encourages growth, risk and the questioning of long-held beliefs about the role of art and the artist in society.

Career Opportunities

Drawing and Painting	3-D Fabrication
Experimental Illustration	Photography
Computer Imaging	Performance Artist
Exhibition Installation	Sculptor
Art Education	Museum Director
Art Therapy	Museum Administrator
Gallery Professional	Curator
Artist's Assistant	Art Historian
Video and Film Editing	

Ashley Landrum, *third term*. Untitled. Instructors: Taft Green, Patrick Hill, Lisa Lapinski

Don Stift, *second term*. "Armario" for the Knoll A3 Office System. Instructors: Karen Hofmann, Norm Schureman

Pengtao Yu, *fourth term*. Freedom Inc. Instructor: Igor Burt

Emi Ishihara, *eighth term*. "Voyage" carrier case for Navigator team project. Instructors: Rob Ball, Lilana Becerra, Todd Belle, Dan Hoy

Jonathan Rowell, *third term*. Teaching Japanese to American children. Instructor: Norm Schureman

The modern product designer is a designer of consumer goods—but also, increasingly, a businessperson or an entrepreneur. At Art Center, we are recognizing and promoting this at exactly the same time that business leaders have acknowledged the importance of good design in corporate success. So while the core mission of the department continues to emphasize that good design can improve lives through a seamless blend of functionality, visual appeal and relevance, we're also expanding our focus. Art Center teaches its Product Design students to develop an entrepreneurial mind-set, which will in turn enable graduates to manage innovation and risk.

Career Opportunities

Consumer Product Design	Automotive Design
Package Design	Model Making
Toy Design	Surface Modeling
Furniture and Lighting Design	Entrepreneur
Exhibition Design	Inventor
Interface Design	Trend Researcher/Forecaster
Entertainment Design	

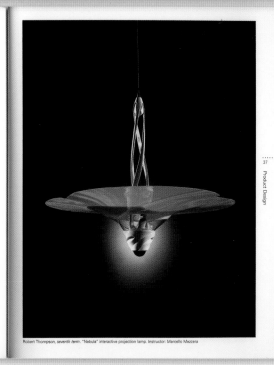

Robert Thompson, *seventh term*. "Nebula" interactive projection lamp. Instructor: Marcello Mezzera

miu miu

過去にもNYやLONDONで発表した経験をもつ、ミュウミュウが今回初めてパリ・コレに参加。"パリっぽさ"を意識した今シーズン、マイクロミニのフレアスカートを基調にした、少し大人びたコケティッシュな女性像を打ち出しました。ぐっとシックになったミュウミュウは今シーズンもトレンド満載です。

ニットのグローブが新鮮!

今シーズンは
マイクロミニにチャレンジ!

夏に引き続きハーフパンツで
キュートなスーツスタイル。

人気のバッグは
ちょっとかっちり目で大人っぽく。

18   19

2006
Galaxy
A/W
COLLECTION

Galaxy men

BALENCIAGA
McQUEEN
JOHN GALLIANO
DOLCE & GABBANA
DSQUARED²
DRIES VAN NOTEN

nylon month_and_year_page
what's up _mania_that's on

good t

BALENCIAGA

今シーズンはニコラゲスキュエールの集大成とでも言うべく、ベストシーズンと呼んでも過言ではない程出来が良いです。品のいいジャケット・コートをはじめ、細身でシャープなシルエットは着ると必ず欲しくなる。そして、シンプルなデザイン故に飽きもこない逸品ばかり。"イチオシ"です!

カジュアルを品良く着こなす
お手本です。

細身のシルエットは
それだけでカッコイイ!欲しい一着。

未だ衰えることのない
人気のバレンシアガのバッグ。
新色も要チェックです。

22   23

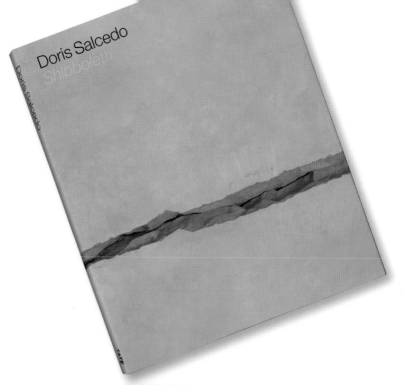

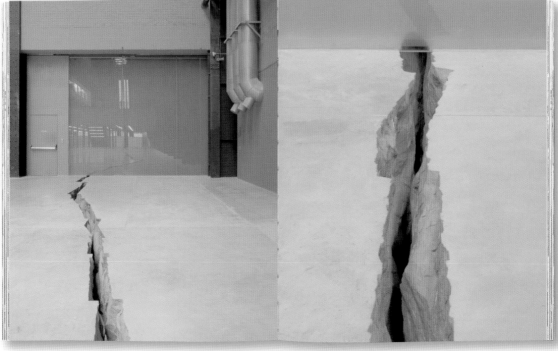

07

BEDDING

Cover up with unison's quilts and duvets.
Inspired by linear forms and patterns, unison bedding complements the contemporary home.

MARTIN DUVET
TATAMI DUVET
PINSTRIPE DUVET
TRACK QUILT
WIDEBAND QUILT

RAISIN B02008
ROYAL B02009
SLATE B02010

Duvets
Twin Duvet 68x88 $120
Queen Duvet 90x94 $142
King Duvet 106x94 $164

Pillowcases
Twin Pillowcase 20x28 (2) $28
Queen Pillowcase 20x32 (2) $33
King Pillowcase 20x32 (2) $38

Sheets
Twin Fitted + Flat $108
Full Fitted + Flat $128
Queen Fitted + Flat $142
King Fitted + Flat $164

Snap closure duvet
100% cotton percale
220 thread count
Made in Portugal

10

PINSTRIPE DUVET

Parallel lines in rhythm. Suits traditional or modern tastes.

MARTIN DUVET

A minimalist's dream come true. Understated stripes with a calming effect. Snap closures for ease and a clean look.

Queen Duvet 90x94 $64
King Duvet 106x84 $74

Snap closure
100% cotton percale
220 thread count
Made in Portugal

Queen Pillowcase 20x32 (2) $15
King Pillowcase 20x38 (2) $17

100% cotton percale
220 thread count
Made in Portugal

CITRUS B01005
LILAC B01006
SKY BLUE B01007

5

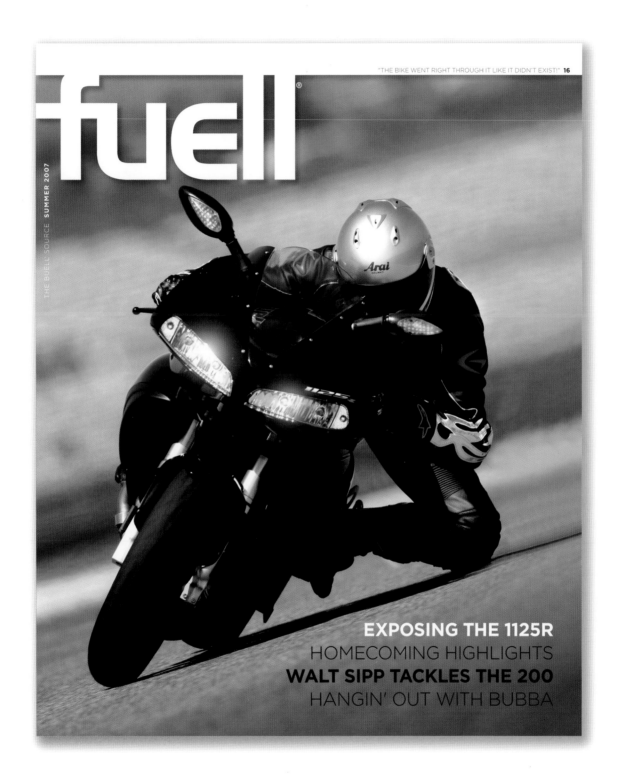

fuell ®

THE BUELL SOURCE **SUMMER 2007**

EXPOSING THE 1125R
HOMECOMING HIGHLIGHTS
WALT SIPP TACKLES THE 200
HANGIN' OUT WITH BUBBA

DOT Magazine 15

Issue 015

● Art Center College of Design

"This photo was an exercise in lighting technique and finesse. The key to this shot was timing. The olive entering the gin had to be synchronized with the release of the shutter."

"Producing this image to satisfy my artistic vision would not have been possible without my friends. Once friends and I built this room in my backyard and attached the yard hose to a fire sprinkler, the fun began. When I developed the film I had a fantastic realization that I would be a photographer for the rest of my life."

"'Depotting' is a condensed urban community experience that promotes Metro ridership by offering an onboard valet of goods and services in addition to choice among public and private spaces."

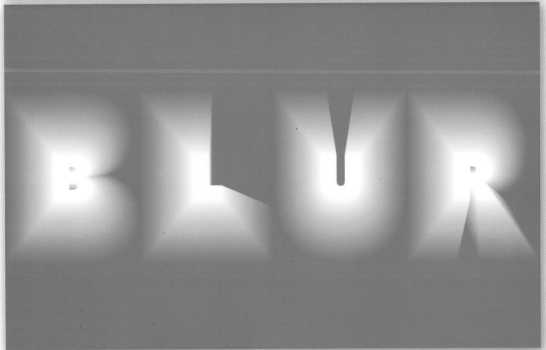

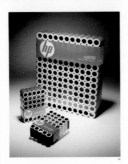

"Soccer is the world's most popular sport. It connects people around the globe and overcomes many of the prevalent economic, cultural, social and religious barriers. I created this piece in a week-long workshop led by Art Center's visionary in residence, Rene Muis of Studio 75B, which took place around the same time as the World Cup."

"Our team set out to reinvent Hewlett-Packard's packaging by positioning HP as a friendly technology company that recognizes its customers' desire for a personal computing experience."

"Images don't act neutrally within the spaces we receive them. Critical awareness of these interactions of meaning is the only way to avoid passive reception of their influence."

"To affect a surface by its meeting with another plane, and the collision of this meeting reverberating indefinitely in all directions. In terms of forces like these, something like a lie is as tangible as a structure's foundation and yet can make that structure disappear."

THE TWO JAKES

BY
MARSHALL
SELLA

PHOTOGRAPHS
BY
NATHANIEL
GOLDBERG

JAKE

— SURE, THERE'S THE AFFABLE, CHARMING YOUNG ACTOR WHOSE —
NAME CROPS UP EVERY NOW AND THEN IN THE GOSSIP PAGES.
AND THEN THERE'S THIS OTHER GUY, THE ONE WHO'S
A LITTLE... *DARKER*. HE'S MUCH MORE INTERESTING

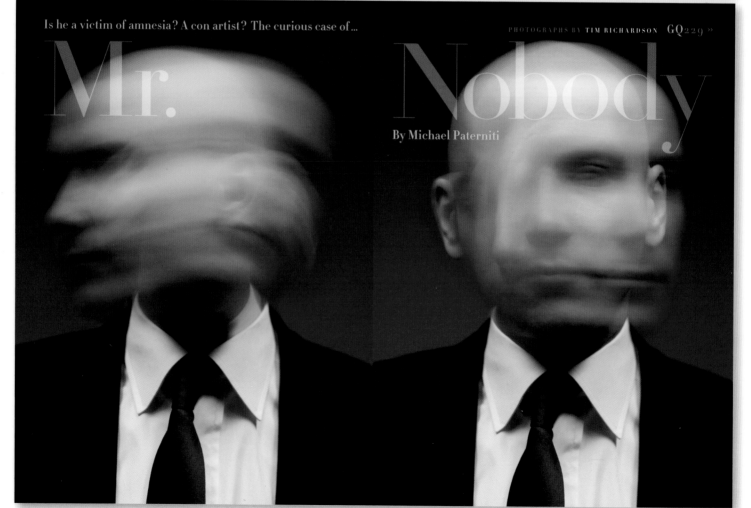

Is he a victim of amnesia? A con artist? The curious case of...

Mr. Nobody

By Michael Paterniti

FOR TWENTY YEARS,
FROM 'EMPIRE OF THE SUN'
TO 'BATMAN BEGINS'
TO HIS NEW FILM,
THE INTENSE AND
PHYSICALLY GRUELING
'RESCUE DAWN,'
CHRISTIAN BALE
HAS BEEN FANATIC
ABOUT HIS
PRIVACY.

GQ
MARCH
274

NOW HE SPEAKS
ABOUT HIS TERROR OF FEELING
"NUMB BEYOND BELIEF,"
THE CHILDHOOD THAT MADE HIM
A "TURBULENCE ADDICT,"
AND THE WEIRDNESS
(JUST ASK HIS WIFE)
OF HIS LIFE BEING TAKEN OVER
BY HIS VERY DARK CHARACTERS

PHOTOGRAPHS BY
NATHANIEL GOLDBERG

162
05-07-GQ

THE GQ PRESIDENTIAL CANDIDATE QUESTIONNAIRE

THE **REAL**
COLBERT REPORT

Let's face it: This country needs a president. And only one man
is fit for the job. The guy you're looking at: Comedy Central pundit
STEPHEN COLBERT. But to be sure that he possesses the moral
authority America so desperately needs, we subjected him
to a highly confidential background check. Then, because we
are the media and have no morals, we decided to betray his
trust and publish his answers

SECTION 1: Candidate Information

1. (a) Last Name   (b) First Name

COLBERT   STEPHEN

2. (a) Office Sought

PRESIDENT OF THE UNITED STATES

(b) Year of Election   3. Photographs by Mark Seliger

2008

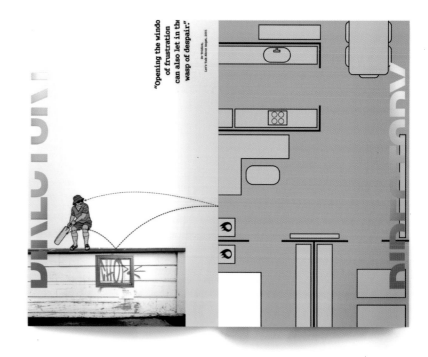

"Opening the windo[w]
of frustration
can also let in th[e]
wasp of despair."

DIRECTORY

DIALOGUE

CLIENT
Tourism Australia

Product
Business Events

Title
Re-energise

Media
Mail, online, podcast, email

Country
Australia

Date
May 2007

BACKGROUND

IDEA

RESULTS

EDITOR'S COMMENTS

AGENCY
M&C Saatchi / Mark, Australia

Creative team
Gavin McLeod
Shane Bradnick
Gavin McLeod
Art Director
Dustin Lane, Dave King, George Show
Copywriters

Production
Josephina Parella
Producer

Other
Kimberlee Wells
Eleni Pelosi, Lara Walsh
Client Service

CLIENT
Terra Spain

Product
Internet Portal

Title
Terra Fighters 2007

Media
Mail

Country
Spain

Date
January 2007 – ongoing

BACKGROUND

IDEA

RESULTS

EDITOR'S COMMENTS

AGENCY
OgilvyOne worldwide
Madrid, Spain

Creative team
Javier Arias
Creative Director
Gerardo Fontanes
Art Director
David Pinel
Copywriter
Marta Gamboa and Celia Martinez
Designers

Production
Yolanda Martin

|DVR| magazine for visual relations |0|

OUT OF SPACE:
PHOUT OF SPACE:PHY
PHOUT OF SPACE:PHY
ANANOUT OF SPACE:PHOTOGRAPHY
SC SC PHOTOGRAPHY
IMAGINATION AND THE
IMAGINATION SCULPTURAL
IMAGINATION

Essay by Susan Edelstein

Out of Space:
Photography
and the
Sculptural
Imagination

A Dazibao Intervention

PREFIX PHOTO

A Publication of Prefix Institute of Contemporary Art

Prefix
Photo
15:
Spectral
Light

HI-SPEED MAGAZINE

LONDON · LOS ANGELES

www.hi-speedmag.com

Big

KNIGHT
VISION

Photography
NICK KNIGHT

Big | 124

SPIN
THE
BOTTLE

PB&J FOR DINNER? PIZZA? MAC AND CHEESE? IF YOU CAN'T THINK OF A GOOD
WINE TO SERVE, YOU NEED TO TALK TO JOSHUA WESSON. BY JENNA SCHNUER.
PHOTOGRAPH BY STEVE MOORS. ILLUSTRATIONS BY JONNY HANNAH.

JULY 1 2007 AMERICAN WAY 63

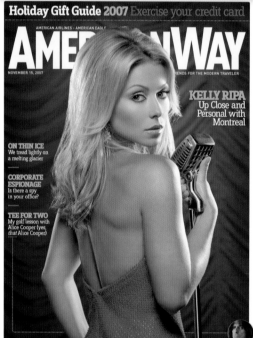

Holiday Gift Guide 2007 Exercise your credit card

AMERICAN AIRLINES · AMERICAN EAGLE

AMERICANWAY

NOVEMBER 15, 2007   TRENDS FOR THE MODERN TRAVELER

KELLY RIPA
Up Close and
Personal with
Montreal

ON THIN ICE
We tread lightly on
a melting glacier

CORPORATE
ESPIONAGE
Is there a spy
in your office?

TEE FOR TWO
My golf lesson with
Alice Cooper (yes,
that Alice Cooper)

ENRIQUE

INSOMNE DE
ALTOS VUELOS

DE ENRIQUE IGLESIAS SE
HA DICHO MUCHO. GRAN
PARTE RELACIONADO
CON SU PADRE, EL
TROVADOR MELÓDICO Y
ETERNO MUJERIEGO,
JULIO IGLESIAS. QUE SI
NO SE HABLAN. QUE SI
SON RIVALES. QUE SI VAN
A CANTAR JUNTOS. EN
OTRAS OCASIONES EL
NOMBRE DEL JOVEN
IGLESIAS HACE PAREJA
JUNTO AL DE SU AMOR,
LA TENISTA ANNA
KOURNIKOVA, CON QUIEN
LA PRENSA COSA LE HA
CASADO TANTAS VECES COMO
LE HA DADO HIJOS. Y TAMBIÉN
HAY VECES EN LAS QUE SU
NOMBRE APARECE EN
SOLITARIO ASOCIADO CON EL
ÉXITO: 40 MILLONES DE
COPIAS VENDIDAS EN
TODO EL MUNDO.

ESCRITO POR: ROCÍO AYUSO

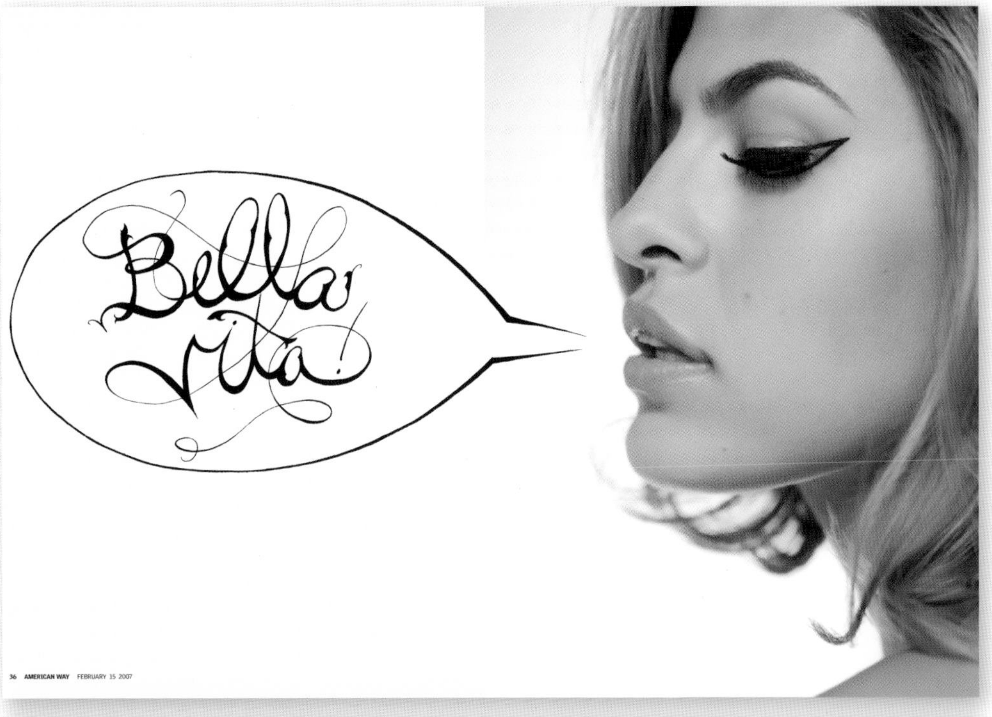
Bella vita!
36 AMERICAN WAY FEBRUARY 15 2007

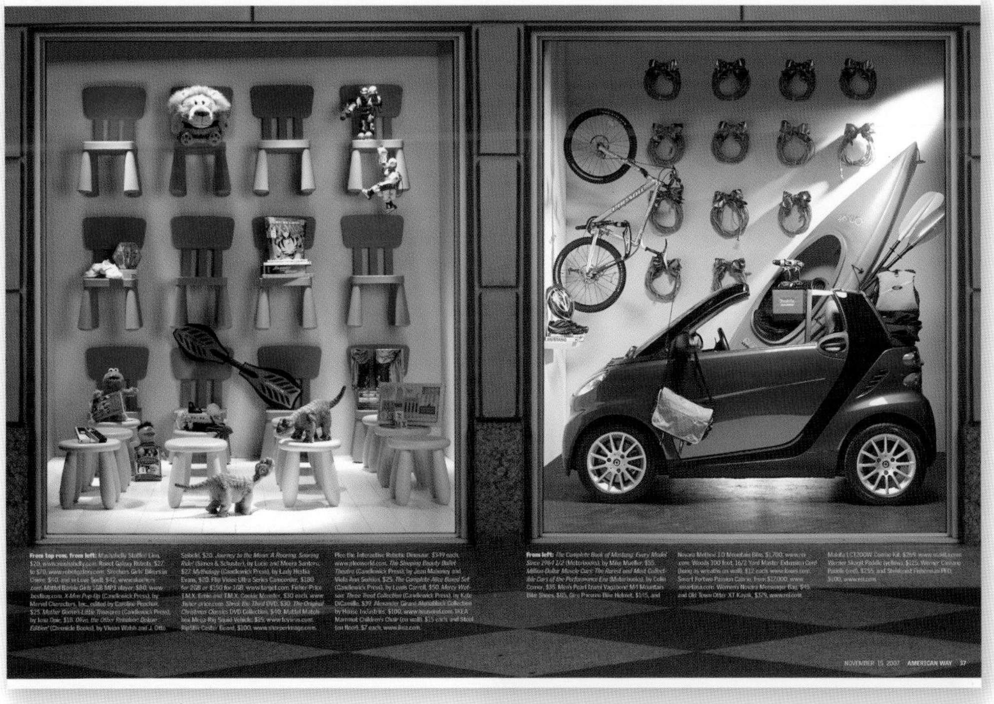
NOVEMBER 15 2007 AMERICAN WAY 37

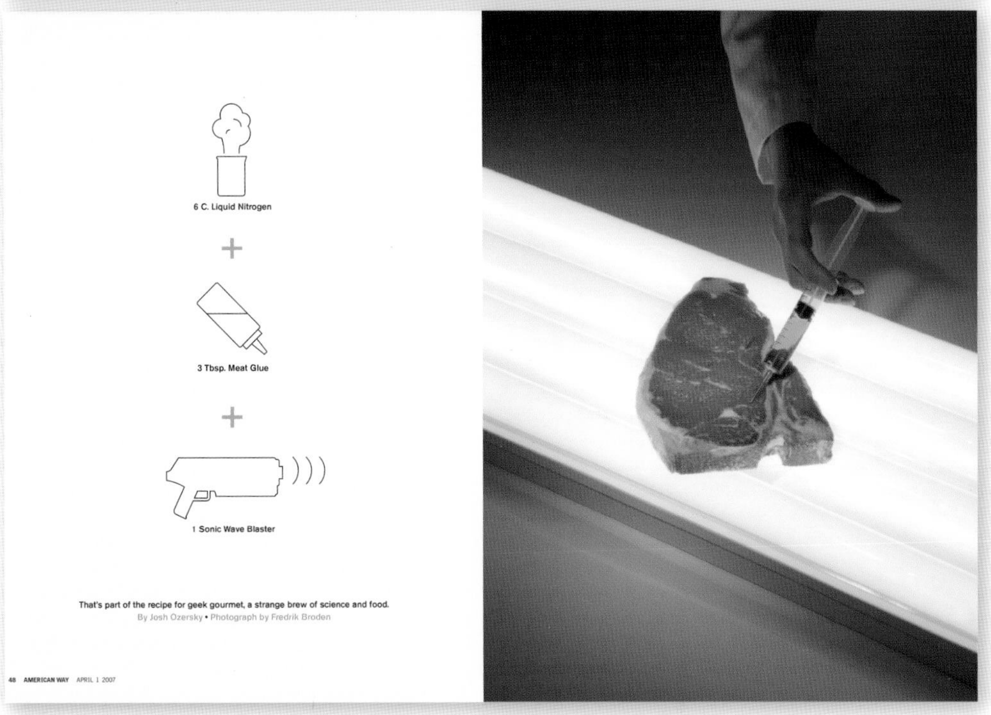
6 C. Liquid Nitrogen
+
3 Tbsp. Meat Glue
+
1 Sonic Wave Blaster
That's part of the recipe for geek gourmet, a strange brew of science and food.
By Josh Ozersky • Photograph by Fredrik Broden
48 AMERICAN WAY APRIL 1 2007

NE⊘2

CREATIVE
GENEORATION
Diciembre 07
+ Enero 08
3€ (Spain)

Austria: 5,15€
Canada: 10,25$Can
England: 4£
España: 3€
France: 6€
Germany: 7,50€
Italy: 4,13€
Mexico: 45P
Morocco: 60Mad
Switzerland: 10Fs
Tahiti: 840 FF
USA: 5?

ESPECIAL
Snow
GENERATION

LÓBULA FREE FONT TIPOGRAFÍA DE REGALO
Tecno Gadgets
DOVER SISTERS
Juliette Lewis
TENDENCIA DEL MES:
EXPLOSION
TRANSFORMER

00069

9 771138 562005

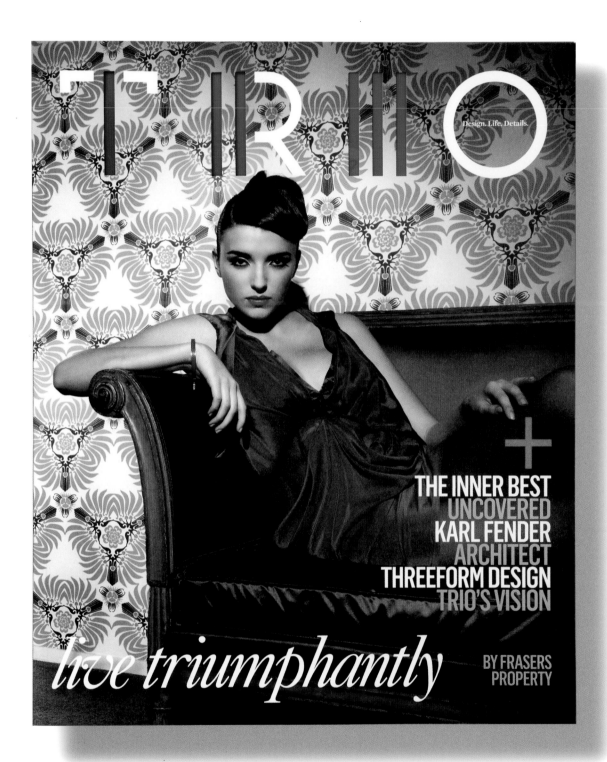

TRIO

Design. Life. Details.

+

THE INNER BEST
UNCOVERED
KARL FENDER
ARCHITECT
THREEFORM DESIGN
TRIO'S VISION

live triumphantly

BY FRASERS
PROPERTY

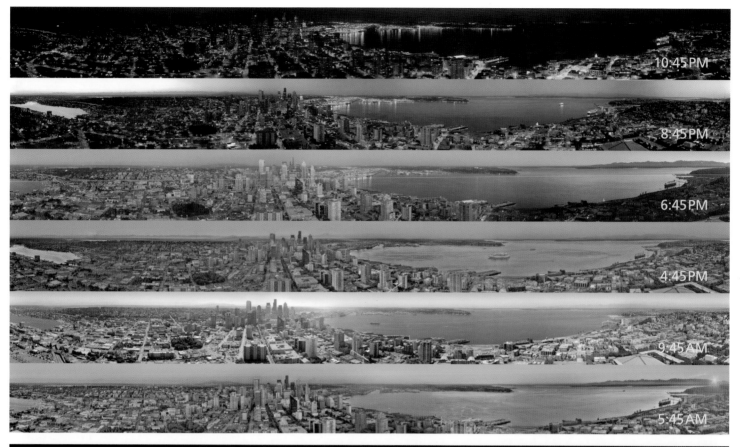

10:45 PM

8:45 PM

6:45 PM

4:45 PM

9:45 AM

5:45 AM

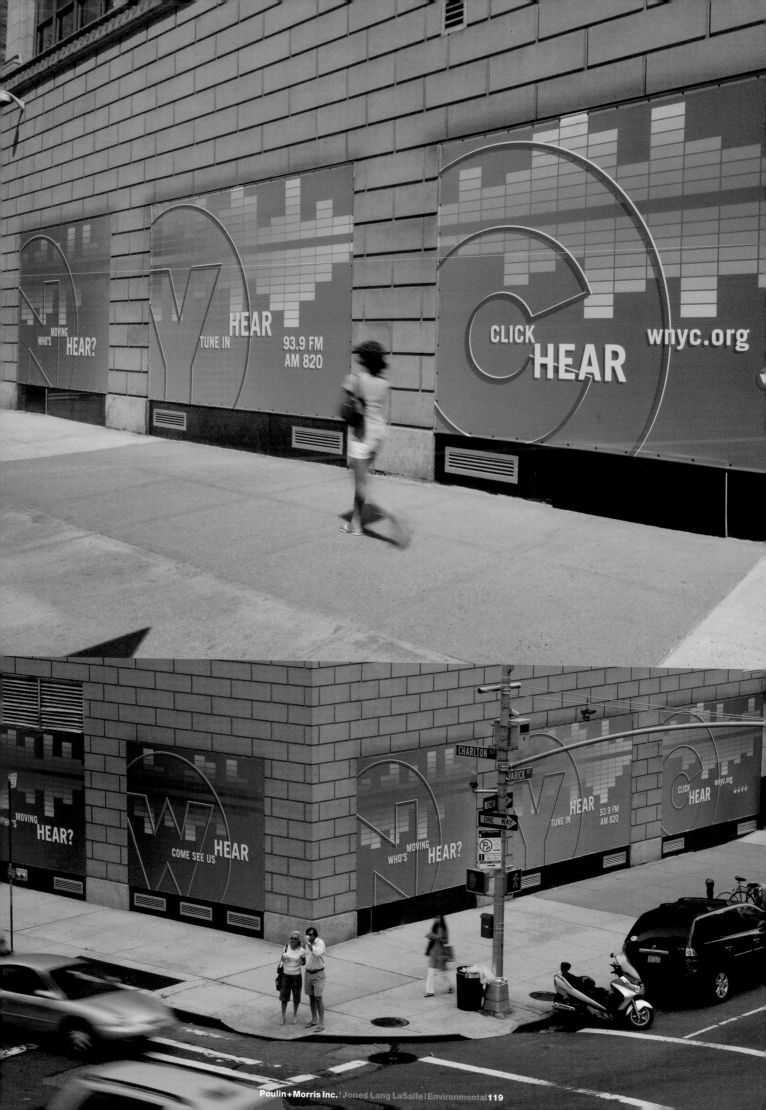

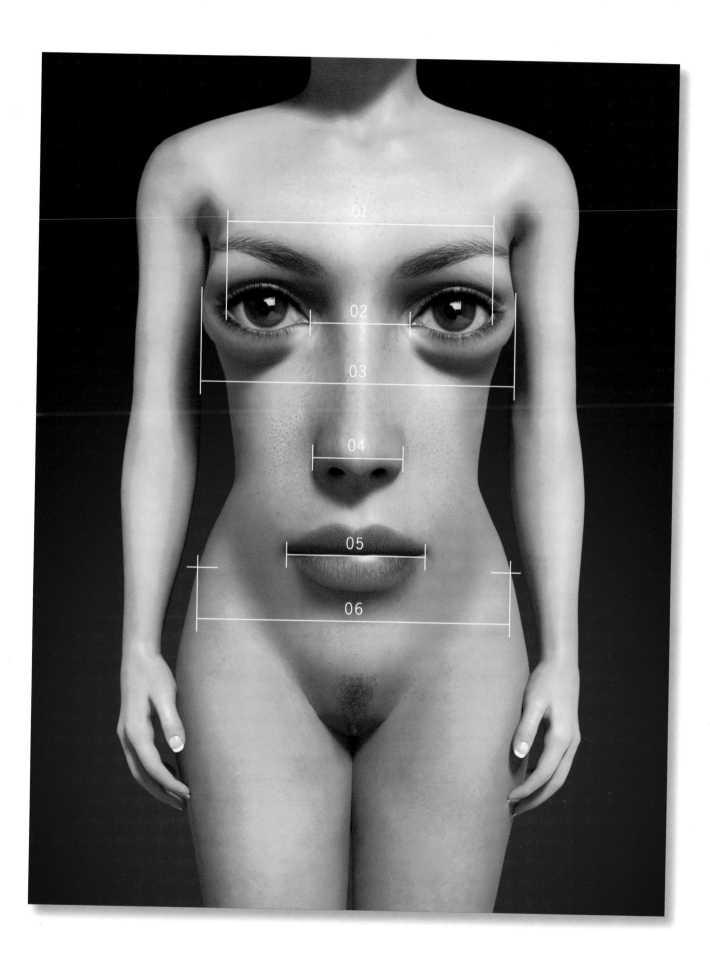

level. vodka
beyond smooth, from Absolut

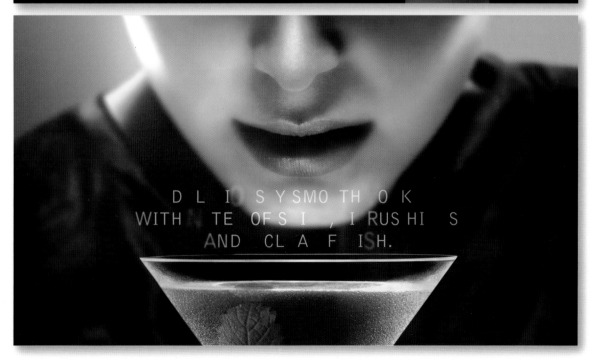

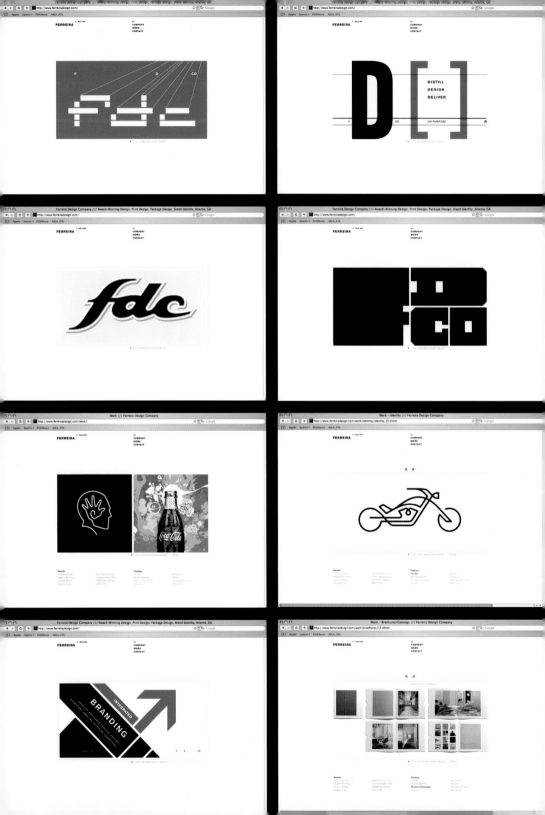

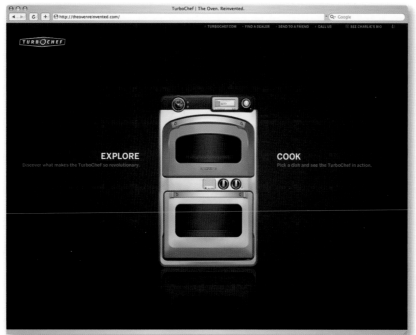

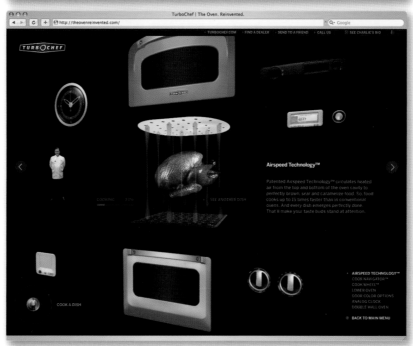

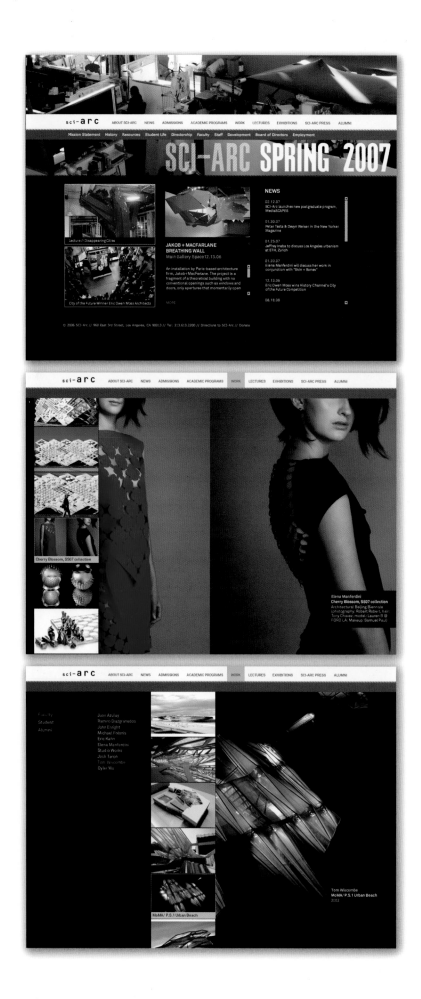

Are You New to ColorCore?

What's New With ColorCore?

Replay intro   Download screensaver Mac PC

OVERVIEW
WHAT'S NEW
FEATURES & BENEFITS
POSTFORMABLE
COLORS & FINISHES

ColorCore 2 SOLID COLOR LAMINATES *from* FORMICA CORPORATION

FULL-LINE   GALLERY   PLAY

The Greenguard Indoor Air Quality certified mark is a certification mark used under the license through the Greenguard Environmental Institute.
Formica Corporation is an official member of the US Green Building Council.
Privacy Statement
©2007 Formica Corporation All Rights Reserved

Postformable

ColorCore®2 is now postformable! This means that the material is now flexible enough to allow you other viable edge treatment options.

squared

beveled

postformed

postformed backsplash

full-line
ARE YOU NEW
WHAT'S NEW
FEATURES & BENEFITS
POSTFORMABLE
COLORS & FINISHES   GALLERY   PLAY THE GAME

ColorCore 2 SOLID COLOR LAMINATES *from* FORMICA CORPORATION

The Greenguard Indoor Air Quality certified mark is a certification mark used under the license through the Greenguard Environmental Institute.
Formica Corporation is an official member of the US Green Building Council.
Privacy Statement
©2007 Formica Corporation All Rights Reserved

< >

full-line
ARE YOU NEW
WHAT'S NEW
FEATURES & BENEFITS
POSTFORMABLE
COLORS & FINISHES   GALLERY   PLAY THE GAME

ColorCore 2 SOLID COLOR LAMINATES *from* FORMICA CORPORATION

The Greenguard Indoor Air Quality certified mark is a certification mark used under the license through the Greenguard Environmental Institute.
Formica Corporation is an official member of the US Green Building Council.
Privacy Statement
©2007 Formica Corporation All Rights Reserved

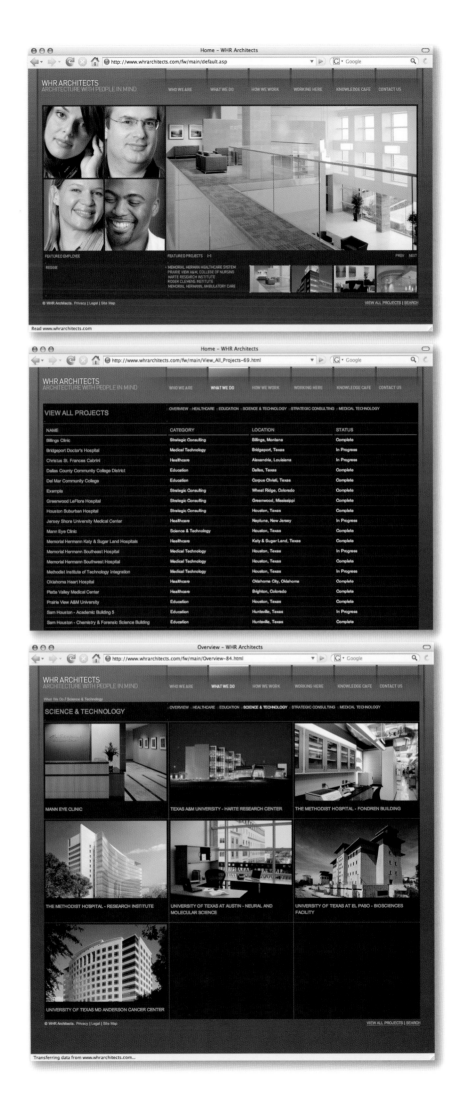

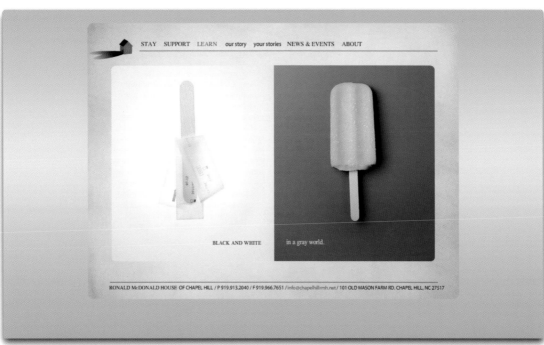

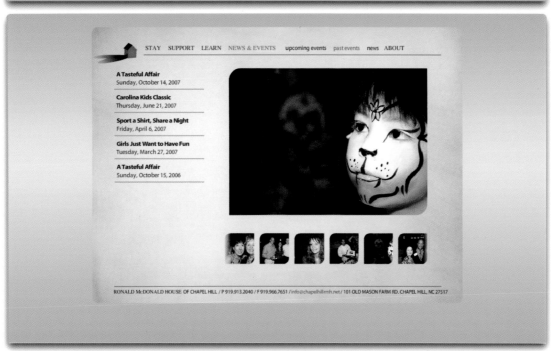

STROUD WAS FAMOUS FOR CLOTH OF EXCEPTIONAL QUALITY. AMONG THEM THE FAMOUS STROUD SCARLET Stroud scarlet clothed the Redcoats who fought rebellious American colonists; the Redcoats of Wellington's army who saw off Napoleon at Waterloo and it clothed the detachment of Welshmen who fought the battle of Rorke's Drift.

THANKFULLY, in more peaceful times there is enough *red* cloth left to keep Santa Claus warm this Christmas.

————

Season's Greetings and Best Wishes for the New Year from Jane, Glenn, Lauren and Leon at High Beeches.

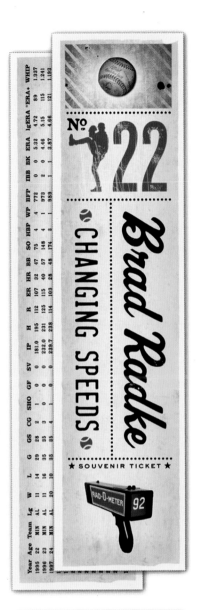

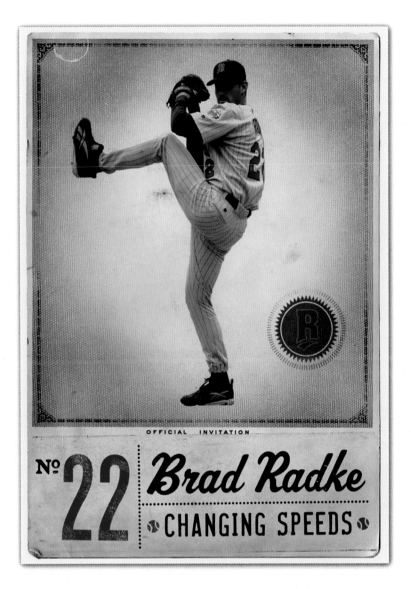

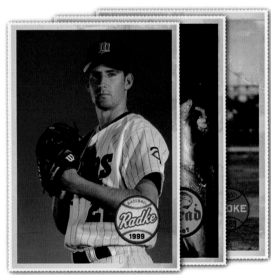

FRIDAY, MARCH 9, 2007

TIME WARNER CABLE and the AUSTIN FILM SOCIETY present the
2007 TEXAS FILM HALL OF FAME AWARDS
a tribute to ANN RICHARDS

austin studios STAGE 2, COCKTAILS, DINNER and AWARDS SHOW

2007 honorees ELIZABETH AVELLÁN, BETTY BUCKLEY,
RICHARD LINKLATER, ANN-MARGRET and BILL PAXTON
presenters ELLEN BURSTYN and JULIE DELPY, emcee LIZ SMITH
with special guests LILY TOMLIN and ANNA DEAVERE SMITH

presenting sponsor **TIME WARNER**
CABLE
Digital Phone
amd live! soundtrack award sponsor AMD
preferred principal sponsor PUBLIC STRATEGIES, INC.
tiffany & co. star of texas award TIFFANY & CO.

DAUGHTER.

MOTHER.

GRANDMOTHER.

GOVERNOR.

FILM AMBASSADOR.

BIKER CHICK.

GET WRANGLED INTO A GOOD TIME
FRIDAY **MARCH 9**TH 2007
AT THE ⟩NINTH⟨ ANNUAL
MAKE-A-WISH FOUNDATION
BLUE JEAN BALL
★ AT THE LIVESTOCK EXCHANGE BUILDING ★
4920 SO. 30TH ST. OMAHA, NEBRASKA
JOIN HONORARY CHAIRMEN GARY & CAROL PERKINS
FOR AN ALL-FIRED GOOD TIME
⟩GUEST SPEAKER: BREANNA GUTHARD⟨
EVENING EVENTS:
6:30
WET YER WHISTLE & BID DURING THE SILENT AUCTION
8:00
HOW FOLLOWED BY PROGRAM & ORAL AUCTION
TAY A SPELL AND MOVE YER BOOTS
O THE KICKIN' COUNTRY SOUNDS OF
★★★ **TAMI HALL** ★★★
BAR AVAILABLE THROUGHOUT T

RE: | COST:
& | $125 PER PERSON
EES | $40 FAIR MARKET VALUE

MAKE A WISH
BLUE JEAN BALL
2007
FOREVER IN BLUE JEANS

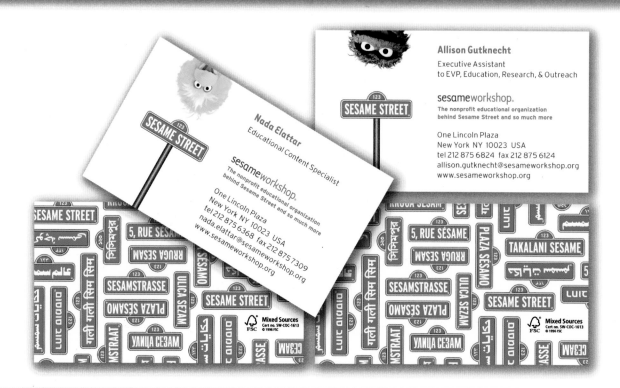

Nada Elattar
Educational Content Specialist

sesameworkshop.
The nonprofit educational organization
behind Sesame Street and so much more

One Lincoln Plaza
New York NY 10023 USA
tel 212 875 6368 fax 212 875 7309
nada.elattar@sesameworkshop.org
www.sesameworkshop.org

FSC **Mixed Sources**
Cert no. SW-COC-1613
© 1996 FSC

Allison Gutknecht
Executive Assistant
to EVP, Education, Research, & Outreach

sesameworkshop.
The nonprofit educational organization
behind Sesame Street and so much more

One Lincoln Plaza
New York NY 10023 USA
tel 212 875 6824 fax 212 875 6124
allison.gutknecht@sesameworkshop.org
www.sesameworkshop.org

FSC **Mixed Sources**
Cert no. SW-COC-1613
© 1996 FSC

One Lincoln Plaza
New York, NY 10023 USA
tel 212 595 3456
www.sesameworkshop.org

One Lincoln Plaza
New York, NY 10023 USA
tel 212 595 3456
www.sesameworkshop.org

sesameworkshop.
**The nonprofit educational organization
behind Sesame Street and so much more**

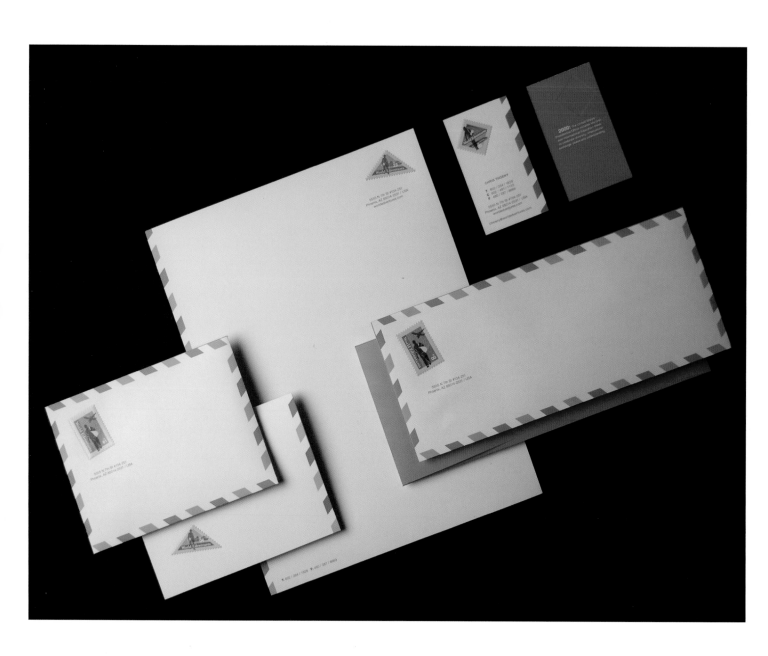

Catapult Strategic Design | City of Phoenix
Brand Envy | Akasha Restaurant
Ogilvy | D'Ambrosio
A3 Design | Bryant & Duffey Optometrist
Graphics & Designing Inc. | World Co., Ltd. | Logos **148**

Hershey|Cause|Hershey|Cause
Sibley/Peteet Design|El Pato Fresh Mexican Food
Graphics & Designing Inc.|Tokyo Good Idea Development Institute Co.,
Catapult Strategic Design|PrismaGraphic Corp.
Jan Šabach|Unilever|Logos**151**

RBMM | Drum Room
RBMM | Dallas Legal Foundation
RBMM | Antler Ranch
RBMM | Lakewood Child Development Center
RBMM | Lobo Tortilla Factory | Logos **152**

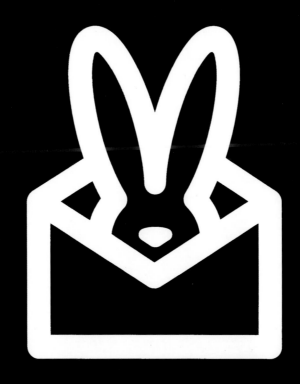

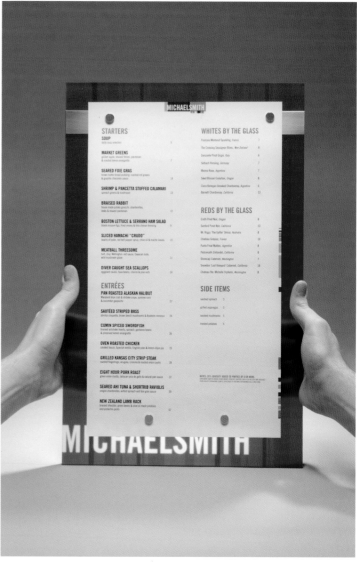

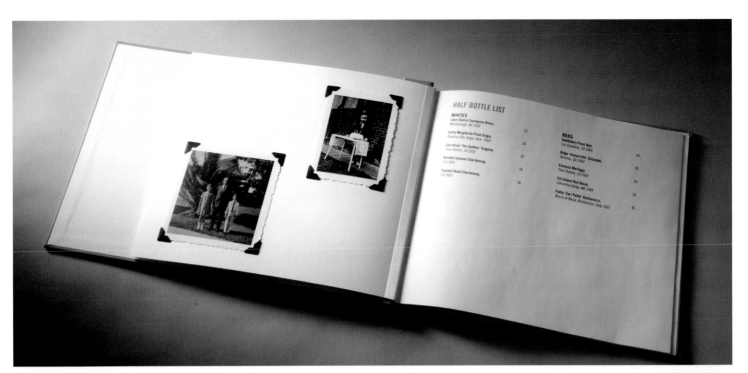

HALF BOTTLE LIST

WHITES
Lake Chalice Sauvignon Blanc,
Marlboro, NZ 2006

Santa Margherita Pinot Grigio,   21
Trentino-Alto Adige, Italy 2004

Carrotton 'The Saothar' Viognier,   34
Paso Robles, CA 2005

Kendall Jackson Chardonnay,   32
CA 2005

Toasted Head Chardonnay,   18
CA 2005
                                                   18

REDS
Sanctuary Pinot Noir,
Los Carneros, CA 2004

Ridge 'Geyserville' Zinfandel,   26
Sonoma, CA 2004

Estancia Meritage,   32
Paso Robles, CA 2004

Col Solare Red Blend,   30
Columbia Valley, WA 1999

Paitin 'Sori Paitin' Barbaresco,   52
Bricco di Neive, Barbaresco, Italy 2001   45

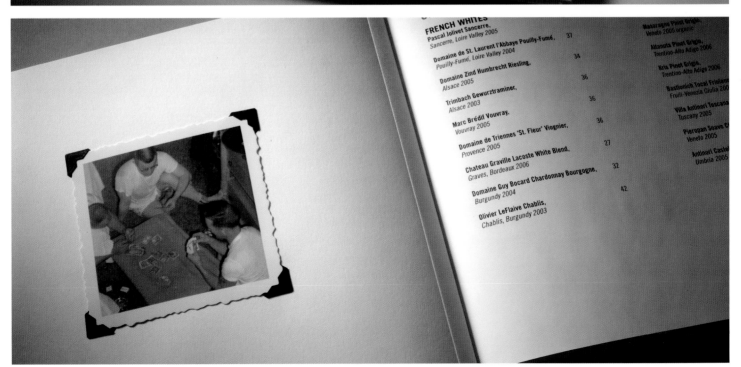

FRENCH WHITES
Pascal Jolivet Sancerre,
Sancerre, Loire Valley 2005

Domaine de St. Laurent l'Abbaye Pouilly-Fumé,   37
Pouilly-Fumé, Loire Valley 2004
                                                   34
Domaine Zind Humbrecht Riesling,
Alsace 2005   36

Trimbach Gewurztraminer,
Alsace 2003   36

Marc Brédif Vouvray,
Vouvray 2005   36

Domaine de Triennes 'St. Fleur' Viognier,
Provence 2005   27

Chateau Graville Lacoste White Blend,
Graves, Bordeaux 2006   32

Domaine Guy Bocard Chardonnay Bourgogne,
Burgundy 2004   42

Olivier LeFlaive Chablis,
Chablis, Burgundy 2003

Masaraona Pinot Grigio,
Veneto 2005 organic

Attanota Pinot Grigio,
Trentino-Alto Adige 2006

Kris Pinot Grigio,
Trentino-Alto Adige 2006

Bastionich Tocai Friulano,
Fruili-Venezia Giulia 2005

Villa Antinori Toscana,
Tuscany 2005

Pieropan Soave C
Veneto 2005

Antinori Castel
Umbria 2005

Roy Harper
The BBC Tapes Vol 1
1969-1973

Roy Harper
The BBC Tapes Vol 2
In Concert 1974

Roy Harper
The BBC Tapes Vol 3
1974

Roy Harper
The BBC Tapes Vol 5
1975 -1978

Roy Harper
The BBC Tapes Vol 4
In Concert 1975

Roy Harper
The BBC Tapes Vol 6
In Concert 1978

uno

DEODORANT
SPRAY

NON FRAGRANCE

SHISEIDO

ICE
DEODORANT
SPRAY

SHISEIDO

DEODORANT
SPRAY

FRESH MARINE

SHISEIDO

DEODORANT
SPRAY

AQUA SOAP

SHISEIDO

DEODORANT
SPRAY

CITRUS SODA

SHISEIDO

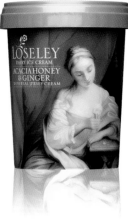

OH, WHAT A BEAU-TIFUL MORNING

MEMPHIS ★ ROASTED
UGLY MUG COFFEE ™

FIRST CUP
EASY
◆ EVEN-BODIED ◆ BERRY OVERTONES ◆
MAKES A GOOD FIRST IMPRESSION

WHOLE BEAN COFFEE

★ ★ ★

PERU / COSTA RICA
Net Weight 12 oz. (340g)

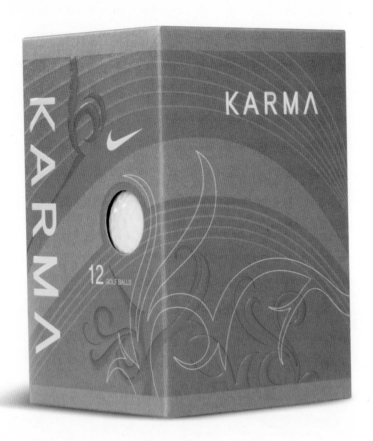

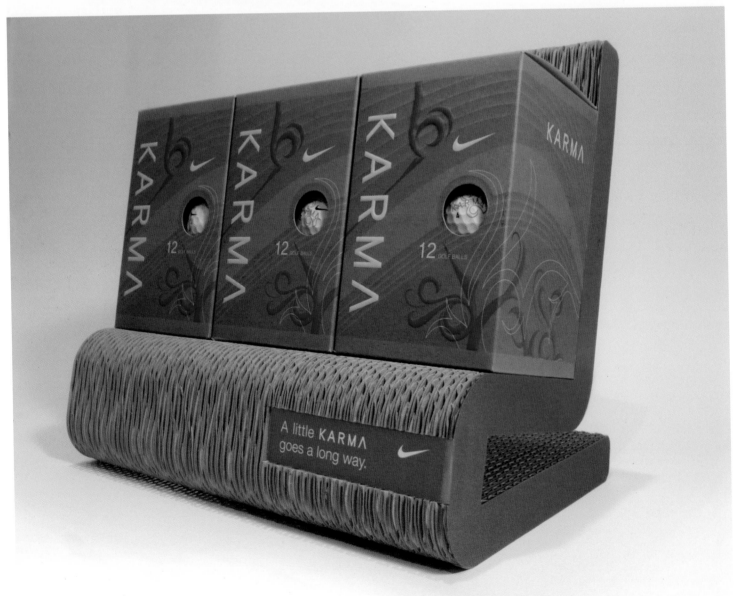

HOMEBASE

Duck Egg

FLAWLESS
SILK FINISH
emulsion for interior walls and ceilings

HOMEBASE

Limestone

FLAWLESS
MATT FINISH
emulsion for interior walls and ceilings

HOMEBASE

Amethyst

FLAWLESS
SILK FINISH
emulsion for interior walls and ceilings

sappi

Proudly Introducing
Lustro Offset Environmental

sappi

Proudly Introducing
Lustro Offset Environmental

This is my work. And, I'm like everybody else—every now and then I like to sit down and look at the results of my labor. Finance guys look at the money they've made. Designers look at their designs. I look at the garbage I've collected.

sappi

Proudly Introducing
Lustro Offset Environmental

While his name may not be Huck or Tom and he is by no means a work of fiction, Chad Pregracke is every bit an American icon. A young man full of endless passion, energy and pluck (yes, pluck), who decided one day, while he was still in his teens, that he wanted to clean up our country's major rivers and watersheds. So on a fateful Thursday morning, Chad set off in his tiny boat down the Mississippi and by day's end he had hauled in a culvert pipe, a refrigerator, three barrels, and as many bottles and cans as his boat would hold. Ten years, six rivers, and millions of pounds of trash later, Chad and his organization, Living Lands and Waters, have—through sheer determination, thousands of volunteers, and a drive to do the right thing—transformed rivers teeming with waste into the beautiful treasures they were intended to be. On the following pages, you'll get a sense of how one man's dream has become a national crusade. You'll also get a sense of how this adventure-filled story prints on Lustro Offset Environmental (LOE), our new paper that embodies Sappi's passion for protecting our environment while preserving the quality and beauty inherent in a great sheet of paper.

Since this is really Chad's story... we thought it would be a good idea to let him tell it to you in his own words.

sappi

Proudly Introducing
Lustro Offset Environmental

HOMELESS
BUT LUCKY

GIVE THEM SHELTER

Sappi Ideas that Matter 2008 Call for Entries

INVINCIBLE
YET POWERLESS

HELP CLEAR THE FOG

YOUNG AND
TRAPPED

HELP THEM SURVIVE

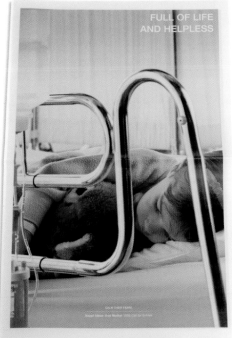

FULL OF LIFE
AND HELPLESS

BREADWINNER
AND HUNGRY

LOVED BUT
ABANDONED

NEIGHBOR
AND NOBODY

Sappi Ideas that Matter 2008 Call for Entries

FAST FOOD
SLOW DECLINE

HOME TURF
DEAD END

LPIE
PA
PRA
CE

DOMENIC LIPPA AND HARRY PEARCE CELEBRATE OVER 20 YEARS OF WORKING TOGETHER
TYPOGRAPHIC CIRCLE 22/02/07

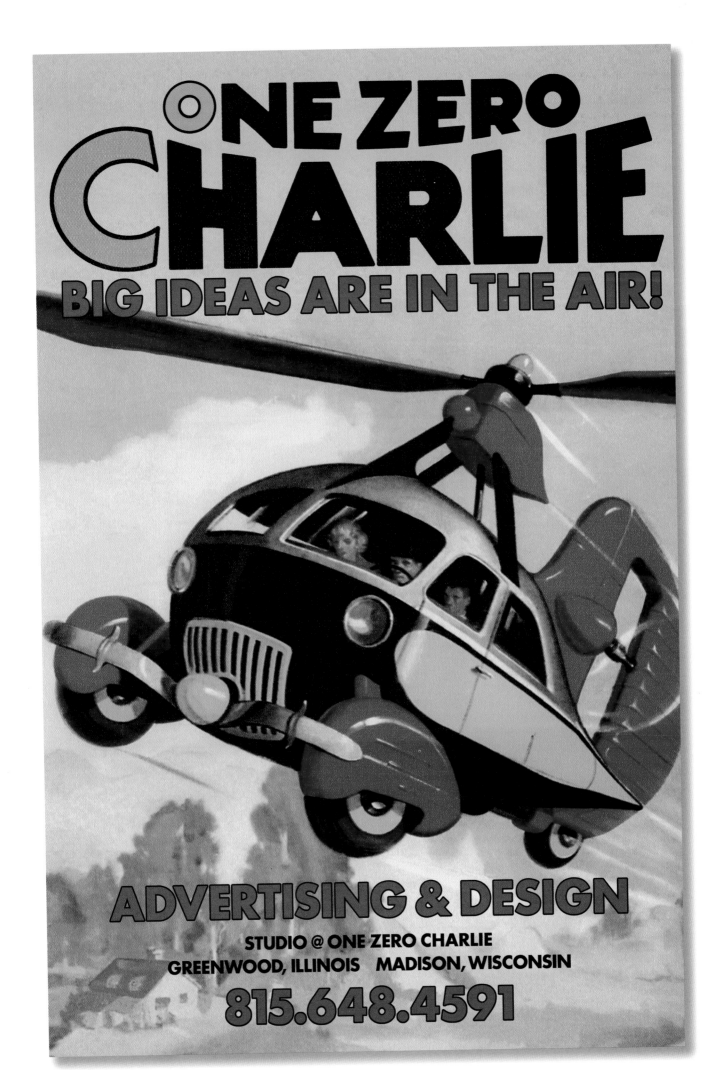

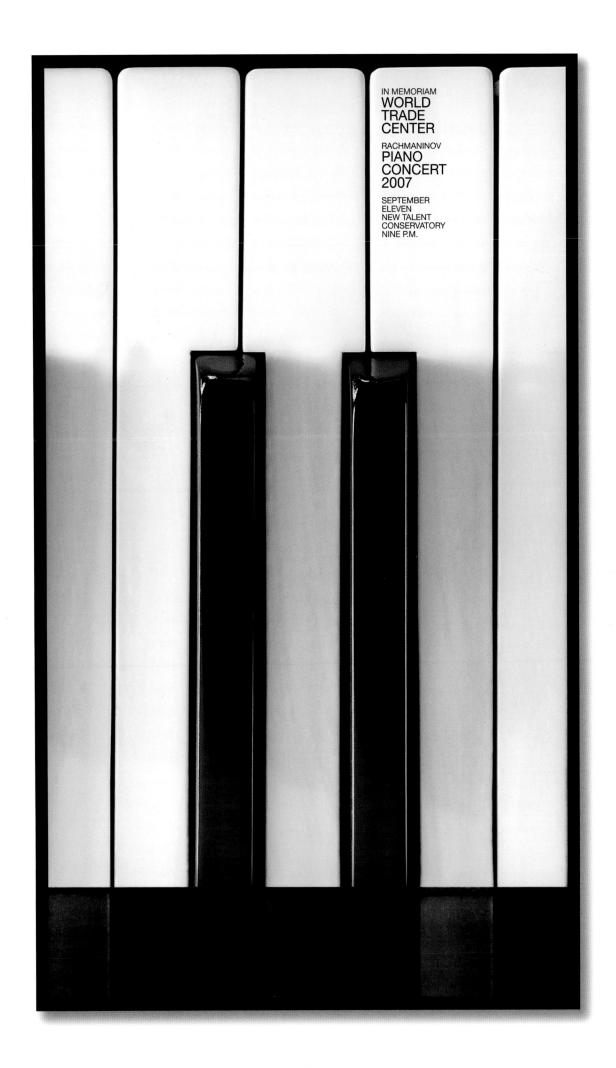

IN MEMORIAM
**WORLD
TRADE
CENTER**

RACHMANINOV
**PIANO
CONCERT
2007**

SEPTEMBER
ELEVEN
NEW TALENT
CONSERVATORY
NINE P.M.

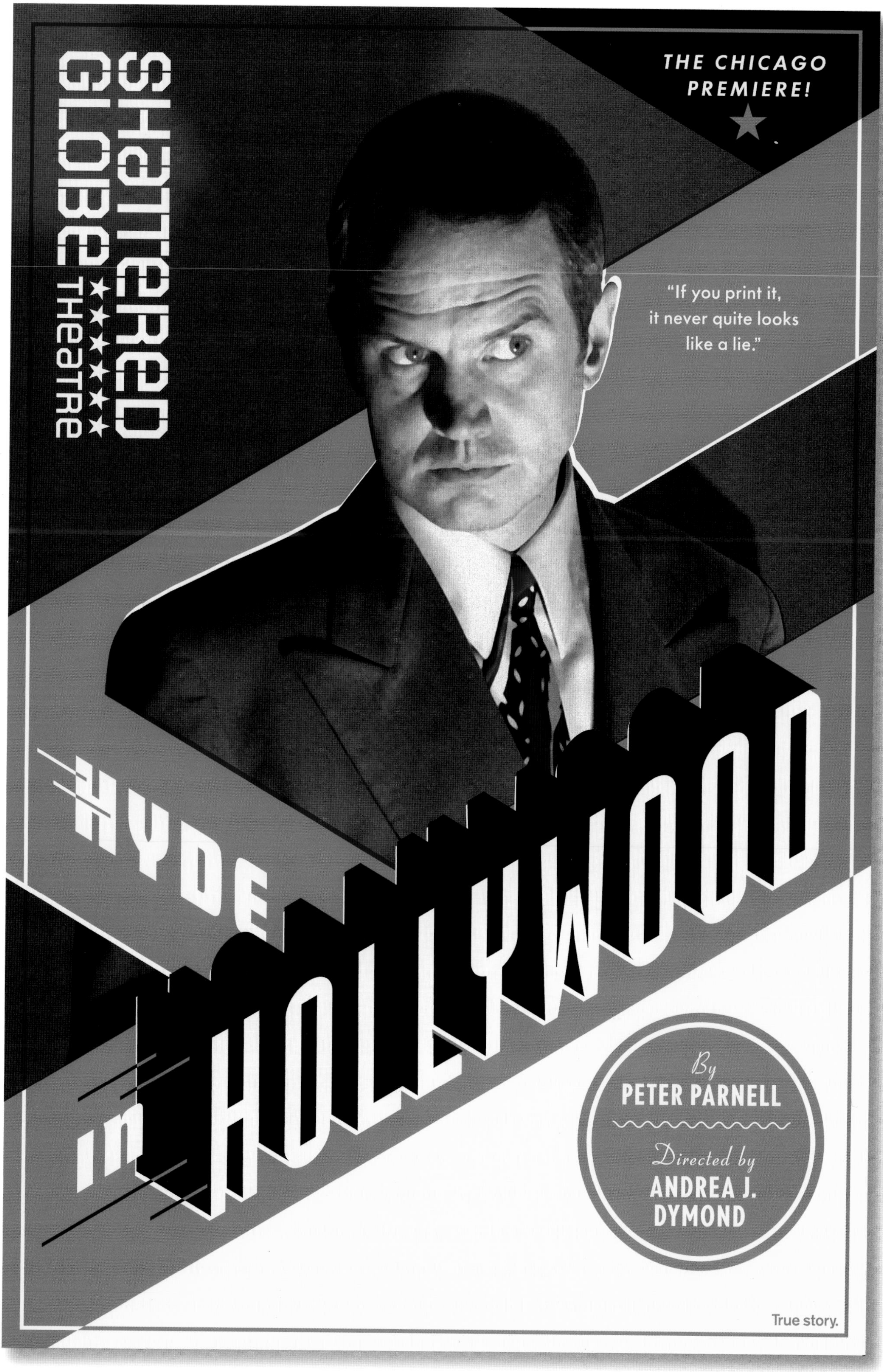

SHATTERED GLOBE THEATRE

THE CHICAGO PREMIERE!

"If you print it, it never quite looks like a lie."

HYDE in HOLLYWOOD

By PETER PARNELL

Directed by ANDREA J. DYMOND

True story.

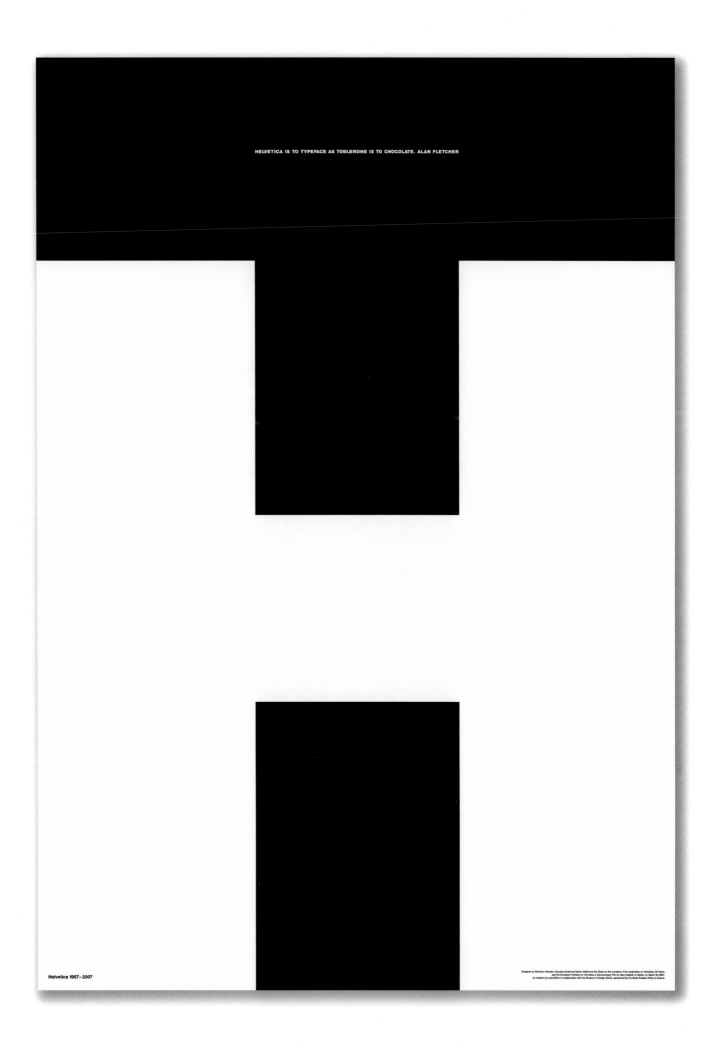

HELVETICA IS TO TYPEFACE AS TOBLERONE IS TO CHOCOLATE. ALAN FLETCHER

Helvetica 1957–2007

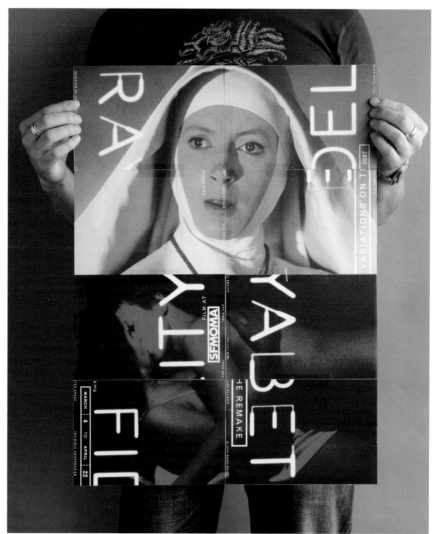

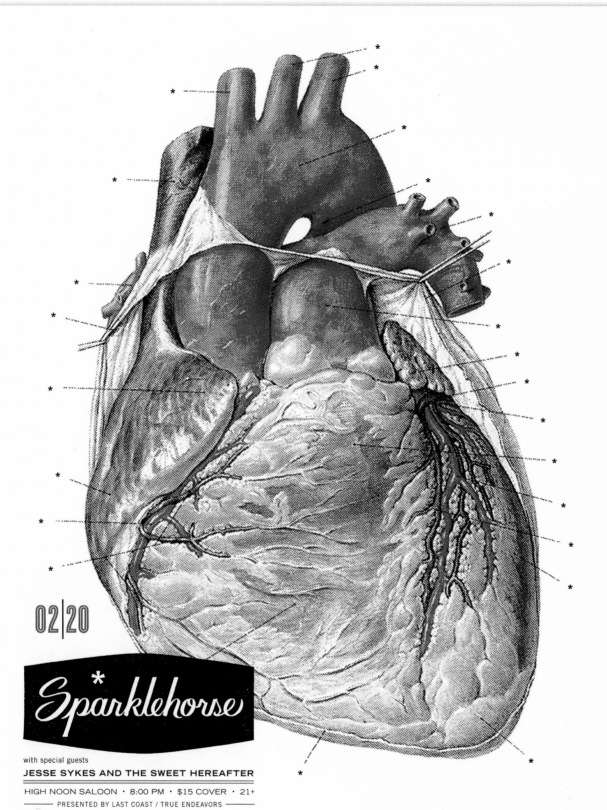

02|20

Sparklehorse

with special guests
JESSE SYKES AND THE SWEET HEREAFTER

HIGH NOON SALOON • 8:00 PM • $15 COVER • 21+
——— PRESENTED BY LAST COAST / TRUE ENDEAVORS ———

PLANET PROPAGANDA

ARCHITECTURE IN HELSINKI

with Glass Candy and Panther

HIGH NOON SALOON | OCTOBER TWENTY-THIRD | 8:00 PM | $12 COVER | 18 AND OVER

PLANET PROPAGANDA

PLANES
MISTAKEN
FOR
STARS

KINGDOM OF MAGIC
RUST BELT SERMON

NOVEMBER 16
HIGH NOON SALOON
10:00 PM
$7 COVER
18 AND UP

PLANET PROPAGANDA

BERLIN

BY GRAEME MURPHY FEATURING ioTA MUSIC DIRECTION & COMPOSITION IVA DAVIES & MAX LAMBERT

"CONTEMPORARY CHOREOGRAPHY THAT IS TOUGH, INTENSE AND CONCISE: SET TO A MONTAGE OF MOODY MUSIC." THE BULLETIN

BOOKINGS: 1300 795 012 6-25 OCTOBER 2007 THEATRE ROYAL
WWW.TICKETEK.COM.AU

SYDANCEY COMPANY

DESIGNED BY FROST* DESIGN SYDNEY, PHOTOGRAPHY JASON CAPOBIANCO

QANTAS   JCDecaux   CITY OF SYDNEY   arts nsw
OFFICIAL AIRLINE   OUTDOOR SPONSOR   COMMUNITY PARTNER

One Devon

More than 5,000
people worldwide

Doing the right thing

We take action

Layers. Depth. Building.

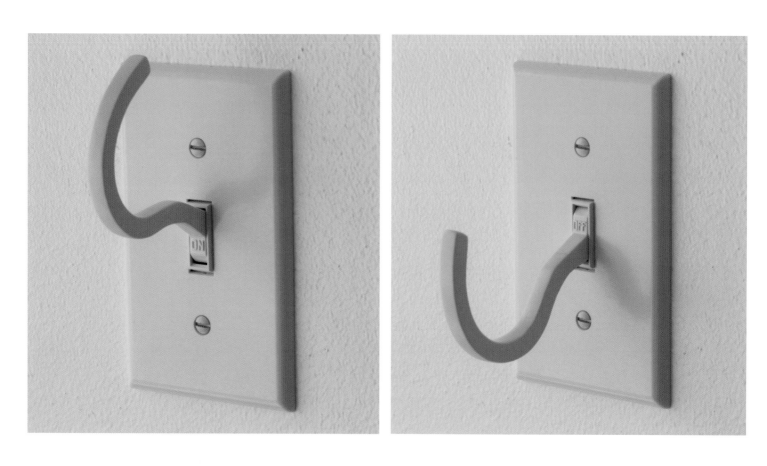

Cocktails, food, fun, grill, patio, and of course, tuna.

THANKSGIVING

Celebrating 50 years of Helvetica

Pat Sloan sends her love.

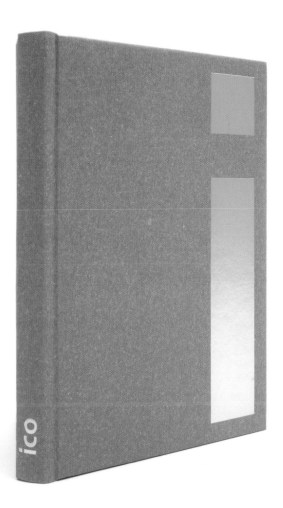

Red, White and ... and Gold

In spite of their use of gold and Americana iconography, the design of this McKinley button conveys a powerful graphic simplicity.

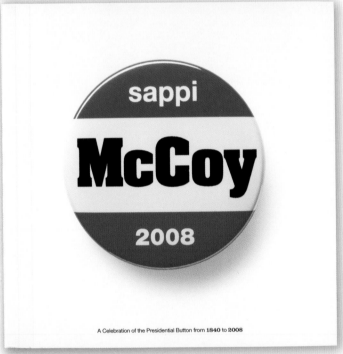

A Celebration of the Presidential Button from 1840 to 2008

Heartthrob Hart

Colorado Senator Gary Hart ran against Michael Dukakis for the Democratic bid in 1988. Almost immediately following the beginning of his campaign, Hart was found to be engaging in an extramarital affair. To prove his "innocence," he invited the news media to follow him around to see the truth for themselves. And so they did – catching him with Donna Rice (not his wife) on the yacht "Monkey Business." The irony is still almost impossible to believe.

"Pop Hart"

This Gary Hart button from 1988 is a classic example of pop art – Andy Warhol meets Robert Indiana. The unconventional visual motifs include a nod to the American flag and no words or photograph of the candidate. The red heart in the center of the star gives the only indication of who this button supports.

From the author of "The Black Light Test."

an
evening
with the
king.

a story by
GEORGE SIMHONI

The Cheektowaga Times Best-seller

MOTEL

DESERT
STAR

MIDWEEK RATE
WEEKLY SPECIAL
Free Cable (22-)

COLOR

MOT

the black
light test.

a story by
GEORGE SIMHONI

"From the author of "An Evening With The King."

a clown scorned.

a story by
GEORGE SIMHONI

the black light test.

Our story begins at the Desert Star Hotel. It wasn't the kind of place you headed for; it was the kind of place you ended up. It never appeared in a single tourist guide and twice it was even left out of the local phonebook. The Desert Star had six different owners, three health advisories, two minor felonies and only one thing that kept it from receding into a comfortable oblivion... one night in 1981 Elvis checked into room 19 and had relations with a slightly chubby, but enthusiastic young woman. For those keeping score, Elvis theoretically died in 1977. This is the story of the investigation of that night – the night we came closest to proving that Elvis had not left the building.

GEORGE SIMHONI 1st EDITION

079 /400

WWW.SIMHONI.COM

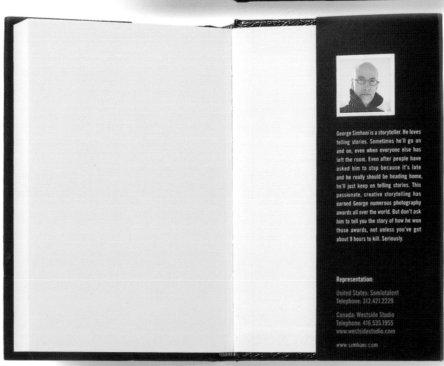

George Simhoni is a storyteller. He loves telling stories. Sometimes he'll go on and on, even when everyone else has left the room. Even after people have asked him to stop because it's late and he really should be heading home, he'll just keep on telling stories. This passionate, creative storytelling has earned George numerous photography awards all over the world. But don't ask him to tell you the story of how he won those awards, not unless you've got about 9 hours to kill. Seriously.

Representation:

United States: Somlotalent
Telephone: 312.421.2229

Canada: Westside Studio
Telephone: 416.535.1955
www.westsidestudio.com

www.simhoni.com

IMAGES
Levitate

OFF THE PAGE

The Great Dynamico summons conventional and "ULTRA-VIOLET" science
to achieve its photomechanical wizardry!
Watch as images leap from ordinary paper —
whether coated or uncoated!
Even the most common of substrates are transformed
through the power of "UV INKS."

Experience the
MAGIC *of*
10
COLORS

METALLIC
Inks
BEND
to our
WILL

Adding MetalFX™ to his repertoire, the magician shall amaze and
delight the senses — seemingly liquefying metal itself!
The Great Dynamico effortlessly yields multiple metallic colors from one
as if through an "inline" connection to the illusionist's mind!

Design for All ⊙

Smart. Simple. Surprising. Great design from A to Z.

BIALETTI

C9 BY CHAMPION™

DYSON

ERGONOMIC

FIREFLY

GRAVES

VICTORIA HAGAN

ISAAC MIZRAHI

JOY

SONIA KASHUK™

LED TEALIGHT

METHOD FLOOR MOP

NATURAL

ORGANIC COOKIES

PÜR

Q-TIPS

RADIO

SUSTAINABILITY

THOMAS O'BRIEN

UNIVERSAL

VIOLIGHT

WINE

CLEAR RX™

YO-YO

LOU GEHRIG HIT 493 HOME RUNS AND BATTED .340 IN 2,130 CONSECUTIVE GAMES.
BUT IN HIS FINAL YEARS HE WAS UNABLE TO TIE HIS OWN SHOES.

HELP FIND A CURE FOR LOU GEHRIG'S DISEASE (ALS). TO DONATE CALL 800-672-8857

ACTUAL SHOE LACES WERE LACED THROUGH DIE-CUT HOLES AND LEFT UNTIED.

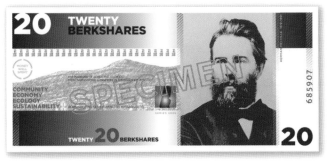

On the bag:

LIFT HANDLES UP
NOT OUT

PLEASE USE
BOTH HANDLES

I AM A BROWN PAPER BAG. MORE THAN LIKELY,
I'LL END UP UNDER YOUR KITCHEN SINK WITH A
FEW OF MY FRIENDS. I MIGHT GET CUT UP AND
WRAPPED AROUND AN OLD TEXTBOOK, OR JUST
STUCK UNDER SOMETHING MESSY. IT WOULD BE
NICE IF SOMEONE MADE ME INTO A KITE. I'D LIKE
TO BE A KITE. BUT WHATEVER HAPPENS, I WILL
NEVER FORGET THE DAY I CARRIED GROCERIES
HOME FROM *Central Market* H·E·B

Phil Jordan and Associates, Inc. (top) | United States Postal Service
q30design inc. (bottom) | Canada Post Corp. | Stamps**224**

OLYMPEX 2008

PORTUGAL

€ 0,75

Des. João Machado   Imp. INCM 08

Jogos da XXIX Olimpíada

Beijing 2008

PORTUGAL

€ 0,75

Des. João Machado   Imp. INCM 08

Jogos da XXIX Olimpíada

Beijing 2008

PORTUGAL

12   108

€ 0,30

Des. João Machado   Imp. INCM 08

OLYMPEX 2008

PORTUGAL

€ 0,75

Des. João Machado   Imp. INCM 08

Jogos da XXIX Olimpíada

Beijing 2008

PORTUGAL

€ 0,30

Des. João Machado   Imp. INCM 08

Mainfranken Theater

Moriori

Nga

Raumahara

YOU ARE NOT FORGOTTEN YOUR SACRIFICE WAS NOT IN VAIN

YOUR LEGACY OF

PEACE & HOPE

ENDURES STILL

HOKOTOHU: TYPEFACE CHARACTER DESIGN FOR MORIORI PEOPLE AND ISLAND OF REKOHU (CHATHAM ISLANDS)

The Hokotohu font has origins in the ancient Moriori tradition of tree carving-Rakau Momori. The Hokotohu font captures the essence of those ancestral designs and presents them to a discerning 21st Century audience as a trading mark of quality, authenticity and unique origin.

{ AaBBbCcDdEeFfGgHhIiJjKkLlMmNn
OoPPpQqRRrSsTtUuVvWwXxYYyZz }

(44°S) 23567890 (176°W)

HOKOTOHU

44°S 176°W

Moriori – we are the first peoples of the remote South Pacific islands of Rekohu and Rangiauria, 800km east of New Zealand, more commonly known as the Chatham and Pitt Islands. We have lived by the peace covenant of our ancestors for over half a millenium. Driven to the brink of extinction in the 19th century by colonisation, invasion, slavery and oppression – the 21st century has seen a revival of our culture and a reinvigoration of our future. Hokotehi Moriori Trust was established in 2001 with a vision of reconnecting and unifying Moriori People and establishing a strong cultural and economic base for the future.

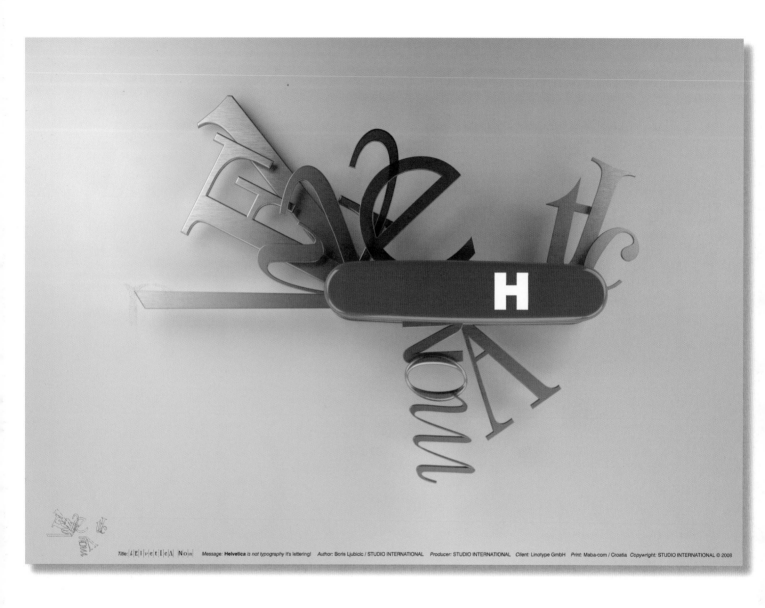

Title: ʰᴱˡᵛᵉᵗⁱᶜᴬ Noⁱⁿ   Message: **Helvetica** *is not typography* it's lettering!   Author: Boris Ljubicic / STUDIO INTERNATIONAL   Producer: STUDIO INTERNATIONAL   Client: Linotype GmbH   Print: Maba-com / Croatia   Copywright: STUDIO INTERNATIONAL © 2008

Credits

AnnualReports

28, 29 Annual Report | Design Firm: Opto Design, New York | Art Director: John Klotnia | Designer: Jared Stone | Executive Creative Director: Camilla Marcus | Executive Creative Strategist: Kelly Atkins | Illustrators: John Hersey, Peter Kramer, Paul Wearing | Photographers: Peter Gregoire, Eric Staudenmaier | Executive Creative Strategist: Nancy Caal Martinez | Client: Alexandria Real Estate Equities, Inc.

30, 31 The Space Between | Design Firm: Dietwee ontwerp en communicatie, Utrecht | Account Director: Joost Hosman | Art Director: Tirso Francés | Artists: Tirso Francés, Dirkjan Brummelman | Author/ Writer: Aquarium Writers (Louise Hide and Charlie Errington) | Designers: Tirso Francés, Dirkjan Brummelman | Client: Bank Insinger de Beaufort NV

Description: Insinger de Beaufort is an Anglo-Dutch private bank and investment house which likes to stand out from the competition by taking an independent and slightly unconventional approach to finance. Every year the company produces an annual review which reflects that approach. The 2006 annual review is the seventh in a series of hardback books. In addition to the report and accounts, it contains a themed section which reflects a topic that is particularly pertinent to the company or the financial markets. The 2006 theme was "uncovering value in the space between." It explores how scientists, writers, sculptors, anthropologists and philosophers have made valuable discoveries in the most unlikely places, implying that value in the financial world is often overlooked. The Dutch design and UK writing teams worked closely together throughout the entire process, from developing concepts to telling stories through prose, musical scores, jokes, political statements, quotations, illustration and (stock) photography. It is the first review in the series where we did not commission a photographer but used existing photography and created our own illustrations, sometimes produced by the designers themselves, to tell the stories in the best way. We wanted to make a book that could be read as a narrative or allow the reader to pick out stories of interest. Creating pace and balancing the stories with the many different visual elements was one of our greatest challenges, as was getting permission to use the portrait and quote of Albert Einstein. As we felt the book would not be the same without him, we believe it was worth the effort.

Books

32, 33 PLATINUM Things I have learned in my life so far | Design Firm: Sagmeister Inc., New York | Art Director/Artist/Author/Creative Director: Stefan Sagmeister | Designer: Matthias Ernstberger | Editor: Deborah Aaronson | Illustrators: Yuki Muramatsu, Stephan Walter | Photographer: Henry Leutwyler | Print Producer: Anet Sirna-Brude | Typographers: Stefan Sagmeister, Matthias Ernstberger | Writer: Stefan Sagmeister | Client: Abrams Inc.

Description: Astonishingly, Stefan Sagmeister has only learned 20 or so things in his life so far. But he did manage to publish these personal maxims all over the world, in spaces normally occupied by advertisements and promotions: as billboards, projections, light-boxes, magazine spreads, annual report covers, fashion brochures, and, recently, as giant inflatable monkeys. In this presentation Sagmeister throws his diary, a lot of design, and a little art together with a pinch of psychology and a dash of happiness into a blender and pushes the button. It tastes surprisingly yummy.

34 The Furniture of Poul Kjaerholm: Catalogue Raisonné | Design Firm: Matsumoto Incorporated, New York | Art Director/Creative Director: Takaaki Matsumoto | Designers: Takaaki Matsumoto, Hisami Aoki | Editor: Amy Wilkins | Photographer: Keld Helmer-Petersen | Writer: Michael Sheridan | Client: Gregory R. Miller & Co., Inc.

Description: This Danish furniture designer is known for severe, pared down elegance. Many of his designs are based on a square, so the book is square to reflect his fundamental aesthetic. The black and white reproductions draw attention to the shape and construction of the minimal, precisely crafted furniture.

35 Nokia Annual Trends 2010 | Design Firm: Nokia, London | Creative Director: Nokia Design/ComLab | Client: Nokia Design

Description:
What is the purpose of the book? To inform Nokia Design about the most important and relevant socio-cultural changes involving consumer, usage, design and technology trends presented in a context of relevance and implications to Nokia.
Who is the customer of the book? Nokia Design is the main customer. The book may also be distributed to other parties in Nokia according to the need. Since the main audience is designers, the book needs to be visually enticing without being too pretty. The design must reflect how trends work/are developed. i.e., the design needs to support the notion of trends being intertwined. Trends are fluid, not subjects working in isolation; they are informed, formed and influenced by many different channels. An emphasis on rich visuals rather than lengthy text is fundamental.

36, 37 Poiret | Design Firm: Matsumoto Incorporated, New York | Art Director/Creative Director: Takaaki Matsumoto | Designers: Takaaki Matsumoto, Hisami Aoki | Editor: Joan Holt | Writers: Harold Koda, Andrew Bolton | Client: The Metropolitan Museum of Art

Description: One of the most important clothing designers of the early 20th century, Poiret is now often overshadowed by Chanel and Schiaparelli. The Met wanted to emphasize the radical nature of Poiret's designs and his importance in the history of fashion in this exhibition catalog. The oversized format and spare photography showcase the garments and their lavish texture and details.

38 64 page book | Design Firm: The Works, Melbourne | Art Director: Jo Waite | Editor: Amy Borrell | Client: RMIT University

Description: The aim was to create a book of 64 pages. The topic was totally left to the student although, it had to be something that inspired them so that the end result was an unique and original piece.

39 YOLK | Design Firm: The Works, Melbourne | Designer: Marianne Saether | Project Manager: Russell Kerr | Client: RMIT University - The Works

Description: Book showcasing the year's work of RMIT Universities Design Consultancy, The Works. The publication is split into two sections, the first showcasing the commercial work undertaking in 2007 and the second section documenting the students' personal research projects.

40, 41 Incognito Royale by Paul Cunningham | Design Firm: punktum design, Copenhagen | Art Director: Søren Varming | Author: Paul Cunningham | Designer: Søren Varming, Graphic Designer MDD | Editors: Majbrit Hansen, JP/Politikens Forlag, Copenhagen | Location: Copenhagen, Denmark | Models: Camilla, Melissa, Daniella, Aston Martin DB5 | Photographer: Andreas Wiking | Photographer's Assistant: Minh Tran | Print Producers: Narayana Press, Denmark | Typographer: Foundry Types, London | Writer: Mia Rudolf | Client: JP/Politikens Publishing

Description: Paul Cunningham is a chef and owns The Paul in Tivoli Gardens in Copenhagen. He has one star in the Guide Michelin and is British born. In the summer 2007 the publisher JP/Politikens Forlag briefed the photographer and us to make a masculine cookbook. We developed a no-nonsense concept called Incognito Royale with full-bleed photography on either red or black background without props. Each chapter has its own colour and the chapters are made as a timeframe rather than traditional cookbook (starters, maincourses, desserts). The typography is Foundry Dit by Freda Sack of the Foundry in London. The gridsystem is seven columns made to feel like a military briefing machine, and remains static throughout the book — again to emphasize the non-nonsense attitude towards cooking that Paul Cunningham wants to get across.

42 (top left) Searching for the new normal | Design Firm: Reed Hill, Castle Rock | Account Director/Creative Director/Designer: Paul Reed | Art Director/Photographer: Joel Hill | Author/Illustrator: Rexanne Williams | Client: Rexanne Williams

Description: The book *Searching For The New Normal* was never supposed to be a book. It was the personal journal of a woman in pain, spawned by the suicide of her son. There is no thought, feeling or emotion that wasn't penned during the three-year span covered in the book's pages.
Near the end of the journal entries, hope and a new happiness returns through small gifts — peculiar yellow butterflies that appear in the most unsuspected times and places, a sublime reminder that her son is still a part of her life and her decisions. This cover is meant to illustrate the complete and utter sorrow the author has borne, with the subtle reference that one can find a new, normal life again after tragedy.

42 (top right) Your Inner CEO | Design Firm: The DesignWorks Group | Art Director: Jeff Piasky | Author: Allan Cox | Creative Director/Designer: Jason Gabbert | Client: Career Press

Description: Helping top executives answer the difficult questions about performance, leadership, relationships, and success.

42 (bottom) African American Bioethics | Design Firm: The DesignWorks Group | Art Director: Debora Weiner | Author: Lawrence Prograis Jr., M.D. | Creative Director/Designer: Tim Green | Client: Georgetown University Press

43 Artists of Invention: A Century of CCA | Design Firm: Volume Inc. | Creative Directors: Adam Brodsley, Eric Heiman | Art Directors: Adam Brodsley, Eric Heiman | Designers: Eric Heiman, Marcelo Viana, Iran Narges | Client: CCA(California College of the Arts)

Description: This volume presents a vivid portrait of Bay Area artists and art movements through the 20th century. With new essays, interviews, and historical texts, the book features more than 100 color illustrations of work by a wide range of artists, including the renegade plein-air painters known as the Society of Six; production ceramists Edith Heath and Jacomena Maybeck; artists of the Bay Area Figurative movement Richard Diebenkorn, Nathan Oliveira, and Manuel Neri; leaders of the studio ceramics movement Peter Voulkos, Robert Arneson, and Viola Frey; minimalist John McCracken and conceptualists David Ireland and Dennis Oppenheim; photorealists Robert Bechtle, Richard McLean, and Jack Mendenhall; and cultural commentators Squeak Carnwath and Raymond Saunders. The book is further enriched by a contemporary section dedicated to work produced in the last 20 years by a new generation: videographers Kota Ezawa, Désirée Holman, and Sergio de la Torre; photographers Larry Sultan, Todd Hido, and Liz Cohen; painter David Huffman; and mixed-media artists Lee Mingwei and Amy Franceschini, among many others.

44, 45 Volume | Design Firm: 3 Deep Design | Art Director/Creative Director/Creative Strategist/Design Director/Designer/Typographer: 3 Deep Design | Authors: Leon van Shaik, Paul Carter, Christopher McAuliffe, Andrew Hutson, Davina Jackson | Client: Thames & Hudson

Description: 3 Deep Design were engaged to conceptualise, art direct and design this monograph on behalf of Australian-based Architectural practice John Wardle Architects (JWA). Published by Thames & Hudson (Australia), the title celebrates 20 years of JWA's practice and reflects on the intricate and finely detailed manner in which each of his buildings is created. As one would imagine, there can be a great deal said about the act of designing 316 pages of information collated from 20 years of an architectural practice. It is a complex and intricate task that requires a methodical, pragmatic and tailored approach. 3 Deep were afforded the scope to craft every aspect of the publication's character, from the art direction and commissioning of visual essays for the publication's end sheets, to the development of bespoke typography reflecting the personality and character of each of the individual authors.

46, 47 Question Everything | Design Firm: mono, Minneapolis | Art Director/Designer/Writer: mono | Client: Science Channel

Description: The Science Channel wanted to announce the brand idea for the re-launch of their network. *Question Everything* is about celebrating intellectual curiosity and the desire to endlessly question and challenge all that we know about our world. And the notion of printing a "Question Everything" manifesto right over the top of an old, existing science book helped to further seed the idea. Each book was created by screenprinting on top of vintage science books. By doing this, we imply that we should always rethink what we've learned.

48, 49 Kristian Kozul | Design Firm: Laboratorium, Zagreb | Art Directors/Creative Directors: Ivana Vucic, Orsat Frankovic | Designers: Ivana Vucic, Orsat Frankovic, Sasa Stubicar | Editor: Jasna Jaksic | Illustrator: Kristian Kozul | Photographers: Tomislav J. Kacunic, Ivana Vucic | Writers: Klaudio Stefancic, Leonida Kovac, Jasna Jaksic | Client: Museum of Contemporary Art Zagreb

Description: A Croatian conceptual artist based in NY wanted a monograph that would represent his art to the international art scene. We designed a book-object for the artist who's dealing with viewers emotions triggered by individual interpretations of transformed ready-made-objects. It's not only a collection of his reproductions, but also, their interpretation. The form and substance conflict of his work is transformed into a book concept. Only by precise observation we find a morbid connection between form and content. Binded in different covers made out of black velvet, red velvet, or limited edition white perforated artificial leather filled with old pins.

50 Anatomy of Design | Design Firm: Mirko Ilic Corp., New York | Art Director/Creative Director/Designers: Mirko Ilic, Kunal Bhat | Client: Rockport

51 2007-2008 Concert Season (The Macao Orchestra) | Design Firm: Kuokwai Cheong, Macau | Creative Director/Designer: Kuokwai Cheong | Client: Cultural Affairs Bureau of the Macao S.A.R. Government

Description: This BOOK is a piece of music. Best music comes from the natural world, from chaos to natural law; from lightness to weight; from white to black; from black & white to color; from repetition to quantum leap — all these elements construct the motif and rhythm of the piece.

Branding

52, 53, 54, 55 PLATINUM Corporate Design for KMS TEAM | Design Firm: KMS TEAM GmbH, Munich | Creative Directors: Knut Maierhofer, Michael Keller | Creative Strategist: Christoph Rohrer | Design Director: Patrick Märki | Print Producer: Chrisina Baur | Web Developer: Bruno Marek | Client: KMS TEAM

Description: KMS TEAM has a new corporate design. It highlights our role as Germany's largest independent design studio and visualizes the method of operation that helped us gain this position. The aim in developing the new design was to step out into public view in an assertive and concise manner, while at the same time remaining neutral with respect to the corporate designs of our clients. Thus, on the whole, we must be perspicuous, but in this perspicuousness we must display the objectivity that is a central component of our consulting service.

The Basic Idea – The corporate design is based on the concept of the "cloud of ideas." It visualizes thoughts, questions and ideas as fields encircling a head and is meant to indicate the method of operation of KMS TEAM. The "cloud of ideas" stands both for the diversity of the activities of the studio, on which we draw in developing a specific design, as well as for the concurrence of all the disciplines involved in the creative process.

The Implementation – The concept of the "cloud of ideas," which is implemented as a rotating bar animation in interactive applications, gives rise to the visual core of the design: an individual black bar. It constitutes the logo and is a clear branding element. At the same time it defines, in analogy to the navigational structure on the Internet, the graphical organizational structure (e.g. forms) and is a playful stylistic device for various applications (e.g. image-film show reel). The color scheme is limited to black and white. This conveys the neutrality and objectivity of KMS TEAM with respect to its clients. The visual language is exclusively derived from the color schemes of clients and is used as a contrastive background in all means of communication. As our font, we chose Universe Black, which is marked by a precise and clear style. The capitalization of the appendage "TEAM" alludes to the importance of our staff members.

56, 57, 58, 59 Mariinsky Festival | Design Firm: Sandra Burch, New York | Creative Director: Harold Burch | Creative Strategist: Elizabeth Segerstrom | Designers: Harold Burch, Sandra Burch | Photographer: Robert Nease (still life) | User Experience Architect: Bob Hernandez | Client: Henry and Elizabeth Segerstrom

Description: Special event branding for a several week–long Gala Festival celebrating the Kirov Orchestra, Kirov Ballet, and Kirov Opera. This was in conjunction with the Grand Opening of The Renee and Henry Segerstrom Concert Hall in Southern California. The events included Wagner's Ring Series, with various performances produced by Mariinsky Artistic Director, Valery Gergiev. The materials included everything from the identifier to brochures, invitations, environmental graphics, and party items such as menus, wine labels, and table cards.

60, 61 Vintage Stripes | Design Firm: TW2, Milano | Account Director: Anna M Massa | Chief Creative Officer/Creative Strategist: Alberto Baccari | Creative Directors: Alberto Baccari, Max Sereno | Design Director: Gianluca Barbero | Writer: Robert Schulman | Client: Riva Yachts

Description: Riva is history, excellence of products. From legend to innovation Riva is a lifestyle. We found a sensual, unique, elegant and strong pattern that represents "Riva's Exclusive Club" colors. It's a chromatic code distinguishing Riva exclusive world. We designed a pattern that reminds clients of Riva legend colors (blue and white stripes) to strengthen the sense of belonging to the club.

62, 63 Corporate Identity System | Design Firm: Landor Associates, San Francisco | Account Director: Mignon Monroe | Creative Directors: Paul Chock, Nicolas Aparicio | Designers: Henricus Kusbiantoro, JJ Ha | Client: First Graduate

Description: Founded in 2000, the former Bay Area Youth Development Fund (b.a.y. fund) is a San Francisco non-profit that believes education is a powerful tool that helps young people overcome adversity, develop character and build community. Their mission is to help young people finish high school and become the first in their families to graduate from college.

The organization was challenged by the confusion and unfamiliarity of its name. Landor aided their rebranding efforts by first assisting in the early stages of the naming development, and later creating their new identity that unified the focus and inspiration they wanted to express in their new name, First Graduate. Based on First Graduate's philosophy of using education to overcome adversity, develop character and build community, the new identity consists of a word mark with a superscripted number one. It clearly communicates the organization's mission to tutor and mentor children so they become the first college graduates in their families. In conjunction with a house style that conveys values like ambition, talent and diversity, the new brand is suited for the various audiences the organization works with, including students as young as 12, academic coaches, volunteers and donors.

The new brand has been implemented across all applications, including the website *www.firstgraduate.org.* Landor also completed brand guidelines.

64, 65 D&AD Identity | Design Firm: Rose, London | Art Director: Simon Elliott | Creative Director: Garry Blackburn | Designers: Garry Blackburn, Simon Elliott, Joseph Luffman | Client: D&AD

Description: D&AD needed to evolve. They wanted to stand for more than just excellence. A new streamlined identity was required to highlight D&AD's multi-faceted nature, along with its charitable status. It was agreed that the typeface family and existing marque would be kept. In addition, the strong association with their corporate yellow had recently been weakened, something D&AD were keen to redress. Given D&AD's increasingly global perspective, it was important to create a marque combining all the elements with a simple idea, helping D&AD position themselves as "the international authority on creativity." We were also asked to introduce the three facets of the organisation, Excellence, Education and Enterprise, and include "not for profit," a gentle reminder that D&AD is a charity.

D&AD's yellow pencil is world-renowned. With this in mind, we combined the original logo with a yellow hexagon — representing the pencil, and communicating the multi-faceted D&AD. The original marque sits in the middle of the hexagon — running though the core. The hexagon marque can also be used in isolation, to act as a seal of quality, providing opportunities for accreditation. It is essential that D&AD practice what they preach and lead by example. We used this as principal to create more interesting solutions, so, as an alternative to the formal business card, we suggested a yellow pencil with contact details on one facet. The membership cards include transparent marques and, when stacked, they make one enormous pencil. Projecting signs protrude from walls like large pencil sections, carrying directional information on their facets. Wall-mounted plaques show a slice of the pencil, with three visible facets. The identity has helped D&AD reconnect with their strong visual heritage, encouraging creative ideas rather than stifling them.

Brochures

66, 67 08 Accord Brochure | Design Firm: Rubin Postaer & Associates, Santa Monica | Art Director: Ron Berry | Creative Director: David Tanimoto | Photographers: Tim Kent, Toshi Oku | Writer: Jon King | Client: Honda

68 Gifts Holiday 2007 catalog | Design Firm: Design Within Reach, San Francisco | Art Director: Michael Sainato | Chief Creative Officer/Creative Director: Jennifer Morla | Designer: Tina Yuan | Writer: Gwendolyn Horton | Photographer: Todd Tankersley | Client: Design Within Reach

Description: A catalog of products for holiday gift-giving.

69 About Face | Design Firm: SamataMason, Dundee | Creative Director/Art Director: Greg Samata | Designer: Beth May | Photographer: Sandro | Writer: Bill Seyle | Client: Sandro

70, 71 PLATINUM Lithographix. Ink, paper and the art of bending light | Design Firm: Robert Louey Design, Santa Monica | Art Director: Robert Louey | Designers: Javier Leguizamo, Christy Thrasher, Vera Kwok | Illustrators: Dana Berry, Joel Nakamura | Photographers: Jeff Corwin, David Emmite, Trevor Pearson, Patrick Messina | Client: Lithographix, Inc.

Description: Bending Light. Designed to celebrate the art of fine lithography through the diverse capabilities of Lithographix Inc., a Los Angeles – based multi media lithographer. An eclectic combination of photographers and illustrators create the stage for the theme of bending light as captured through the eyes of those who view the world in their own unique way. Use of special inks, papers and production techniques display the ages-old alchemy of applying ink on paper.

72 Ultra | Design Firm: Centerpoint Design, New York | Account Director/Design Director: Jean Shin | Artist: Jan Gronvold | Creative Director: Shanley Jue | Creative Strategist: Jean Shin | Designer: Natasha Samoylenko | Photographer: Bret Wills | Writer: Donna La Brecque | Client: Samsung

Description: A brochure for Samsung's Ultra Edition of mobile phones:
– For global launch (created in English for local adaptation).
– To capture the essence of the entire lineup and provide product concepts for sub-categories.

Credits

73 PLATINUM Lida Baday Spring 2008 | Design Firm: Concrete Design Communications Inc., Toronto | Art Directors: Diti Katona, John Pylypczak | Designer: Leticia Luna | Client: Lida Baday

Description: Hyper-seductive photography, dramatic understatement and simple but calculated pacing are the hallmarks of the Lida Baday Spring 2008 Collection brochure. With offices in Toronto and New York, Lida Baday designs and produces well-detailed, beautiful clothing that capture the essence of thoughtful, discerning, modern women. The brochure uses clothing, not for the purposes of documentation, but as an expression of the woman who is intelligent, feminine, confident and ultimately modern.

74 stories 01 | Design Firm: feldmann + schultchen design studios GmbH, Hamburg | Designers: Florian Schoffro, Kati Lust, Ralf Höpfner, André Feldmann, Arne Schultchen | Client: feldmann + schultchen design studios

Description: "Stories 01" is the first volume in a series of narratives about the work of feldmann + schultchen. Freshly and joyfully, this book focuses on the designers' work. The ten stories describe visually and tangibly how successful branding grows out of healthy common sense. The nature of this interaction describes and illustrates with a poetic directness the creative interplay and collaboration inherent in this work. But its relevance extends well beyond the 10 cases; it provides a breviary for a sensible and meaningful approach to working in design.

75 Ronald McDonald House Brochure | Design Firm: Ogilvy, Durham | Art Directors: Noah Rosenberg, Amy Mastroguiseppe | Creative Director: Jeff Dahlberg | Associate Creative Directors: Noah Rosenberg, Michael Gorelic | Photographer: Bruce Peterson | Writers: Michael Gorelic, Leslie Gray | Client: Ronald McDonald House

Description: The Ronald McDonald House of Chapel Hill (RMH) is a non-profit organization that provides a home for sick children and their families while they are being treated at local hospitals. RMH operates entirely on donations from individuals and corporations. Their goal was to increase donations by bringing in new donors or by increasing the donations of those who were already involved. The big idea for the work was to show the balance in the house. However bad these families' situations are, the RMH has to be that much better. They have to counter the sickness and the sadness with as much joy and happiness as possible.

76, 77 Speaker Brochure | Design Firm: Sabatino/Day, Miamisburg | Design Director: Gary W. Hinsche | Designer: Hugo Chang | Photographer: Don Miller | Print Producer: Tony Fleet | Client: Pioneer Mobile

78 Niki in the Garden. The Extraordinary Scupltures of Niki de Sainte Phalle | Design Firm: Birkdesign Inc., Chicago | Art Director/Creative Director/Creative Strategist/Designer/Print Producer/Project Manager/Typographer: JinJa Davis-Birkenbeuel | Artist: Niki de Sainte Phalle | Author: Chicago Office of Tourism | Editors/Writers: Chicago Office of Tourism, Niki de Saint Phalle Foundation | Photographer: Thomas Marlow | Client: Chicago Office of Tourism

Description: First book of Niki de Saint Phalle's American sculptures published in the United States. The Department of Cultural Affairs and the Chicago Office of Tourism published the book. Book showcases the Niki de Saint Phalle exhibition at Chicago's Garfield Park Conservatory, which took place during the summer of 2007.

79 SADI newspaper 2006 fall | Design Firm: SADI (Samsung Art & Design Institute) | Art Director/Creative Director/Designer: Han Kyu | Copywriter/Editor: Jae-Kyung, Jeon | Client: SADI

Calendars

80, 81 Everlasting Adhesive Calendar | Design Firm: Laboratorium, Zagreb | Art Directors/Creative Directors/Designers: Ivana Vucic, Orsat Frankovic | Client: Laboratorium

Description: Everlasting Calendar is multi-functional adhesive tape which functions at the same time as organizer/planner/post-it/tape/sticker... It's limited only by its own length. You can create each month in any time by the day and date combination of two separate rolls (different widths) and stick them together at any place you need (different surfaces, wall, table, toilet walls...). The calendar was produced as a promotional gift/Christmas card for Laboratorium clients and friends.

82, 83 zweinullnullacht | Design Firm: Glanzmann Schoene Design, Loerrach | Art Directors: Cornelia Glanzmann Schoene, Markus Schoene | Artist/Designer/Illustrator: Cornelia Glanzmann Schoene | Print Producer: Hornberger Druck | Paper: Winter&Company, Loerrach | Client: Self promotion

Description: This calendar is a co-operation of our design company with a manufacturer, very special paper materials and a premium printing press. It was a Christmas gift for all clients of these three companies. The illustrations were all influenced by the paper materials.

84 Work/Life 2008 | Design Firm: CIA, Baltimore | Creative Director/Writer: Kurt Thesing | Designers: Kurt Thesing, Rebecca Hrizuk | Client: Creative Intelligence Agency (C.I.A)

Description: A self-promotional calendar/planner book.

Catalogues

85 Kobe Ink Brochure | Design Firm: Paul Lam Design Associates, Hong Kong | Creative Director: Paul Lam | Designers: Patrick Chan, Queenie Shek | Illustrators: Or Hoi Kit, Chui Ka Ying | Photographers: Lester Lee, Jennifer Chau | Print Producer: Wide Ocean Printing Company Ltd. | Client: Gang Ri Development Company Ltd.

86 N/A | Design Firm: Spark Studio, Melbourne | Art Director/Creative Director/Designer: Gary Domoney | Client: Watches of Switzerland

Description: 2008 Prestige Swiss Watch catalogue for Watches of Switzerland Australia.

87 Designer Book | Design Firm: Nordstrom, Seattle | Client: Nordstrom

88, 89 View 2008/9 | Design Firm: Art Center College of Design, Pasadena | Creative Directors: Takaaki Matsumoto, Amy Wilkins, Hisami Aoki | Design Director: Steve Sieler | Photographers: Steven A. Heller, Vahe Alaverdian | Client: Art Center College of Design

Description: View 2008/9 provides a general overview of Art Center College of Design, its programs and admissions guidelines in a compact booklet. View 2008/9 is distributed primarily to high school students who are just beginning to explore educational and career opportunities in art and design. As such, easy-to-read department summaries are accompanied by a list of career opportunities and a portfolio of student work. In order to make a strong impact in very few pages, the publication itself exemplifies, inside and out, the high caliber of student Art Center attracts and produces.

90 2006 Galaxy A/W Collection | Design Firm: Penguin Graphics | Creative Director: Tomiko Nakamura | Art Director: Kazuto Nakamura | Designers: Kazuto Nakamura, Tomokazu Yamada, Ryuji Mizuoka | Writer: Tomiko Nakamura | Client: EVE GROUP CO., LTD.

Description: This is a direct-mail, original catalog for the Fall/Winter collection of a select shop. This product was made with the consumer's way of thinking in mind. Flipping through fashion magazines at the begining of a season thinking. "What should I buy this season?" and marking potential items with sticky notes. Each original sticky note is printed and carefully placed by hand in each of the 1,000 copies of the catalog. We aimed to create an illusory experience for consumers that receive this product, that shop staff have placed the sticky notes especially for them, one by one.

91 Shibboleth Catalogue | Design Firm: Rose, London | Artist: Doris Salcedo | Authors: Achim Borchardt-Hume, Paul Gilroy, Eyal Weizman, Mieke Bal | Creative Director: Simon Elliott | Designer: Terry Stephens | Editor: Achim Borchardt-Hume | Photographers: Sergio Clavijo, Stephen White, Marcus Leith, Andrew Dunkley | Project Manager: Alice Chasey | Client: Tate Publishing

Description: We were asked to create the exhibition catalogue for Shibboleth: the 8th installation in the Unilever Series at Tate Modern. The series has built up a reputation for being one of the most eagerly anticipated arts events in the world. Previous artists in the series include Louise Bourgeois, Annish Kapoor, Bruce Nauman and Rachel Whiteread, the most recent installation being the phenomenally successful slides by Carsten Holler. Columbian-born Salcedo is now widely recognized as one of the leading sculptors of her generation. Her work is highly charged with political and social significance, and she has now completed several large-scale projects around the world. Shibboleth is her first public commission in the UK. The designers began the project by examining the meticulous attention to detail inherent in Doris's work, and specifically Shibboleth, where individual sections of the chasm's interior were hand-made in Bogota and shipped across to London. Swiss-binding — exposing the natural thread-sewn sections of the catalogue — was subsequently chosen to reflect the raw materials and wire mesh used in the construction of the artwork. 40gsm bible-paper pages were tipped in at the beginning of each section to reiterate the contrast in materials used by the artist. The first four of these feature duo-tone ghosted images of Shibboleth, the remainder housing explanatory texts relating to six of Doris's previous installations also featured in the catalogue. The cover idea came from direct dialogue with the artist. Owing to the sheer size of the installation, it's impossible to see the entire installation in one take. With this in mind, Salcedo and the designers became interested in the idea of conveying a perspective on the artwork that the public would never otherwise have the opportunity to see. Consequently Rose commissioned a birds-eye photograph of the work, which would run across both front and back covers and the inside cover flap. The cover treatment opens up to expose a large detail of the interior of the crack running across the interior of the covers.

92 (top) Unison 07 | Design Firm: IA Collaborative, Chicago | Creative Director: Dan Kraemer | Designer: Olivia Samson | Client: Unison

92 (bottom), **93** Unison 06/07 | Design Firm: IA Collaborative, Chicago | Creative Director: Dan Kraemer | Designer: Jason Eplawy | Client: Unison

DVDs

94 4 by Agnes Varda | Design Firm: Neil Kellerhouse, Mar Vista | Art Director/Artist/Creative Director/Designer/Typographer: Neil Kellerhouse | Chief Creative Officers: Neil Kellerhouse, Sarah Habibi | Photographer: Agnes Varda | Client: The Criterion Collection

Description: 4 DVDs in individual packages, SlipCase, and 60-page book.

Editorial

95 Fuell Magazine | Design Firm: GS Design, Inc., Milwaukee | Creative Director: Steve Radtke | Designer: Matt Fleming | Writers: Mike Zimmerman, Charles Nevsimal | Client: Buell Motorcycle Company

96, 97 Dot Magazine #15 | Design Firm: Art Center College of Design, Pasadena | Creative Directors: Takaaki Matsumoto, Amy Wilkins, Hisami Aoki | Photographers: Steven A. Heller, Vahe Alaverdian, Dennis Keeley | Project Manager: Jered Gold | Client: Art Center College of Design

Description: DOT is Art Center's biannual magazine that is distributed to the Art Center community (which includes students, faculty and alumni) and those who are interested in the college and the art and Design world.

98 (top) The Two Jakes | Design Firm: GQ magazine/Conde Nast, New York | Design Director: Fred Woodward | Designer: Anton Ioukhnovets | Photographer: Nathaniel Goldberg | Client: GQ magazine

98 (bottom) Mr. Nobody | Design Firm: GQ magazine/Conde Nast, New York | Design Director: Fred Woodward | Designer: Delgis Canahuates | Photographer: Tim Richardson | Client: GQ magazine

99 (top) Christian Rocks | Design Firm: GQ magazine/Conde Nast, New York | Design Director: Fred Woodward | Designer: Anton Ioukhnovets | Photographer: Nathaniel Goldberg | Client: GQ magazine

99 (bottom) The Real Colbert Report | Design Firm: GQ magazine/Conde Nast, New York | Design Director: Fred Woodward | Designer: Thomas Alberty | Photographer: Mark Seliger | Client: GQ magazine

100 DIRECTORY 5 | Design Firm: SVIDesign, London | Creative Director: Sasha Vidakovic | Designers: Sasha Vidakovic, Sarah Bates, Julia Cheftel | Client: Extreme Information

Description: Quarterly magazine/catalogue of best direct marketing campaigns from around the world, available only by subscription.

101 DVA (TWO) MAGAZINE | Design Firm: Design Center Ltd., Ljubljana | Art Director/Artist: Eduard Cehovin | Authors/Chief Creative Officers/Creative Directors/Creative Strategists/Design Directors/Editors/Executive Creative Directors/Executive Creative Strategists: Eduard Cehovin, Fedja Vukic | Print Producers: Gorenjski Tisk, Slovenia | Client: Design Center Ltd.

Description: DVA (TWO) Magazine is about:
– Today and tomorrow
– Past and future
– West and East
– Made in two sheets of paper (B1)
– Written in two languages (English and Serbian/Croatian)
– Created by two friends (Eduard Cehovin and Fedja Vukic)
– Who live in two countries (Slovenia and Croatia)
Sharing the same thoughts about Design in the so-called Eastern Europe.

102 Prefix Photo 15 | Design Firm: Underline Studio, Toronto | Art Directors: Fidel Pena, Claire Dawson, Scott McLeod | Designers: Fidel Pena, Claire Dawson | Client: Prefix Institute of Contemporary Art

Description: Prefix Photo is an engaging magazine that presents contemporary Canadian photography in an international context. Characterized by innovative Design and outstanding production values, it features photography portfolios and critical essays.

103 Hi-Speed Magazine/The Art of Speed | Design Firm: Hans Heinrich Sures, London | Art Director/Creative Director/Designer: Hans Heinrich Sures | Photographers: Hans Heinrich Sures, Elke Bock | Print Producer: Paul Foote | Printer: Assignments UK | Client: Hi-Speed Magazine

Description: Series of on-demand printed posters for a new magazine on the subject of motoring in the widest sense (incl. flying, boating and motorcycling) in Photography and art in general. It will also feature the development of alternative energy sources (like Hydrogen) for vehicles. The magazine will be published bi-annually from 2008.

104, 105 Swarovski | Design Firm: Big Magazine, New York | Creative Director: Daren Ellis | Art Director/Designer: Sy-Jenq Cheng | Photographers: Warren du Preez, Nick Thornton-Jones, Andrew Bettles, Christopher Bucklow, Simen Johan, Christian Coinbergh, André Wolff, Albrecht Kunkel, Nick Knight, Marcus Tomlinson, Benedict Redgrove, Koichiro Doi | Client: Swarovski

106 (top) Spin the Bottle | Design Firm: American Way, Fort Worth | Art Director: Carrie Olivier | Design Director: J.R. Arebalo, Jr. | Photographer: Steve Moors | Client: American Airlines

106 (middle) November 15, 2007 cover | Design Firm: American Way, Fort Worth | Art Director/Design Director: J.R. Arebalo, Jr. | Photographer: Sarah A. Friedman | Client: American Airlines

106 (bottom) Enrique | Design Firm: American Airlines Publishing, Fort Worth | Design Director/Designer: Marco Rosales | Client: American Airlines Publishing

107 (top) Bella Vita! | Design Firm: American Way, Fort Worth | Art Director: Samuel Solomon | Design Director: J.R. Arebalo, Jr. | Photographer: Don Flood | Typographer: Darren Booth | Client: American Airlines

107 (middle) What's In Store for the Holidays | Design Firm: American Way, Fort Worth | Art Director/Design Director: J.R. Arebalo, Jr. | Photographer: Arturo Rodriguez | Client: American Airlines

107 (bottom) 6 C. Liquid Nitrogen + 3 Tbsp. Meat Glue + 1 Sonic Wave Blaster | Design Firm: American Way, Fort Worth | Art Director: Samuel Solomon | Design Director: J.R. Arebalo, Jr. | Photographer: Fredrik Broden | Client: American Airlines

108 December Cover | Design Firm: IPSUM PLANET, Madrid | Art Director: IPSUM PLANET | Creative Director: IPSUM PLANET | Designer: IPSUM PLANET | Photographer: Angelika Buettner | Client: NEO2

109 Trio magazine | Design Firm: Frost Design, Surry Hills | Account Director: Catriona Burgess | Creative Director: Vince Frost | Design Director: Anthony Donovan | Designer: Adrian Hing | Photographer: James Cant | Project Manager: Ellie Bradley | Client: Frasers Property

Description: Property marketing tends to be full of cliches and meaningless superlatives, so when the opportunity came to develop the promotional brochure and campaign for Trio in Sydney's inner west, we wanted to create something not only different but also rich in substance. Our idea was to create a promotional magazine, and to use all of the typical contents of a magazine — fashion spreads, location reviews, interviews and features — to tell the Trio story. The 60-page magazine opens with a stunning fashion feature with single models caught in triplicate, shot by leading fashion Photographer James Cant, with interior styling by Inside Out Style Director Glen Proebstel. Each image was painstakingly styled and art directed to capture a moment that would intrigue readers as well as display an innate understanding of prestige brands through the fashion and product selection. The unspoken message is that this is a development for people who truly know and understand style. The magazine format allowed us to give potential purchasers a much richer understanding of the development, and for its creators to give in-depth interviews about their approach. Architects Fender Katsalidis describe their vision for the new apartments-which will set new benchmarks in style in Sydney's inner west — as well as setting out in detail the features that make it distinctively desirable. Other sections provide top tips about living in the inner west, as well as reviewing local cafés, shops and galleries. Keen to make the magazine a good read in its own right, we commissioned *Vogue Living* contributor Robert Bevan and *Harper's Bazaar* Associate Editor Margaret Merten to write copy. The magazine approach has been extended to the project website and display suite.

Environmental

110, 111 SkyQ Experiential Branding System Installation | Design Firm: Hornall Anderson Design Works, Seattle | Creative Director: Jamie Monberg | Designers: Nathan Young, Joseph King, Hans Krebs, Adrien Lo, Corey Paganucci | Programmers: Ryan Hickner, Jordan Lee | Project Manager: Chris Monberg | Client: Space Needle

Description: Overlooking Seattle's beautiful Elliott Bay, Cascade and Olympic mountain ranges and the city's magnificent skyline, is where Hornall Anderson delivered on the Space Needle's tagline of "Live the View!" positioning, by creating a guest experience unlike those typically found at view-oriented tourist attractions. Interactive designers and technicians built a series of intuitive, highly user-friendly stations that extend the 360-degree view — not just visually, but experientially — as people learn about the many treasures of the Emerald City. The branded experience is called SkyQ.

112, 113 PLATINUM alternative | Design Firm: love the life, Tokyo | Creative Directors: Akemi Katsuno, Takashi Yagi | Designesr: Akemi Katsuno, Takashi Yagi, Kaname Aratame | Photographer: Shinichi Sato | Project Manager: Toshiyuki Kiyohara | Client: Yoshinori Watanabe

Description: "alternative" is a restaurant of contemporary Japanese-style foods. It is on the second floor of in small building at a popular commercial district in Tokyo. There are steps in the center of the floor. The reception and the kitchen are at the one side, the hall at the other side. Those areas are arranged very simply. The partitions of frosted glass divide the hall vaguely. The indirect lighting is in the top and center of the wall. Those aspects of absent-minded colors influence the whole space as "blank with high density." The curved stainless pipes are arranged on the line of flow. The matte black reception counter has sculptural form. The designs of those fixtures are motifs of "Waves at Matsushima" drawn by Korin Ogata.

114, 115 EFD Interior Wall Graphics | Design Firm: Catapult Strategic Design, Phoenix | Account Director: Dave Duke | Art Director: Spencer Walters | Creative Director: Art Lofgreen | Designers: Spencer Walters, Jeff McKee | Client: EFD

Description: Interior graphics program to promote company strategy and fun to both employees and visitors. EFD is a payments solutions company. With the unique ability to take an integrated view of enterprise payments and data & decisioning, EFD provides financial services companies and other large enterprises with business insight to make better new-account decisions, improve fraud detection and management and streamline payment processing. Large images look out of focus with a separate, offset layer of frosted plex. Tiny windows cut through the frost give viewers insight to what is "behind the glass."

116 Museum of the City of New York Construction Barricade | Design Firm: Poulin + Morris Inc., New York | Designers: Richard Poulin, Brian Brindisi, Sarah Meyer | Photographer: Deborah Kushma | Client: Polshek Partnership Architects

Description: In 2006, the Museum of the City of New York's first expansion and renovation project, a three-phase, $80 million effort, was launched. While the Museum's landmark Georgian Revival building has been largely unaltered since 1932, the project includes updating the physical plant, creating new galleries and public program spaces, and renovating the entire facility. The Museum will be open throughout construction and renovation.
The initial phase of work comprises 23,000 square-feet of new space, including the Museum's first climate-controlled gallery, a restored and updated lobby with enhanced visitor amenities, the renovation and restoration of the Fifth Avenue Terrace to improve visitor access, and a crucially needed climate-controlled curatorial center to further preserve the Museum's precious collections. Subsequent phases include the reorganization of the building into public and private spaces, establishing new exhibition galleries and new curatorial and administrative offices. These subsequent phases will also be built to ensure that the building receives the silver certification of the LEED Green Building Rating System, the national benchmark for high-performance green buildings. Poulin + Morris worked closely with the building architect and Museum senior staff members on the programming, design, documentation, and implementation supervision of a comprehensive environmental graphics, donor recognition, and wayfinding sign program that responds to specific requirements of the newly expanded facility. An initial element of the program was the design and implementation supervision of a construction barricade blocking the Fifth Avenue main entrance and surrounding the existing building. The large-scale, brightly colored panels, using the same color and typography found in the existing Museum logotype, identify the Museum to visitors and direct them to a temporary entrance on 103rd Street. The completed program includes building identification, directional, informational, office identification, classroom identification, and regulatory signs relating to building, health, accessibility, fire, and accessibility codes.
The success of the expansion and renovation project will ensure that the City's heritage is available to inspire, entertain, and educate future generations.

117 Samsung Rising Hand Sculpture, Frankfurt Airport | Design Firm: Lorenc + Yoo Design, Roswell | Designer/Artist: Jan Lorenc | Account Director: Cheil Communications in Seoul, Korea - Marketing firm | Design Director: Jan Lorenc / Lorenc+Yoo Design | Location: Frankfurt Airport, Frankfurt, Germany | Photographer: Cheil Communications | Print Producer: Studio Sungshin Fabrication – Studio Sungshin is a company located in Seoul, Korea which specializes in art products fabrication, such as public sculptures and special structures. Studio Sungshin has been working with a lot of Korean and international artists and companies for the last 20 years. It is a total manufacture company with experts in various fields. Its qualified technicians have a deep understanding about the aesthetic aspects of products as well as the materials and techniques to realize the basic concept. | Project Management: Box&Cox in Seoul, Korea | Client: Samsung, Seoul, Korea

Description: Jan Lorenc of Atlanta, Georgia has a reputation for uniting eastern and western traditions to solve sculptural and other artistic challenges. A native of Poland, Lorenc has used this approach to design sculptures for firms in the U.S. and internationally. Entitled "Rising Hand," the painted high-gloss metallic silver with accent red aluminum sculpture rises 50 feet (15 meters). It features a hand holding a Samsung mobile phone. The sculpture has a powerful upward thrust that is futuristic and dynamic. Rather than a realistic hand, Lorenc created an abstract form, one that represents people all over the world. According to Lorenc, the work suggests energy, triumph and the power of global communications. Lorenc views the Rising Hand as a symbol for a world united by global communication and tools such as those that Samsung famously delivers.

118 The Rocket | Design Firm: Young and Laramore, Indianapolis | Artist: David Young | Location: Indianapolis, Indiana | Project Manager: Malissa Cooper | Client: Young and Laramore Advertising

Description: The Rocket is a jungle gym — the gathering point of the playground, located in the uniquely renovated School No. 9. The installation fosters a sense of play throughout the offices of Young & Laramore Advertising. It embraces the spectrum of intelligence between math and art, designed entirely with a compass, where the distances between the rings are proportional to the diameter of the rings (and descending in scale to the infinite).

119 WNYC Radio Broadcast Studios Construction Barricade | Design Firm: Poulin + Morris Inc., New York | Designers: Douglas Morris, Moonsun Kim | Photographer: Deborah Kushma | Client: Jones Lang LaSalle

Description: WNYC New York Public Radio is America's most listened-to public radio station, reaching over one million listeners each week. WNYC FM and AM are New York's premier public radio stations, broadcasting the finest programs from National Public Radio and Public Radio International, as well as a wide range of award-winning signature local programming. In 2006, construction started on WNYC's new broadcast studios located in the Hudson Square neighborhood of Lower Manhattan. WNYC's new home divides 71,900 square-feet between two-and-a-half floors of a 12-story building in the former hub of the city's printing industry. The number of recording studios has been doubled, and a ground-floor, glass-enclosed auditorium and performance space provides the public with a glimpse inside to the inner workings of this popular public radio station.

Initially, WNYC commissioned Poulin + Morris to design and supervise the implementation of a construction barricade covering their street-level space windows. Large-scale, digital vinyl murals pop with a full-color spectrum of bright fuschia, blue, red, and green, combining imagery and typography to announce the station's upcoming arrival. This initial installation uses a visually kinetic graphic equalizer continuing across five windows with the WNYC identity represented at an extreme scale. Additionally, the passer-by is invited to consider typographic statements relying on a play on words of "here" and "hear." Poulin + Morris was also asked to develop, design, document, and supervise the implementation of a comprehensive environmental graphics, wayfinding, and donor recognition program. The visual elements used for all project components are derived from words and visual metaphors of sound. Sound waves, graphic equalizers, voice patterns, and related visual technology all play a major role in this program's realization.

Exhibits

120, 121 National World War I Museum | Design Firm: Ralph Appelbaum Associates, New York | Art Director: Fabio Gherardi | Chief Creative Officer: Ralph Appelbaum | Creative Directors: Chip Jeffries, Tim Ventimiglia | Design Directors: Joshua Dudley, Scott Simeral | Designers: Tana Green, Luka Kito, Jande Wintrob, Josh Hartley, Aki Carpenter | Editors: Nikki Amdur, Christine Valentine | Models: Don MacKinnon, Jan Pietruska, George Robertson, Scott Shepard | Project Managers: Kate Cury, Judy Vannais | Writer: Mary Shapiro | Client: Liberty Memorial Association

Description: The Liberty Memorial Association charged us with creating a museum that, like the memorial itself, would honor "those who served in the World War in defense of liberty and our country." This exhibition shares the stories of those men and women and chronicles one of our nation's central epics, World War I, which brought the United States onto the world stage and marked the beginning of the American century.

122, 123 DLC Trade Show Booth for 2007 ICSC Convention | Design Firm: Lorenc + Yoo Design, Roswell | Account Director: Beth Cochran/Journey Communications | Design Director: Jan Lorenc | Designers: Chung Yoo, Sora Cin, David Park, Steve McCall | Photographer: Rion Rizzo/Creative Sources Photography | Print Producer: ID3 | Project Manager: Beth Cochran/Journey Communications Inc. | Location: Las Vegas Convention Center, Las Vegas, NV | Client: DLC Management Company, Tarrytown, NY

Description: Trade Show Booth for the International Council of Shopping Centers 2007 Convention. The concept was to reintroduce this Maverick company and its real estate holdings in a bold and unique fashion. The User was greeted by large-scale letters and had to venture into the space to get the whole picture. We used the company's unique ads over the past years as an accent to the space.

Illustration

124 Designer | Design Firm: Peter Kraemer, Duesseldorf | Art Director: Peter Kraemer | Artist/Designer/Editor/Illustrator: Peter Kraemer | Client: Peter Kraemer

Description: Illustration for a greeting card that shows a cactus in shape of a pencil (self-promotion).

125 Great Expectations | Design Firm: Ogline Design, Marlton | Editors: Chris Satullo, John Timpane | Illustrator: Tim E. Ogline | Writers: Chris Satullo, Tom Ferrick Jr., Dave Boyer, Russell Cooke | Client: The Philadelphia Inquirer

Description: "Great Expectations," an eight-week series for *The Philadelphia Inquirer* was a joint project of *The Philadelphia Inquirer* Editorial Board and the Project on Civic Engagement at the University of Pennsylvania. This series (comprised of 15 installments — each with an accompanying illustration by Tim E. Ogline) discussed the issues and challenges that the City of Philadelphia faced as it prepared for the Mayoral election on November 6, 2007. The project also featured a website and blog, candidate forums as well as citizen, neighborhood, and issue forums. Pieces submitted from this series include illustrations on the themes of city services (Philadelphia's infrastructure), crime (focusing on the escalating murder rates in the City of Brotherly Love), ethics (the rampant pay-to-play culture that plagues City Hall), environment (green initiatives for Philadelphia), and arts & culture (discussing Philly's rich historic legacy and arts experiences).

126 Vogue Magazine Insert | Design Firm: Nordstrom, Seattle | Client: Nordstrom

Description: Nordstrom's *Vogue* magazine Insert for September *Vogue*.

127 Look of Love | Design Firm: Mirko Ilic Corp., New York | Art Director: Rob Wilson | Illustrator: Mirko Ilic | Client: Playboy

Interactive

128 Tommy Bahama Web Site | Design Firm: Hornall Anderson Design Works, Seattle | Creative Directors: Jamie Monberg, Greg Quist | Designers: Nathan Young, Joseph King, Hans Krebs, Adrien Lo, Corey Paganucci | Programmers: Gordon Mueller, Matt Frickelton | Project Manager: Erica Goldsmith | Client: Tommy Bahama

Description: Bringing the in-store experience online. That was the objective of Tommy Bahama when they approached Hornall Anderson seeking to evolve their online shopping process. Through a new, richer web presence, visitors are offered a true digital "experience" that mirrors the Tommy Bahama signature brand offerings. This site redesign marries the extension of their products, retail look & feel, and customer service to the creation of a new e-commerce platform with intuitive buy-flow, all designed to seamlessly launch their products online. The result is a deep on-brand consumer experience backed by a robust design and technology solution, enabling guests to shop and take part in the Tommy Bahama community in a refined and relaxed manner — the Tommy Bahama way of life. *www.tommybahama.com*

129 LEVEL Loop | Design Firm: G2 Branding and Design, New York | Creative Director: Phil Koutsis | Designer: Maria Samodra | Motion Grpahics: KC Tagliareni | Client: LEVEL Vodka

130 ferreiradesign.com | Design Firm: Ferreira Design Company, Alpharetta | Creative Director/Designer: Lionel Ferreira | Programmer: Neil Gamradt/inovaone.com | Client: Ferreira Design Company

Description: Self-promotional site.

131 TheOvenReinvented | Design Firm: mono, Minneapolis | Art Director/Creative Director/Writer: mono | Web Developer: Your Majesty | Client: TurboChef

Description: An interactive site that brings to life why the TurboChef is the oven reinvented. Utilizing an "explode" mode, you're able to see how the oven works and learn more about the controls and functions, as well as swap out door colors. You can also have four-star chef Charlie Trotter cook any one of five dishes for you. This site gives you the ability to see and interact with the oven, much like you would on a high-end automobile site. *www. theovenreinvented.com*

132 SCI-Arc | Design Firm: Hello Design, Culver City | Account Director: Anna Simonse | Chief Creative Officer: David Lai | Creative Director: Hiro Niwa | Design Director: Ron Thompson | Designers: KunChe Lu, Midori Yamanaka | Programmers: Brian Johnson, Jessica Shao, Jason Taylor | Web Developer: Hugo Zhu | Client: Southern California Institute of Architecture

Description: The Southern California Institute of Architecture (SCI-Arc) is an independent, avant-garde architecture school in downtown Los Angeles. The new website embodies the vibrant atmosphere for prospective students and keeps currently enrolled students up-to-date with events and news. The course structure for all degree programs is accessible through the Flash-based navigation, providing not only course descriptions but linking instructors and relevant work. Over 30 years of the school's history is archived on the web, including full-length video lectures and gallery exhibitions by world-renowned architects, designers and writers such as Norman Klein, John Maeda, Rudolph Schindler and Eric Owen Moss. *www.sciarc.edu*

133 ColorCore 2 Microsite | Design Firm: Kuhlmann Leavitt Inc., St. Louis | Design Director: Deanna Kuhlmann-Leavitt | Designer: Krista Hoppe | Photographer: Scott Dorrance | Stylist: Vivian Ogier | Typographer: Kulhmann Leavitt, Inc. | Web Developer: Propaganda 3 | Writer: Penny Benda | Client: Formica Corporation

Description: The ColorCore® 2 microsite was created for the Formica Corporation re-launch of the product they first introduced over 25 years ago. Through improved technology, ColorCore® was ready to come back as a modern solution to the dark lines of today's laminates and it needed a fresh campaign to reach specifiers in Canada, the USA and Mexico. A direct mailer and an email blast increased awareness of the launch, and the microsite provided additional relevant information regarding the product, as well as a photo gallery, a competitive game to share with co-workers and the ability to order samples or contact a representative through the site. The campaign was considered a great success when the clients received a large quantity of positive feedback and new job leads within hours of the launch.

134 WHR Architects Web Site | Design Firm: Savage, Houston | Account Director: Doug Hebert | Art Director/Designer: Daren Guillory | Chief Creative Officer/Creative Director: Dahlia Salazar | Creative Strategist/Design Director/Project Manager: Doug Hebert | Location: Houston, Texas | Photographer: Drew Donovan | Programmers: Chris MacGregor, Jonathan Thompson, Craig Tooms | Typographer/Web Developer: Savage | Writer: Scott Redepenning | Client: WHR Architects

Description: The site's primary objective was to allow access to WHR's extensive portfolio while portraying the personality of its employees. The portfolio section gives one the ability to scan thumbnails and large images while keeping project specific-details a click away, and is balanced with a featured employee section with interviews, testimonials and portraits. The site utilizes Flash, XML, AJAX, XSLT and ASP within a content-managed system for ease of updating.

135 Ronald McDonald House web site | Design Firm: Ogilvy, Durham | Art Directors: Sara Mc-Creary, Callie Peck | Creative Director: Jeff Dahlberg | Associate Creative Director: Noah Rosenberg | Programmers: Craig Mann, Callie Peck | Writer: Heather Apple, Laura Rudolph | Client: Ronald McDonald House

Description: The Ronald McDonald House of Chapel Hill (RMH) is a nonprofit organization that provides a home for sick children and their families while they are being treated at local hospitals. RMH operates entirely on donations from individuals and corporations. Their goal was to increase donations by bringing in new donors or by increasing the donations of those who were already involved. The big idea for the work was to show the balance in the house. However bad these families' situations are, the RMH has to be that much better. They have to counter the sickness and the sadness with as much joy and happiness as possible. The RMH web site extends the same dual message in a flash-based interface. Its design is clean and functional, with an easy-to-use backend so the RMH staff can update their news and events sections and change out photos or staff bios without having to format them. The site includes a game, a place to sign up to become a volunteer and an interactive, printable shopping list.

Invitations
136 "Stroud" Christmas Card | Design Firm: The Brand Union, London | Art Director/Creative Director/Design Director/Executive Creative Director: Glenn Tutssel | Designers: Glenn Tutssel, Lauren Tutssel, Anthony Clayton | Client: Jane Tutssel

Description: Every year, the Tutssel family send out a Christmas card based on the culture of their surrounding neighborhood in Gloucestershire, England. Last year (December 2007) was the story of local cloth relating to Santa Claus.

137 Brad Radke Retirement Party | Design Firm: Parachute design, Minneapolis | Creative Director: Bob Upton | Designer: Charlie Ross | Client: Brad Radke

Description: Decorations were created for a private party to celebrate the retirement of Minnesota Twins' pitcher, Brad Radke. The pieces were created to transform a sparse Marriott Hotel reception hall into a historical salute to Brad's life and career.

138 Ann Rides Again Invitation | Design Firm: GSD&M's Idea City, Austin | Art Director: Marty Erhart | Artist: Anne Rix Sifuentez | Creative Directors: Tim McClure, Marty Erhart | Designers: Marty Erhart, Marc Ferrino | Writer: Tim McClure | Illustrator: Marc Ferrino | Print Producer: Diane Patrick | Project Manager: Mara Truskoloski | Client: Austin Film Society

Description: To promote the 2007 Texas Film Hall of Fame Awards by honoring the late Ann Richards (who was scheduled to host the previous year's award show but could not, due to being diagnosed with cancer.) Inspired by the classic Texas Monthly shot of Ann Richards on a motorcycle, we came up with the theme "Ann Rides Again," rendering it as a motorcyclist's tattoo.

139 Blue Jean Ball Event Materials | Design Firm: Webster Design Associates, Omaha | Account Director: Lisa Hug | Creative Director: Dave Webster | Designer: Karen Koch | Client: Make A Wish Foundation of Nebraska

Description: The Blue Jean Ball was the 2007 annual fundraising event for the Make A Wish Foundation of Nebraska. We designed and produced the belt buckles for the cover photo, which then became auction items at the event.

Letterhead
140, 141 Corporate Stationery | Design Firm: SamataMason, Dundee | Art Director: Dave Mason | Designers: Beth May, Skot Waldron | Client: Sesame Workshop

142 World Edventures Stationery System | Design Firm: Catapult Strategic Design, Phoenix | Account Director: Brad Ghormley | Art Director/Illustrator: Spencer Walters | Creative Director: Brad Ghormley | Designers: Spencer Walters, Gini Price | Printer: Oneil Printing | Client: World Edventures

Description: Higher education study abroad program: Education meets Adventure!

143 Creative Director | Design Firm: Finished Art, Inc., Atlanta | Creative Directors: Donna Johnston, Kannex Fung | Designer: Kannex Fung | Illustrators: Barbara Dorn, Luis Fernandez, Mary Jane Hasek, Kevin Inglls, Cory Langner, Sutti Sahunalu | Client: Kannex Fung

Description: Finished Art, Inc. created a set of unique business cards to showcase the talents of the diverse illustration and Design studio in Atlanta, GA. Creative die-cuts and folds make a series of cards that reveal a variety of artwork created by staff artists. The design allows for use as a traditional business card or a stand-up card for display.

Logos
144 Logotype for campaign "Germany produces more..." | Design Firm: WAJS, Hoechberg | Art Director/Designer: Joachim Schmeisser | Client: VDMA - Verband Deutscher Maschinen- und Anlagenbau e.V.

Description: Logotype for the VDMA campaign "Germany produces more..." which means in the figurative sense "beyond producing."
VDMA – the German engineering federation.

145 PLATINUM Olynthia Olive Oil | Design Firm: SVIDesign, London | Creative Director: Sasha Vidakovic | Designers: Sasha Vidakovic, Sarah Bates | Client: Olynthia

Description: Branding and packaging of organic olive oil from a small island in the Adriatic sea.

146 Shiner Black Lager Packaging Campaign | Design Firm: McGarrah/Jessee, CHAOS, Austin | Design Director/Designer: David Kampa | Client: Spoetzl Brewery

147 (top) The Wine Tie Logo | Design Firm: Lam Design Group, Arlington | Account Director/Art Director/Artist/Chief Creative Officer/Creative Director/Illustrator/Typographer: Linda T. Lam | Client: Kyriakos and Megan Pagonis

Description: Neck tie for a wine bottle. A neck tie that sits on the neck of a wine bottle and catches the drips.

147 (second) Time Travelers logo | Design Firm: Pennebaker, Houston | Creative Director/Designer: Jeffrey McKay | Client: Time Travelers

147 (third) Zwick Construction Company Logo | Design Firm: Catapult Strategic Design, Phoenix | Account Director: Dave Duke | Art Director/Creative Director/Designer: Art Lofgreen | Illustrator: Jon Arvizu | Client: Zwick Construction Company

Description: Hands-on, one-on-one, customer – service – oriented construction management.

147 (fourth) Tokyo Food Museum "Tower logo" | Design Firm: Graphics & Designing Inc., Tokyo | Art Director/Designer: Toshihiro Onimaru | Creative Director: Takanori Aiba | Client: Tokyo Good Idea Development Institute Co., Ltd.

Description: Facility based on a theme of the food culture in Tokyo. In the logo, Tokyo Tower — a symbolic structure of the city — is expressed in Japanese kanji character.

147 (bottom) BlackDog monogram | Design Firm: BlackDog, San Francisco | Designer/Illustrator: Mark Fox | Client: BlackDog

Description: A BD monogram for a San Francisco Graphic Design studio.

148 (top) Phoenix Convention Center Logo | Design Firm: Catapult Strategic Design, Phoenix | Account Director: Brad Ghormley | Art Director/Designer/Illustrator: Spencer Walters | Creative Director: Art Lofgreen | Client: City of Phoenix

Description: Mark created for new Phoenix Convention Center — a place where people come together for business and commerce.

148 (second) Southern California Restaurant | Design Firm: Brand Envy, Seattle | Art Director/Designer: Nadine Stellavato | Client: Akasha Restaurant

Description: Located in the historic Hull Building in downtown Culver City, AKASHA restaurant/bar/bakery features New American cuisine, offering comfort food with big flavors and sustainable ingredients for carnivores and herbivores alike. Keeping the principles of sustainability in mind, the building's original steel, wood, concrete and brick arches were restored while the design materials pair with a 70s modernity to exude an inviting and lively atmosphere.

148 (third) D'Ambrosio logo | Design Firm: Ogilvy, Durham | Creative Director: Jeff Dahlberg | Associate Creative Director: Noah Rosenberg | Designer: Carolin Harris | Client: D'Ambrosio

Description: Otto D'Ambrosio is a luthier by trade and heart. His guitars are hand-crafted and made to fit the owner's personality, making them more than just an instrument. Otto was in need of an identity that would represent the harmony of craft, music and beauty reflected in his guitars. The resulting design mimicks guitar strings, the movement of sound and traditional guitar logos. It speaks to Otto's heritage of craftsmenship and the delicate curves present in his product. This identity departs from existing ones in that it takes a step forward while not neglecting tradition. It is handcrafted, as are Otto's guitars, and created to be timeless, as are the guitars. The logo's dynamism lies within its upward movement and highly varied line weights, as if it had been written in musical notes.

148 (fourth) Bryant & Duffey | Design Firm: A3 Design, Charlotte | Art Director/Designer: Alan Altman | Client: Bryant & Duffey Optometrist

Description: This optometrist practice was looking (ahem!) for a simple, memorable logo. After pages of sketches and ideas, we discovered a similarity between a *b*, a *d*, and a pair of eyeglasses. Then it all came into, um, focus. The clean, bold line illustration is the very model of classic understatement, and the "bridge" between the two letters implies a partnership of strength and, yes, vision (okay, we'll stop now).

148 (bottom) Fashion Building "DooRooMoo" | Design Firm: Graphics & Designing Inc., Tokyo | Art Director/Designer: Toshihiro Onimaru | Creative Director: Takanori Aiba | Client: World Co.,Ltd.

Description: The fashion building owned by World, the general apparel maker. The logo consists of an *R* and *M* framed by a *D*. It depicts the expanse of the interior of the facility beyond the doors. It was designed to evoke feelings of gentleness and pleasure, graceful movement and modern sharpness. The graphic's apparent complexity is offset by the fact that it was made to be reproduced on paper and cloth clothing tags in monochrome.

149 Cafy's logo | Design Firm: Ventress Design Group, Franklin | Designer: Tom Ventress | Client Cafy's Roast House Cafe

150 Logo | Design Firm: Bailey Lauerman, Lincoln | Art Director: Ron Sack | Creative Director: Carter Weitz | Designers: Ron Sack, James Strange | Illustrator: Gayle Adams | Client: International Quilt Study Center

Description: Logo for International Quilt Study Center in Lincoln, Nebraska.

151 (top) Eye-Q Logo | Design Firm: Hershey|Cause, Santa Monica | Creative Director: R. Christine Hershey | Design Director: Joanna Lee | Designer: Jerry Lazaro | Client: Hershey|Cause

Description: Eye-Q Logo – The Eye-Q concept which includes tests, webinars and classes, was recently developed in collaboration by Hershey|Cause founder R. Christine Hershey and writer Andy Goodman to train nonprofit veterans, newbies, and anyone in between to know what it takes to develop effective communications materials for their organization. A play on the word I.Q. the Eye-Q helps identify and sharpen a person's marketing design I.Q and helps one develop the keen eye of an expert when evaluating visual elements in marketing materials. Hershey|Cause developed a logo to support this fun, informative concept. The resulting logo combines creative design and a play on the eye image, ideal for representing the Eye-Q concept.

151 (second) Pato Zazo Logo | Design Firm: Sibley/Peteet Design, Austin | Art Director: Rex Peteet | Designers: Rex Peteet, David Kampa | Client: El Pato Fresh Mexican Food

Credits

Description: Pato (meaning duck in Spanish) is the mascot and symbol for this fresh food Mexican restaurant. "Pato," a term of endearment coined by the childhood friends of the owner, stuck with him. The mark is inspired by the Mola art of South America.

151 (third) Tokyo Food Museum | Design Firm: Graphics & Designing Inc., Tokyo | Art Director/Designer: Toshihiro Onimaru | Creative Director: Takanori Aiba | Client: Tokyo Good Idea Development Institute Co., Ltd.

Description: Facility based on a theme of the food culture in Tokyo. In the logo, Tokyo Tower — a symbolic structure of the city — is expressed in Japanese kanji character.

151 (fourth) PrismaGraphic Logo | Design Firm: Catapult Strategic Design, Phoenix | Account Director: Brad Ghormley | Art Director/Creative Director/Designer: Art Lofgreen | Client: Prisma-Graphic Corp.

Description: Full-service printing company.

151 (bottom) Window On Women | Design Firm: Jan Šabach, Munich | Art Director/Designer: Jan Šabach | Project Managers: Jaroslav Cir, Joanne Loader | Client: Unilever

Description: Logo for an online-based community.

152 (top) Drum Room Logo | Design Firm: RBMM, Dallas | Designer/Illustrator: Brian Owens | Client: Drum Room

Description: Restaurant, casual nightclub and lounge located in the historic Hilton President Kansas City.

152 (second) Dallas Legal Foundation Logo | Design Firm: RBMM, Dallas | Designer: Kevin Bailey | Client: Dallas Legal Foundation

Description: Effecting systemic change through representation, advocacy and community education.

152 (third) Antler Ranch Logo | Design Firm: RBMM, Dallas | Creative Director: Dick Mitchell | Designer/Illustrator: Brian Owens | Client: Antler Ranch

Description: Whitetail deer breeding ranch.

152 (fourth) Lakewood Child Development Center Logo | Design Firm: RBMM, Dallas | Account Director/Designer/Illustrator: Yvette Wheeler | Location: Dallas, Texas | Client: Lakewood Child Development Center

Description: Daycare facility for children ranging in age from 6 weeks to 5 years old.

152 (bottom) Lobo Tortilla Factory Logo | Design Firm: RBMM, Dallas | Designer: Kevin Bailey | Client: Lobo Tortilla Factory

Description: A manufacturer of flour and corn tortillas and pre-cut corn chips.

153 Mailer Magic Logo | Design Firm: RBMM, Dallas | Designer: Brian Owens | Client: Williamson Printing Corporation

Description: Self-promotion for printing company, promoting their state-of-the-art, in-line direct mail printing capabilities.

Menus

154, 155 Michael Smith Wine Menu | Design Firm: Barkley, Kansas City | Chief Creative Officer: Brian Brooker | Creative Director: Craig Neuman | Design Director: Travis Kramer | Designers: Travis Kramer, Jennifer Jacquinot, Kathy Johnson, Ai Osada | Print Producer: Shelley Schulenberg | Client: Michael Smith

MusicCDs

156 OHM+ CD and DVD set | Design Firm: Stoltze Design, Boston | Art Director: Clifford Stoltze | Designers: Clifford Stoltze, Tammy Dotson, Soe Lin Post | Client: Ellipsis Arts

Description: This collection is a humble but bold attempt to give form to the wonderful, multi-directional, inevitable birth of electronic music. A three-CD set with bonus DVD and 96-page book in a transparent slipcase cover, OHM+ explores the work of the pioneers of electronic music. The intended audience is anyone with an interest in eclectic, experimental music of historical and artistic significance. It should also appeal to anyone interested in the history and evolution of contemporary electronic music. The packaging, designed with intricate patterns of connecting lines, circles and squiggles that resemble bolts of electrical activity between two conductors, was intended to suggest the inner workings of an electric device, possibly an unusual musical instrument.

157 The BBC Tapes Vol 1-6 | Design Firm: Pentagram Design, London | Art Director: Harry Pearce | Client: Roy Harper

Description: Harry Pearce has designed the sleeve art for the re-issue of The BBC Tapes, a set of CDs by cult singer/songwriter Roy Harper, released by Harper's Science Friction Records. Pearce's design for the series emulates Harper's subtle poetry in its central motif. Portraits of Harper, taken during the period the recordings were made, have been cropped so that the singer's eyes are the same size within each image, evoking the intensity and intimacy of the recordings. The simple, vertical typography, set in Akzidenz Grotesk, and monochromatic treatment of the photographs means that the most direct way of differentiating between CDs at a glance is through Harper's facial expressions. Recorded at sessions for the BBC between 1969 and 1978, The BBC Tapes is a record of some incredible live performances by a legendary English maverick who has collaborated with Led Zeppelin, Kate Bush and Pink Floyd, amongst others.

Harper writes of the design – "To maximise an original intention, its packaging; the vehicle of its presentation to the world, should always aim to be more than the sum of the design. At best, it should always have its own complimentary but very separate meaning, which should transcend written explanation. "I've known Harry for the past 27 years. Our friendship has developed in the crucible of many shared views of the nature of humanity and our response to it. The purity of the palette we have generally chosen to use for my work

over the years exemplifies our shared belief in allowing images to speak for themselves. A lot of content that would seem to be inaccessible can be made more available with the help of commiserate imagery."

Outdoor

158, 159 "PENCIL TRAFFIC CONES" | Design Firm: KNARF, New York | Art Directors: Jeseok Yi, Andrew Seagrave, Frank Anselmo | Creative Director/Illustrator: Frank Anselmo | Designers: Andrew Seagrave, Jeseok Yi, Frank Anselmo | Photographer: Billy Siegrist | Writers: Frank Anselmo, Andrew Seagrave, Jeseok Yi | Client: D&AD

Packaging

160 (top left, top right) Alchera | Design Firm: RBMM, Dallas | Account Director: Michele Crick | Creative Director: Yvette Wheeler | Designer: Yvette Wheeler | Illustrator: Yvette Wheeler | Photographer: John Wong | Client: Domistyle

Description: Home fragrance line.

160 (bottom left, bottom right) Atmosphere | Design Firm: RBMM, Dallas | Account Director: Michele Crick | Designer: Yvette Wheeler | Photographer: John Wong | Client: Domistyle

Description: Home fragrance line.

161 Bohéme | Design Firm: RBMM, Dallas | Account Director: Michele Crick | Art Director/Creative Director: Yvette Wheeler | Designer: Christy Gray | Photographer: John Wong | Client: Domistyle

Description: Home fragrance line.

162 Banana Republic Discover Collection | Design Firm: Desgrippes Gobé, New York | Account Director: Renee Peet | Creative Director: Sam O'Donahue | Design Director: Lela Houston | Designer: Iwona Waluk | Executive Creative Director: David Israel | Executive Creative Strategist: Judd Harner | Writer: Laura Fitzgerald | Client: Banana Republic

Description: After an impressive launch ten years earlier, Banana Republic's line of personal care products had been languishing. With over 400 retail outlets, they knew that there was a huge opportunity to completely re-imagine their approach to personal care. In 11 short months, we helped Banana Republic create 5 beautiful new fragrances — three scents for women; Rosewood, Alabaster, and Jade; and two scents for men: Slate and Black Walnut. The bottle for Jade is shaped like an acorn. Alabaster is modeled after a teardrop, and the inspiration for Rosewood was a pebble. The men's fragrances are of similar design but use a more masculine, square shape.

163 uno | Design Firm: Shin Matsunaga Design Inc., Tokyo | Art Director: Shin Matsunaga | Creative Director: Taisuke Kikuchi | Designers: Shinjiro Matsunaga, Mao Komai | Client: Shiseido Co., Ltd.

Description: Cosmetics for men.

164 (top) Loseley Ice Cream Tubs | Design Firm: Pemberton & Whiteford Design Consultants, Marylebone | Art Directors: Simon Pemberton, Adrian Whiteford | Designer: Lee Newham | Illustrators: Lee Newham, Anne Sharpe, Sharif Tarbay, Martin Hargreaves, Warren Madill, Jon Rogers | Writers: Lee Newham, Gina Hall | Client: Hill Station

Description: Loseley is an old English brand of premium Ice Cream that desperately needed revitalizing. Often found in theatres, cinemas and National Trust sites, it was once owned and produced in the grounds of Loseley Park by the Loseley family themselves. The solution was to go back to the origins of the brand, to use portraits based on the pictures hanging in Loseley House. At first look they appear deadpan but on scrutiny reveal a subtle humorous twist (and they are all enjoying their ice cream). Back of pack copy is as if it was written by the characters in the portraits (each flavour is written in a different style, right down to the ingredients), singing the praises of the subjects favourite flavour.

Loseley Brief – Packaging should reflect English heritage of brand, give good standout and be clearly different from other brands. Packaging should reflect premium positioning but inject ownable personality to brand.

164 (middle) Seeds of Change Simmer Sauces | Design Firm: Sandstrom Design, Portland | Creative Director/Design Director: Marc Cozza | Designers: Chris Gardiner, Marc Cozza | Illustrator: Howell Golson | Print Producer/Project Manager: Kelly Bohls | Writer: Mark Waggoner | Client: Seeds of Change

Description: The challenge was to create a visual story that conveys the richness-of-place and depth-of-flavor that is inherent in these sauces. The bottles themselves are designed to be clean and simple cylinders around which a rich-colored ribbon of label depicts scenery, ingredients and a short history of the sauce itself. This package jumps off the shelf at retail because of its bright and exotic personality.

164 (bottom) Waitrose High Fruit Jams | Design Firm: Turner Duckworth, San Francisco | Account Director: Moira Riddell | Creative Directors: David Turner, Bruce Duckworth | Designer: Mike Harris | Photographer: Andy Grimshaw | Photographer's Assistant (Retouching and Artwork): Reuben James | Client: Waitrose

Description: Waitrose briefed us to redesign their High Fruit Jams range to coincide with a product reformulation. The range now contains the highest level of fruit content within the reduced sugar sector of the market. Our brief was to communicate the deliciously fruity jam to be found in each jar. The result is an uncluttered label which heroes each of the fruits. The images are placed "high" on the label, and with a name like "High Fruit" the message cannot be missed!

165 Gateau Breton package | Design Firm: Tracy Sabin, Carlsbad | Art Director: Bridget Sabin | Designer/Illustrator: Tracy Sabin | Client: Seafarer Baking Company

Description: Label and package design for Gateau Breton, a shortbread that originates from Brittany, France.

166, 167 PLATINUM Ugly Mug Coffee Packaging | Design Firm: Young and Laramore, Indianapolis | Account Directors: Margit Fawbush, Christian Mehall | Art Director: Trevor Williams | Creative Director: Charlie Hopper | Designer: Yee-Haw Industries | Photographer: Harold Lee Miller | Writer: Bryan Judkins | Client: Ugly Mug Coffee

Description: Capturing the feel of a brand as unpretentious as Ugly Mug, yet retaining enough sophistication to reassure that this is indeed premium coffee (and confirm that the "ugly" joke is deliberate), a high-end silver background was combined with letterpress, actually-funny humor, and ugly mugshots of people right out of bed and in desperate need of good coffee.

168 (top) India Pale Ale Packaging | Design Firm: tbdadvertising, Bend | Account Director: Rene Mitchell | Creative Director: Paul Evers | Designer: David Carlson - Gearbox | Illustrator: Mona Caron | Writer: Frank Gjata | Client: Odell Brewing, Co.

Description: The packaging for this special line of beers was designed to help elevate Odell Brewing Co. It brings sophistication and conveys their handcrafted approach and passion for brewing. The image of the casual contemporary west coast character riding a bucking elephant captures the spirit of this Western-American variation of the traditional India Pale Ale.

168 (bottom) 2007 Jubelale | Design Firm: tbdadvertising, Bend | Account Director: Kevin Smyth | Creative Director: Paul Evers | Designer: Benjamin Kinzer | Illustrator: Lindy Gruger | Client: Deschutes Brewery

Description: This packaging for Deschutes Brewery's Jubelale is unique from year to year and is designed using paintings by local Northwest artists that convey the celebration of winter and the holiday spirit.

169 Gran Centenario Leyenda | Design Firm: Klim Design, Inc., Avon | Art Directors/Illustrators: Matt Klim, Marcus Klim | Designers: Matt Klim, Marcus Klim, Peter Klimkiewicz | Client: Jose Cuervo International

170 Belvedere IceTower | Design Firm: mass, New York | Chief Creative Officer: Stephan Valter | Designers: Stephan Valter, Kai Zimmermann | Client: LVMH

Description: BELVEDERE ICETOWER, a retail packaging for LVMH that turns into a sleek and functional product for clubs and homes: a high-presentation ice container that lets the bottle be the star of the entertainment. The intriguing design adds a sensual and playful element: on store shelves the acrylic packaging visually distorts the shape of the super-premium vodka bottle; by adding ice and water the bottle magically regains its shape.

171 10 Year Old - White Porto | Design Firm: Wren and Rowe Ltd, London | Account Director: Paul Foulkes - Arellano | Author/Creative Director: Michael Rowe | Location: London | Photographer: Andy Atkinson | Project Manager: Alex Kontetski | Client: JH Andresen

Description: Andresen 10 Year Old White Port is a new product in the market. Whilst there have been matured white Ports issued before, classified as "Reserve" Ports, only recently has the IVDP (the Douro & Port Wine Institute, regulators of the Port industry) allowed an age statement to be included. A new classification in Port is very rare indeed, and took three years of lobbying by Carlos Flores, MD of Andresen, before he was allowed to issue this Port. He plans 20, 30 and 40 Year Olds next! The design reflects the heritage of the company, founded back in 1845, and has the gravitas necessary to justify the premium price. It is, however, modern in execution and materials. The clear bottle, two-part cream labels, cream capsule and the premium gift carton are finished in a unique, matching paper texture to the label. JH Andresen successfully communicates the originality of a new product with fresh and modern credentials. The new product was launched to the French Horeca trade in Autumn 2006 and is now listed in top hotels and restaurants across Paris. France has taken several thousand cases already. In 2007 the global rollout to other white Port markets — particularly USA and Canada — begins, as well as the listings in European Duty Free.

172 Miletta Vista Campaign | Design Firm: Bailey Lauerman, Lincoln | Art Directors/Designers: Ron Sack, James Strange | Creative Director: Carter Weitz | Illustrator: Gayle Adams | Photographer: Scott Dobry | Client: Miletta Vista

Description: A winery located on the Nebraska prairie.

173 Snowy Egret White | Design Firm: Bailey Lauerman, Lincoln | Art Directors: James Strange, Ron Sack | Creative Director: Carter Weitz | Illustrator: James Strange | Client: Lincoln Childrens Zoo

Description: Wine sold locally in Lincoln to support the children's zoo. The bottle features one of the zoo's birds.

174 (middle) Keyboards | Design Firm: Graphic Design, Apple Computer, Cupertino | Creative Director: Apple Graphic Design, Apple Industrial Design, Apple Packaging Engineering | Client: Apple

Description: The box was designed as a slim package mirroring the thinness of the product and saving storeroom space.

174, 175 (top) iPhone | Design Firm: Graphic Design, Apple Computer, Cupertino | Creative Director: Apple Graphic Design, Apple Industrial Design, Apple Packaging Engineering | Client: Apple

Description: From the moment the box is opened, the iPhone packaging is designed to deliver an elegant presentation of the product and all its components, while making the most economical use of space possible.

174, 175 (bottom) iPhone Bluetooth Headset Package | Design Firm: Graphic Design, Apple Computer, Cupertino | Creative Director: Apple Graphic Design, Apple Industrial Design, Apple Packaging Engineering | Client: Apple

Description: The iPhone Bluetooth headset is intended to present the product with as much consideration as iPhone packaging itself. The singular focus on the headset is elegant, while discreetly packing away the cable, dock, and printed materials.

176 Karma | Design Firm: Nike Golf Image Design, Beaverton | Account Director: Mark Alan | Art Director/Creative Director: Satoru Igarashi | Designer: David Creech | Project Manager: Liza Blackwell, Nola Jensen | Client: Nike Golf Inc

Description: Display for the Karma ball packaging.

177 Dunhill Tribute Packaging | Design Firm: G2 Branding and Design, New York | Creative Director: Ed Taussig | Designer: Sara Press | Client: Dunhill

178 40th Anniversary Packaging | Design Firm: MiresBall, San Diego | Creative Director: John Ball | Designer: Dylan Jones | Photographer: Marc Tule | Project Manager: Holly Houk | Client: Shure Microphone

Description: Marking the 40th anniversary of the legendary Shure SM58 microphone, MiresBall designed limited edition packaging that evokes the rugged durability that has made it a mainstay among performers worldwide. With a chiseled anniversary seal and bold application of Shure color, the packaging helped spark an up-tick in sales of the classic mic.

179 Flawless Paint | Design Firm: Turner Duckworth, San Francisco | Account Director: Moira Riddell | Creative Directors: David Turner, Bruce Duckworth | Designers: Emma Thompson, Mike Harris | Photographer: Andy Grimshaw | Photographer's Assistant (Retoucher): Matt Kay | Print Producer (Artworker): Reuben James | Client: Homebase Ltd

Description: Leading British DIY chain Homebase has created a range of wall paints with a distinct usp within the market-the paint dries to a perfect finish whether applied by an amateur or professional decorator. Designed and named by Turner Duckworth, our solution is based on the range usp of perfection. Thus the range has the biggest possible paint swatch (in the world!) to show the customer exactly what they want to see, the color and finish.

PaperCompanies

180 Sappi Proudly Introducing Lustro Offset Environmental | Design Firm: VSA Partners, Chicago | Art Director: Jason Kriegler | Author: Jonathon Turitz | Creative Director: Dana Arnett | Photographers: Francios Robert, Mark Smalling | Client: Sappi Fine Papers of North America

181 Sappi Ideas that Matter direct mail | Design Firm: Weymouth Design, San Francisco | Art Director: Arvi Raquel-Santos | Creative Director: Bob Kellerman | Designer: Arvi Raquel-Santos | Photographers: Various from Getty and Corbis, Michael Weymouth (judge photography) | Writers: Jean Gogolin, Wordwright | Client: Sappi Fine Paper

Description: In order to gain more visibility for Sappi's Ideas that Matter campaign, we decided to break the traditional format of Sappi's single call for entry brochure into three separate direct-mail pieces, which will mail out six weeks apart from each other.

The world's problems aren't pretty, so why do designers feel that they need to sugarcoat it when approaching a design project such as this? This year, we designed the piece to take on a grittier approach, alluding to the look and feel of an editorial piece. There are a ton of problems in the world and it needs all the help it can get to fix it. All it takes is one good and meaningful idea.

Posters

182 Lippa Pearce Talk | Design Firm: Pentagram Design, London | Art Director: Harry Pearce | Client: Pentagram

Description: Domenic Lippa and Harry Pearce produced this poster to celebrate over 20 years of working together. The Typographic Talk was held at the Typographic Circle on the 22nd of February, 2007.

183 Burma | Design Firm: Pentagram Design, London | Art Director: Harry Pearce | Client: WITNESS

Description: This poster was designed for an event organized by NY-based charity WITNESS to raise awareness about human rights violations in Burma. It has been used by WITNESS and Burma Issues to raise awareness of the crisis displacing rural civilians in eastern Burma whose homes are burnt.

184 Big Ideas Are In The Air | Design Firm: Studio @ One Zero Charlie, Greenwood | Account Director: Laura Witlox | Art Director/Content Strategist/Copywriter/Creative Director/Creative Strategist/Design Director: Michael Stanard | Designer: James Westwood | Paper Type: Cougar | Poster Size: 24 x 36 | Printer: Ace Graphics | Production Company: One Zero Charlie | Typographer: James Westwood | Client: One Zero Charlie

185 PLATINUM In Memoriam: World Trade Center | Design Firm: Volt Positive, Ottawa | Designer: Ziad Alkadri | Creative Director: Ziad Alkadri | Poster Size: 12 x 20.375 inches | Client: New Talent Conservatory

Description: The New Talent Conservatory's mandate is to promote and support new talent musicians in concerts. In tribute to the victims of September 11, the New Talent Conservatory organized a piano concert led by different rising young pianists. The poster designed for this event is entitled "In Memoriam: World Trade Center." The two black piano keys represent the World Trade Center Twin Towers.

186 Things I have learned in my life so far | Design Firm: Sagmeister Inc., New York | Art Director: Stefan Sagmeister | Creative Director: Stefan Sagmeister | Designer: Mathias Ernstberger | Copywriter: Stefan Sagmeister | Photographer: Henry Leutwyler | Illustrators: Yuki Muramatsu, Stephan Walter | Typographer: Mathias Ernstberger | Editor: Deborah Aaronson | Client: Abrams Inc.

Description: Astonishingly, Stefan Sagmeister has only learned 20 or so things in his life so far. But he did manage to publish these personal maxims all over the world, in spaces normally occupied by advertisements and promotions: as billboards, projections, light-boxes, magazine spreads, annual report covers, fashion brochures, and, recently, as giant inflatable monkeys. In this presentation Sagmeister throws his diary, a lot of design, and a little art together with a pinch of psychology and a dash of happiness into a blender and pushes the button. It tastes surprisingly yummy.

187 Hyde in Hollywood | Design Firm: True story., Chicago | Designer: Eric Wagner | Paper Type: French Speckletone | Photographer: Eric Wagner | Poster Size: 16 x 24 inches | Printer: True story. | Special Process: Hand silkscreened | Client: Shattered Globe Theatre

Description: This poster advertised Shattered Globe Theatre's production of "Hyde in Hollywood," set in the Golden Age of Hollywood. The lead character, Julian Hyde, a famous movie star/director/producer with a career-threatening secret, is determined to manipulate the media to protect his image and his livelihood.

188 Christian Finnegan Promotional Campaign | Design Firm: the decoder ring design concern, Austin | Designer/Illustrator: Christian Helms | Client: Christian Finnegan

Description: The group's newest album has drawn comparisons to The Cure, and rightfully so — they craft beautiful, poppy melodies juxtaposed with lyrics exploring darker subjects. The quote featured on the poster is a central lyric from their current album, and the poster's concept is based directly on the quote. The poster was placed at the music venue and other strategic locations to promote the show and was also sold by the band as merchandise at the event. To push the idea even further, we designed custom whoopee cushions to unexpectedly show up at venues a few weeks before each show.

189 HELVETICA 50 | Design Firm: Melchior Imboden, Buochs | Designer: Melchior Imboden | Poster Size: 90.5 x 128 cm | Print Producer: Bösch Siebdruck AG Stans | Client: Initiative by Lars Muller in collaboration with the Museum of Zurich

190 SFMOMA "Remakes" Film Series Poster | Design Firm: Volume Inc., San Francisco | Creative Directors/Art Directors: Adam Brodsley, Eric Heiman | Designers: Adam Brodsley, Eric Heiman, Marcelo Viana | Client: SFMOMA

Description: This poster was commissioned to promote SFMOMA's film series Fidelity and Betrayal: Variations on the Remake, which explores the relationships between film remakes and their source material.

191 Our Dark Twin | Design Firm: Pentagram Design, London | Art Director: Harry Pearce | Poster Size: A1 | Client: The Tagman Press

Description: A poster to promote a new book that explores the darker side of the subconscious.

192 Sparklehorse poster | Design Firm: Planet Propaganda, Madison | Creative Director: Kevin Wade | Designer: Curtis Jinkins | Client: High Noon Saloon

193 Architecture in Helsinki poster | Design Firm: Planet Propaganda, Madison | Creative Director: Kevin Wade | Designer: Curtis Jinkins | Client: High Noon Saloon

194 Planes Mistaken for Stars poster | Design Firm: Planet Propaganda, Madison | Creative Director: Kevin Wade | Designers: Mike Krol, Travis Cain | Client: High Noon Saloon

195 Man | Design Firm: WAX partnership, Calgary | Copywriter: Trent Burton | Creative Director/Designer: Monique Gamache | Illustrator: Tara Hardy | Printer: CSM Media | Client: Honens International Piano Competition

196 Berlin | Design Firm: Frost Design, Surry Hills | Creative Director: Vince Frost | Designer: Caroline Cox | Photographer: Jason Capobianco | Client: Sydney Dance Company

Description: Seductively theatrical, *Berlin* is a production exploring the city of Berlin as a symbol of decline and resurrection. Its innovative score includes an astonishing variety of songs made famous by David Bowie, Lou Reed, Frank Sinatra and more. Throughout the production singer iOTA wanders the stage dressed in wings — an angel of Berlin reminiscent of its famous victory column. Frost worked with photographer Jason Capobianco to create an image expressive of the emotional range of the production, later adding the ghost-like wings in Photoshop. The powerful, distressed letterpress typography adds to the moody and emotive design. The design appeared in posters as well as the program and other promotional collateral for the event.

197 Ronald McDonald House of Chapel Hill Posters | Design Firm: Ogilvy, Durham | Account Director: Heather Engard | Associate Creative Directors: Noah Rosenberg, Jeff Van Zandt, David Eller | Copywriter: Michael Gorelic | Creative Director: Jeff Dahlberg | Designer: Kyle Jackson | Photographer: Bruce Peterson | Poster Size: 20 | Fabricator: Otto D'Ambrosio, A.J. Rosenberg | Client: Ronald McDonald House of Chapel Hill

Description: The posters reuse the images from the brochure. They execute the message on one single page by adding headlines that remark on the joy and sadness within the RMH. The posters were sent out, given away at tradeshows and given to prospective donors and people who stayed at the house.

198, 199 Brand Book Poster | Design Firm: Landor Associates, San Francisco | Account Director: Bob Kersten | Creative Director: Christopher Lehmann | Designers: Ken Frederick, Gaston Yagmourian, Jo Clarke, E. Gilliam | Project Manager: Jennifer Suchor | Paper Type: 80# Jefferson Gloss Text | Poster Size: 22 x 34 inches | Print Run (Quantity): 5,000 | Printer: California Lithographers | Special Process: 5C + Flood varnish | Client: Devon

Description: Devon Energy is one of the world's leading independent oil and gas companies. Having grown exponentially over the past ten years through mergers and acquisitions, future growth will be organic. Historically shying away from branding efforts, Devon recognized that to better communicate with internal and external audiences, it would need to more actively manage its brand. So Landor developed positioning that focused on Devon's strength of acting with integrity, found throughout its organization, across cultures and geographies. Landor created a brandline, 'Commitment Runs Deep,' and an identity system that are inspired by the earth and geology-specifically, the idea of strata as a metaphor for building upon past experiences. By knowing their past and taking action in the present, Devon builds on a strong foundation to create a successful future. Visually, this comes to life in various strata graphic shapes and a color palette inspired by energy and the earth. When combined as layers of visual and verbal messages, each resulting communication piece is familiar yet becomes its own unique variation of elements.

As part of an employee launch program, a poster was created that highlights the new identity, captures key positioning messages and invites each employee to engage with the new Devon brand by taking the poster apart via a series of perforated strata shapes that can be combined or reconfigured into unique shapes and messages.

Products

200 BARE | Design Firm: Duffy & Partners LLC, Minneapolis | Creative Director: Dan Olson | Designer: Candice Leick | Account Director: Tricia Davidson | Project Manager: Jen Jagielski | Client: Myndology

Description: Bare. Just the essentials. Recycled paper. Soy ink. Clean energy. Acid-free. The new environmentally friendly line of disc-bounds. Free your mind. Jot down your notes. Feel good about doing your part. Cleaner earth. Clearer thoughts.

201 GOE | Design Firm: G2 Branding and Design, New York | Designers: Pablo Pineda (CD/Design, Industrial Design), Jeff Brant (Industrial Design) | Copywriter: Megan Trinidad | Client: Pantone

202 Cook-n-Serve Tongs | Design Firm: Stuart Karten Design, Marina Del Rey | Chief Creative Officer: Stuart Karten | Design Director: Eric Olson | Designers: Michael Rocha, Simon Sollberger | Photographer: Carin Krasner | Client: Zyliss

Description: The Cook-n-Serve Tongs introduce a new form factor to a tired kitchen tool, adding superior function and a lively new appearance. From the graceful curve of the tongs' stainless steel body to their uniquely shaped silicone tips, smart design details provide comfortable ergonomics and better grips for different types of food.

203 Dry Vase | Design Firm: Amron Experimental, Westbury | Account Director/Art Director/Artist/Author/Chief Creative Officer/Creative Director/Creative Strategist/Design Director/Designer/Editor/Executive Creative Director/Executive Creative Strategist/Illustrator/Photographer/Print Producer/Programmer/Project Manager/Set Designer&Props/Typographer/Web Developer/Writer: Scott Amron | Location: New York | Client: Handled w/ Care

Description: Dry Vase is a pressed vase for the romantic display of pressed flowers (rubber coated earthenware).

204, 205 Die Electric | Design Firm: Amron Experimental, Westbury | Account Director/Art Director/Artist/Author/Chief Creative Officer/Creative Director/Creative Strategist/Design Director/Designer/Editor/Executive Creative Director/Executive Creative Strategist/Illustrator/Photographer /Print Producer/Programmer/Project Manager/Set Designer&Props/Typographer/Web Developer /Writer: Scott Amron | Client: The FLICK OFF Movement

Description: A dielectric is an insulating material. It does not conduct electricity. The 'Die Electric' Experiment makes use of AC power plugs and sockets less the flow of electricity. Die Electric is an environmentally conscious experimental product design campaign. It was intended to promote mindful energy use by offering alternative non-electrical utility as an incentive. This series of dielectric objects force us to reevaluate our relationship with point of release power terminals and to consider the environmental cost of flipping a switch or plugging in an electric device.

The burning of fossil fuels to generate electricity contributes substantially to global warming and poor air quality. You can pump fuel into and see exhaust exit a car... But, turning ON a light or plugging in a device seems clean — it's not. We turn ON lights and plug things in without thinking. We are rarely reminded of the environmental impact of our own electric usage. Putting AC power plugs, sockets and switches to non-electrical use makes people stop and think.

Promotions/Designer

206 Origami Tuna Party Invite: "Tunagami" | Design Firm: Wallace Church, Inc., New York | Creative Director: Stan Church | Designer: Chung-Tao Tu | Client: Wallace Church, Inc.

Description: Every year Wallace Church throws a Tuna Party where we grill up fresh tuna for clients and friends. For 2007, we created a unique invitation: an origami fish. We printed our invitation as a small poster, black on black, and folded it into a fish. We then tucked the fish into a clear plastic pillow envelope and sent it "swimming" through the mail to its recipient. Upon receipt, the guests would tug at the designated fin to unfold the fish, revealing the invitation.

207 PLATINUM Wallace Church Thanksgiving Wine | Design Firm: Wallace Church, Inc., New York | Creative Director: Stan Church | Designers: Bird Tubkam, Chung-Tao Tu | Client: Wallace Church, Inc.

Description: Every year Wallace Church designs a Thanksgiving wine bottle as a gift for clients and friends. Here, a simple twist on a classic fork suggests all things Thanksgiving: a turkey feast with a good wine.

208 Celebrating 50 years of Helvetica | Design Firm: Ken-Tsai Lee design studio, Taipei | Art Director/Creative Director/Design Director/Designer: Ken-Tsai Lee | Client: Helvetica

209 Webster the Promotional Pachyderm | Design Firm: Websiter Design Associates, Omaha | Account Director: Lisa Healy, Nicole Dixon | Creative Director: Dave Webster | Designer: Lucinda Hamling | Writers: Bob Gardner, Lisa Healy, Dave Webster | Client: Webster Design Associates

Description: This is a holiday promotion we mailed to friends, clients, and prospective clients.

210 Valentine Self Promotion | Design Firm: Pat Sloan Design, Fort Worth | Designer: Pat Sloan | Client: Pat Sloan

211 ico Book | Design Firm: ico Design Consultancy, London | Account Director: Niall Henry | Art Director: Steve Lloyd | Creative Director: Ben Tomlinson | Design Director: Andy Spencer | Designer: Akira Chatani | Photographers: Fernando Manoso Borgas, Steve Lancefield | Writer: Gerald Ivall | Client: ico Design Consultancy

Description: This book has been produced to complement and contrast with our highly-functional and comprehensive web site. As a multi-disciplinary design company, print design and production aesthetics are equally important. Entitled *Various Artists*, the book illustrates our unselfconscious and unprescriptive creative approach. It's a journey through a rich collection of diverse projects and the pace is kept fresh with varied layouts, photographic styles and image crops.

The small-format hardback book is bound with a traditional book-binding material and features an unusual round spine. Print production techniques include foil-blocking and a metallic ink which lift the intentionally restrained design. Content is predominantly image-led, accompanied by limited and concise text. Two eight-page sections are printed black only on newsprint and are dedicated to ideas and sketches. The book is an honest insight into how we work and think, and a real reflection of our values.

Promotions/Paper

212 McCoy 2008 A Celebration of the Presidential Button from 1840 to 2008 | Design Firm: VSA Partners, Chicago | Art Director: Jason Kriegler | Authors: Jonathon Turitz, Daniel Harmon | Creative Director: Dana Arnett | Photographer: Mark Smalling | Client: Sappi Fine Papers of North America

Promotions/Photographer
213 Alan Kaplan Direct Mail | Design Firm: TODA, New York | Art Director/Creative Director: Marcos Chavez | Designer: Dory Pogers | Print Producer (Production): Gillian Spilchuk | Project Manager: Lasse Martinussen | Client: Alan Kaplan

Description: Alan Kaplan's promo piece is intended to bring interest to his range as a lifestyle photographer by revealing the concept behind several case studies. The piece allows destruction (ripping along the perforations), which is in keeping with his photographic style: raw, real, not too precious. The poster folds down to a mailable size and unfolds to be a poster showing his range. The folds are perforated so that the poster can be divided up into individual case study panels.

214, 215 George Simhoni Books | Design Firm: TAXI Canada Inc, Toronto | Artist (Mac): Peter Hodson | Creative Director/Designer: Dave Watson | Writer: Jason McCann | Client: George Simhoni

216 Hot Dog Promo | Design Firm: William Huber Productions, Inc., Boston | Designer: Rick Rawlins / WORK | Photographer: William Huber | Project Manager: Christina Regon | Writer: Rick Rawlins / WORK | Client: William Huber Productions

Promotions/Printer
217 Experience the Magic of 10 Colors | Design Firm: Squires & Company, Dallas | Creative Director: Brandon Murphy | Designers: Laura Root, Brandon Murphy | Photographer: Doug Davis | Writer: Wayne Geyer | Client: Color Dynamics

Description: Promotional brochure for Color Dynamics' new ten-color press. Various printing techniques used throughout.

Promotions
218 Design For All Insert | Design Firm: Peterson Milla Hooks, Minneapolis | Account Director: Marcia Asch | Art Director: Monika Kim | Chief Creative Officer/Creative Director: Dave Peterson | Photographer: Lars Hansen | Print Producer: Christine Moe | Project Manager: Steve Carlson | Writer: Jenny Shears | Client: Target

219 Get Out of Jail Free | Design Firm: Esparza Advertising, Albuquerque | Art Director: Cyndi Penn | Creative Director/Writer: Adam Greenhood | Client: Geoff Scovil

Description: A local Public Defender wanted a business card that quickly communicated the key benefit of his services to his clients.

220 "LOU GEHRIG" | Design Firm: BBDO New York, New York | Art Directors: Jeseok Yi, Jayson Atienza | Chief Creative Officers: David Lubars, Bill Bruce | Creative Directors: Frank Anselmo, Jayson Atienza | Designers/Writers: Jayson Atienza, Jeseok Yi, Frank Anselmo | Client: ALS Association (Lou Gehrig's Disease)

Description: Goal: Encourage people to donate money for ALS (Lou Gehrig's disease).
Background – ALS rapidly robs your body of all physical movement, causing patients to eventually lose their ability to breathe. New York Yankees great Lou Gehrig, who the ALS disease is named after, was the first known celebrity/athlete to be diagnosed with ALS, giving the disease a face.
Execution – We demonstrated one of the horrible effects of this disease, still without a cure. The cropped photograph of the baseball cleat is an actual photo of Lou Gehrig. The existing laces were retouched out of the photograph. Then actual shoelaces were laced through die-cut holes and left untied, making the experience both interactive and personal.
Location – The ad ran on the back cover of the annual Lou Gehrig's Disease Benefit Program. 1000-plus people who attended the event organized to raise money for ALS research were given a copy of the program.

221 President | Design Firm: John Isaacs, Claverack | Designer: John Isaacs | Client: Birkshares, Inc.

Description: BerkShares (*www.berkshares.org*) is a local currency that circulates in the Berkshires region of Massachusetts. The current exchange rate for BerkShares is 1 BerkShare for 90 U.S. cents. BerkShares are traded for US dollars at 12 local bank locations in the area. As of August 2007, 280 businesses were formally listed on the BerkShares website to accept the currency. Other businesses participate informally. Listed businesses are identified by window stickers and joint promotional material. Exchange occurs between customers and businesses and between businesses. Excess BerkShares may be traded in for US dollars at participating banks at the current exchange rate. Approximately 1,095,000 BerkShares were issued through participating banks in the first 11 months of operations, worth $985,500

ShoppingBags
222 Grocery Bag | Design Firm: McGarrah/Jessee, CHAOS, Austin | Designer/Writer: Ben Harman | Design Director: David Kampa | Client: Central Market

Signage
223 Signage Program | Design Firm: Regina Rubino/IMAGE: Global Vision, Santa Monica | Creative Directors: Regina Rubino, Robert Louey | Design Director: Regina Rubino | Designers: Robert Louey, Javier Leguizamo, Daniela Fahrig, John Starkweather | Client: Hyatt Regency O'Hare

Description: Created, produced and installed a signage program for the newly renovated iconic Hyatt Regency O'Hare Airport Hotel that captured its modern and contemporary feel. Layered colored acrylic panels with silkscreened and cut metal graphics on different levels bolted at corners and mounted away from the wall. Each meeting room named after an airport and floorplan used as backdrop to create interest. Each level is color-coded (purple for level one, orange for level two and yellow for lover level for ease in navigating the convention hotel).

Stamps
224 (top) James Stewart Stamp | Design Firm: Phil Jordan and Associates, Inc., Falls Church | Art Director/Designer: Phil Jordan | Illustrator: Drew Struzan | Client: United States Postal Service

224 (bottom) International Polar Year Stamps | Design Firm: q30design inc., Toronto | Art Director: Peter Scott | Creative Director: Glenda Rissman | Designer: Gildo Martino | Photographers: Michel Lamarche, Kevin Raskoff, Elizabeth Calvert | Client: Canada Post Corp.

Description: 2007 marked the advent of the International Polar Year, a multi-nation collaborative scientific study of the polar ecosystem. 8 countries, including Canada, issued commemorative stamps to inform and educate people about the sensitivity of the northern environment. Many stamps have been done internationallyl, featuring arctic animals and landscapes. Our challenge was to find a unique and visually dynamic approach that included additional bilingual educational information within a very small area. Canada Post also requested a multilingual approach for the stamp title, with translation into eight languages. Our research uncovered that a deep-sea jellyfish was recently discovered in northern Canadian waters. We found a beautiful color photo for which we secured reproduction rights. The jellyfish is pictured floating in deep black water (at actual size!), and we contrasted the image with a colorful crown of a King Eider, an indigenous arctic bird, on the second stamp. Surrounding the stamps is additional educational information that presents up-to-date data on research initiatives about the shrinking polar ice cap. The stamps bleed across the centre and isolate a custom die-cut maple leaf perforation in the centre.

225 Jogos Olímpicos de Pequim 2008 (2008 Olympic Games) | Design Firm: João Machado, Porto | Account Director/Art Director/Creative Director/Design Director/Designer/Illustrator: João Machado | Client: CTT Correios de Portugal

Description: This series of eight stamps was created for the Portuguese post office to celebrate the 2008 Olympic Games.

226 PLATINUM Landmark Modernist Architecture | Design Firm: Spark Studio, Melbourne | Creative Director /Typographer: Gary Domoney | Client: Australia Post

Description: Series of four stamp designs celebrating Modernist Architecture in Australia. Minisheet features all four stamps in a newly developed presentation (star configuration).

T-Shirts
227 Barcode | Design Firm: Heye Group, Unterhaching | Art Director/Designer: Volker Heuer | Creative Director/Executive Creative Director: Norbert Herold | Client: Theater Mainfranken

228 "SWEATY T-SHIRT" | Design Firm: KNARF, New York | Art Directors/Designers: Kevin Honneger, Martin Durkin, Frank Anselmo | Creative Director/Illustrator: Frank Anselmo | Photographer: Billy Siegrist | Writers: Kevin Honneger, Martin Durkin, Frank Anselmo | Client: Derby Energy Drink

Description: Derby Energy Drink needed a promotional item to hand out to customers. The beverage is made for active people who play sports, run, exercise, thus frequently breaking out with sweat. Hence the T-shirt always looks as if the person is sweating. The silkscreen process used actually printed underneath and around the armpit area to create the realistic effect.

229 Bike Jersey | Design Firm: Duffy & Partners LLC, Minneapolis | Creative Director: Dan Olson | Designer: Brad Surcey | Client: Duffy & Partners

Description: Hors Categorie is French for "beyond category," which could be a motto at Duffy & Partners, a vision for what we do and how we endeavor to do our work. The lion is a modern interpretation from the Duffy Irish crest, a symbol of our clan. Our team is comprised of a rare combination of biking fans and participants. This jersey was designed for summer road trips.

Transportation
230 Deschutes Brewery Truck | Design Firm: tbdadvertising, Bend | Account Director: Rene Mitchell | Creative Director: Paul Evers | Illustrator: Tim Lee | Photographer: Steve Tague | Designer: Chad DeWilde | Client: Deschutes Brewery

Description: The strategy was to convert a standard delivery truck into something that conveys the spirit of this craft brewer. The image of an antique beer crate carries emblems from packaging labels depicting their flagship brands. As new beers are released, new emblems are applied.

231 Big Barrel | Design Firm: tbdadvertising, Bend | Account Directors: Kevin Smyth, Rene Mitchell | Executive Creative Strategists: Paul Evers, David Jenkins | Set Designer & Props: Eddie Paul, EP Industries/Fabricator | Chief Creative Officer: Paul Evers | Creative Director: David Jenkins | Designer: Sebastian Schroeder | Client: Deschutes Brewery

Description:
Challenge – How do you convey the passion of a craft brewery to markets outside the region?
Solution – Bring the brewery and pub experience to them.
Execution – Create one-of-a-kind giant traveling beer barrel (essentially a traveling pub) that holds 12 kegs and 16 taps. Create a series of traveling beer festivals that tours neighborhoods celebrating the craft of great beer making and the spirit of the local community. All proceeds benefitted local charities.

Typography
232, 233 Hokotohu typeface design | Design Firm: DNA Design, Wellington | Design Director/Designer: Charlie Ward | Typographer: Kris Sowersby | Client: Hokotehi Moriori Trust Board

Description: Moriori are the first people of the remote Pacific Island of Rokoho (The Chatham Islands), 800 kilometres off the coast of New Zealand. The Hokotohu font originates in the ancient Moriori tradition of tree carving-Rakau Momori. The Hokotohu font captures the essence of those ancestral designs and presents them to a discerning 21st-century audience as a trademark of quality, authenticity and unique origin.

234 Helvetica Now | Design Firm: STUDIO INTERNATIONAL, Zagreb: Creative Director/Designer/Art Director/Designer/Chief Creative Officer/Copywriter/Typographer: Boris Ljubicic | Account Director/Executive Creative Strategist: Igor Ljubicic | Illustrators: Boris Ljubicic, Igor Ljubicic | Paper: Zanders, 170 g | Poster Size: 118 x 84 cm | Print Producer: Svebor, Zagreb, Croatia | Special Process: 3D Max | Client: STUDIO INTERNATIONAL

Description: Every day designers make new typography. Why? Types A to Z in latin letters are communication code worldwide! Helvetica is best because Helvetica is not typography; it is lettering!

Index

AccountDirectors

Alan, Mark 176
Amron, Scott 203, 204, 205
Asch, Marcia 218
Burgess, Catriona 109
Cheil Communications in Seoul 117
Cochran, Beth / Journey Communications 122, 123
Crick, Michele 160, 161
Davidson, Tricia 200
Dixon, Nicole 209
Duke, Dave .... 114, 115, 147 (third)
Engard, Heather 197
Fawbush, Margit 166, 167
Foulkes, Paul - Arellano 171
Ghormley, Brad .... 142, 148 (top), 151 (fourth)
Healy, Lisa 209
Hebert, Doug 134
Henry, Niall 211
Hosman, Joost 30, 31
Hug, Lisa 139
Kersten, Bob 198, 199
Korea - Marketing firm 117
Ljubicic, Igor 234
Lam, Linda T. .... 147 (top)
Machado, João 225
Massa, Anna M. 60, 61
Mehall, Christian 166, 167
Mitchell, René .... 168 (top), 230, 231
Monroe, Mignon 62, 63
Peet, Renee 162
Reed, Paul .... 42 (top left)
Riddell, Moira 164, 179
Shin, Jean 72
Simonse, Anna 132
Smyth, Kevin .... 168 (bottom), 231
Wheeler, Yvette .... 152 (fourth)
Witlox, Laura 184

ArtDirectors

3 Deep Design 44, 45
Altman, Amanda .... 148 (fourth)
Anselmo, Frank 158, 159, 220, 228
Arebalo, Jr., J.R. .... 106 (middle), 107
Atienza, Jayson 220
Brodsley, Adam 43, 190
Cehovin, Eduard 101
Cheng, Sy-Jenq 104, 105
Davis-Birkenbeuel, JinJa 78
Dawson, Claire 102
Domoney, Gary 86
Gherardi, Fabio 120, 121
Glanzmann Schoene, Cornelia 82, 83
Guillory, Daren 134
Heiman, Eric 43, 190
Hill, Joe .... 42 (top left)
IPSUM PLANET 108
Jordan, Phil .... 224 (top)
Katona, Diti 73
Klotnia, John 28, 29
Kriegler, Jason 180, 212
Kyu, Han 79
Ljubicic, Boris 234
Lofgreen, Art .... 147 (third), 151 (fourth)
Machado, João 225
Mason, Dave 140, 141
Mastroguiseppe, Amy 75
Nakamura, Kazuto 90
Olivier, Carrie .... 106 (top)
Pearce, Harry 157, 182, 183, 191
Peck, Callie 135
Pena, Fidel 102
Penn, Cyndi 219
Piasky, Jeff .... 42 (top right)
Raquel-Santos, Arvi 181
Šabach, Jan .... 151 (bottom)
Sabin, Bridget 165
Sagmeister, Stefan 186
Samata, Greg 69
Schmeisser, Joachim 144
Seagrave, Andrew 158, 159
Stoltze, Clifford 156
Strange, James 172, 173
Sures, Hans Heinrich 103
Tutssel, Glenn 136
Vucic, Ivana 48, 49, 80, 81
Weiner, Debora .... 42 (bottom)
Yi, Jeseok 158, 159, 220

ChiefCreativeOfficers

Amron, Scott 203, 204, 205
Appelbaum, Ralph 120, 121
Baccari, Alberto 60, 61
Brooker, Brian 154, 155
Bruce, Bill 220
Cehovin, Eduard 101
Evers, Paul 231
Habibi, Sarah 94
Karten, Stuart 202
Kellerhouse, Neil 94
Lai, David 132
Lam, Linda T. .... 147 (top)
Ljubicic, Boris 234
Lubars, David 220
Morla, Jennifer 68
Peterson, Dave 218
Salazar, Dahlia 134
Valter, Stephan 170
Vukic, Fedja 101

CreativeStrategists

3 Deep Design 44, 45
Amron, Scott 203, 204, 205
Baccari, Alberto 60, 61
Cehovin, Eduard 101
Davis-Birkenbeuel, JinJa 78
Hebert, Doug 134
Rohrer, Christoph 52, 53, 54, 55
Segerstrom, Elizabeth 56, 57, 58, 59
Shin, Jean 72
Stanard, Michael 184
Vukic, Fedja 101

CreativeDirectors

3 Deep Design 44, 45
Aiba, Takanori .... 147 (fourth), 148 (bottom), 151 (third)
Alkadri, Ziad 185
Amron, Scott 203, 204, 205
Anselmo, Frank 158, 159, 220, 228
Aoki, Hisami 88, 89, 96, 97
Aparicio, Nicolas 62, 63
Apple Graphic Design 174, 175
Apple Industrial Design 174, 175
Apple Packaging Engineering 174, 175
Arnett, Dana 180, 212
Atienza, Jayson 220
Baccari, Alberto 60, 61
Ball, John 178
Blackburn, Garry 64, 65
Brodsley, Adam 43, 190
Burch, Harold 56, 57, 58, 59
Cehovin, Eduard 101
Chavez, Marcos 213
Cheong, Kuokwai 51
Chock, Paul 62, 63
Church, Stan 206, 207
Cozza, Marc 164
Dahlberg, Jeff .... 75, 135, 148 (third), 197
David Turner 164, 179
Davis-Birkenbeuel, JinJa 78
Domoney, Gary 86, 226
Duckworth, Bruce 164, 179
Elliott, Simon 91
Ellis, Daren 104, 105
Erhart, Marty 138
Evers, Paul .... 168 (bottom), 168 (top), 230
Ferreira, Lionel 130
Frankovic, Orsat 48, 49, 80, 81
Frost, Vince 109, 196
Fung, Kannex 143
Gabbert, Jason .... 42 (top right)
Gamache, Monique 195
Ghormley, Brad 142
Green, Tim .... 42 (bottom)
Greenhood, Adam 219
Heiman, Eric 43, 190
Herold, Norbert 227
Hershey, R. Christine .... 151 (top)
Hopper, Charlie 166, 167
Igarashi, Satoru 176
Ilic, Mirko 50
IPSUM PLANET 108
Jeffries, Chip 120, 121
Jenkins, David 231
Johnston, Donna 143
Jue, Shanley 72
Katsuno, Akemi 112, 113
Keller, Michael 52, 53, 54, 55
Kellerhouse, Neil 94
Kellerman, Bob 181
Kikuchi, Taisuke 163
Koutsis, Phil 129
Kraemer, Dan 92, 93
Kyu, Han 79
Lam, Linda T. .... 147 (top)
Lam, Paul 85
Lee, Ken-Tsai 208
Lehmann, Christopher 198, 199
Ljubicic, Boris 234
Lofgreen, Art .... 114, 115, 147 (third), 148 (top), 151 (fourth),
Louey, Robert 223
Machado, João 225
Maierhofer, Knut 52, 53, 54, 55
Matsumoto, Takaaki 34, 36, 37, 88, 89, 96, 97
McClure, Tim 138
McKay, Jeffrey .... 147 (second)
Mitchell, Dick .... 152 (third)
Monberg, Jamie 110, 111, 128
mono 131
Morla, Jennifer 68
Murphy, Brandon 217
Nakamura, Tomiko 90
Neuman, Craig 154, 155
Niwa, Hiro 132
Nokia Design/ComLab 35
O'Donahue, Sam 162
Olson, Dan 200, 229
Peterson, Dave 218
Quist, Greg 128
Radtke, Steve 95
Reed, Paul .... 42 (top left)
Rissman, Glenda .... 224 (bottom)
Rosenberg, Noah (Associate Creative Director) .... 75, 135, 148 (third)
Rowe, Michael 171
Rubino, Regina 223
Sagmeister, Stefan 32, 33, 186
Salazar, Dahlia 134
Samata, Greg 69
Sereno, Max 60, 61
Stanard, Michael 184
Sures, Hans Heinrich 103
Tanimoto, David 66, 67
Taussig, ED 177
Thesing, Kurt 84
Tomlinson, Ben 211
Tutssel, Glenn 136
Upton, Bob 137
Ventimiglia, Tim 120, 121
Vidakovic, Sasha 100, 145
Vucic, Ivana 48, 49, 80, 81
Vukic, Fedja 101
Wade, Kevin 192, 193, 194
Watson, Dave 214, 215
Webster, Dave 139, 209
Weitz, Carter 150, 172, 173
Wheeler, Yvette 160, 161
Wilkins, Amy 88, 89, 96, 97
Yagi, Takashi 112, 113

DesignDirectors

3 Deep Design 44, 45	Gorelic, Michael 75	Lee, Joanna .... 151 (top)	Spencer, Andy 211
Amron, Scott 203, 204, 205	Hebert, Doug 134	Lorenc, Jan 117, 122, 123	Stanard, Michael 184
Arebalo, Jr. J.R. .... 106 (top, middle), 107	Hinsche, Gary W. 76, 77	Machado, João 225	Thompson, Ron 132
Barbero, Gianluca 60, 61	Houston, Lela 162	Märki, Patrick 52, 53, 54, 55	Tutssel, Glenn 136
Cehovin, Eduard 101	Jue, Shanley 72	Olson, Eric 202	Vukic, Fedja 101
Cozza, Marc 164	Kampa, David 146, 222	Rosales, Marco .... 106 (bottom)	Ward, Charlie 232, 233
Donovan, Anthony 109	Kramer, Travis 154, 155	Rubino, Regina 223	Woodward, Fred 98
Dudley, Joshua 120, 121	Kuhlmann-Leavitt, Deanna 133	Sieler, Steve 88, 89	
Eller, David 197	Lee, Ken-Tsai 208	Simeral, Scott 120, 121	

ExecutiveCreativeDirectors

Amron, Scott 203, 204, 205	Herold, Norbert 227	Marcus, Camilla 28, 29	Vukic, Fedja 101
Cehovin, Eduard 101	Israel, David 162	Tutssel, Glenn 136	

ExecutiveCreativeStrategists

Amron, Scott 203, 204, 205	Evers, Paul 231	Ljubicic, Igor 234	
Atkins, Kelly 28, 29	Harner, Judd 162	Martinez, Nancy Caal 28, 29	
Cehovin, Eduard 101	Jenkins, David 231	Vukic, Fedja 101	

Designers

3 Deep Design 44, 45	Fung, Kannex 143	Lazaro, Jerry .... 151 (top)	Saether, Marianne 39
Alkadri, Ziad 185	Gabbert, Jason .... 42 (top right)	Lee, Ken-Tsai 208	Samodra, Maria 129
Altman, Alan .... 148 (fourth)	Gamache, Monique 195	Leguizamo, Javier 70, 71, 223	Samoylenko, Natasha 72
Amron, Scott 203, 204, 205	Gardiner, Chris 164	Leick, Candice 200	Samson, Olivia 92
Anselmo, Frank 158, 159, 220, 228	Gilliam, E. 198, 199	Ljubicic, Boris 234	Schmeisser, Joachim 144
Aoki, Hisami 34, 36, 37	Gray, Christy 161	Lo, Adrien 110, 111, 128	Schoffro, Florian 74
Aratame, Kaname 112, 113	Green, Tana 120, 121	Lofgreen, Art .... 147 (third), 151 (fourth)	Schroeder, Sebastian 231
Atienza, Jayson 220	Green, Tim .... 42 (bottom)	Lorenc, Jan 117	Schoene, Cornelia Glanzmann 82, 83
Bailey, Kevin .... 152 (Second)	Guillory, Daren 134	Louey, Robert 223	Schultchen, Arne 74
Bates, Sarah 100, 145	Hamling, Loucinda 209	Lu, KunChe 132	Seagrave, Andrew 158, 159
Bhat, Kunal 50	Harman, Ben 222	Luffman, Joseph 64, 65	Shek, Queenie 85
Blackburn, Garry 64, 65	Harris, Carolin .... 148 (third)	Luna, Leticia 73	Sloan, Pat 210
Brant, Jeff (Industrial Design) 201	Harris, Mike 164, 179	Lust, Kati 74	Sollberger, Simon 202
Brindisi, Brian 116	Hartley, Josh 120, 121	Machado, João 225	Starkweather, John 223
Brodsley, Adam 190	Heiman, Eric 43, 190	Martino, Gildo .... 224 (bottom)	Stellavato, Nadine .... 148 (second)
Brummelman, Dirkjan 30, 31	Helms, Christian 188	Matsumoto, Takaaki 34, 36, 37	Stephens, Terry 91
Burch, Harold 56, 57, 58, 59	Heuer, Volker 227	Matsunaga, Shinjiro 163	Stoltze, Clifford 156
Burch, Sandra 56, 57, 58, 59	Hing, Adrian 109	May, Beth 69, 140, 141	Stone, Jared 28, 29
Cain, Travis 194	Honneger, Kevin 228	McCall, Steve 122, 123	Strange, James 150, 172
Canahuates, Delgis .... 98 (bottom)	Höpfner, Ralf 74	McKay, Jeffrey .... 147 (second)	Stubicar, Sasa 48, 49
Carlson, David / Gearbox .... 168 (top)	Hoppe, Krista 133	McKee, Jeff 114, 115	Surcey, Brad 229
Carpenter, Aki 120, 121	Hrizuk, Rebecca 84	Meyer, Sarah 116	Sures, Hans Heinrich 103
Chan, Patrick 85	Ilic, Mirko 50	Mizuoka, Ryuji 90	Thesing, Kurt 84
Chang, Hugo 76, 77	Imboden, Melchior 189	mono 46, 47	Thompson, Emma 179
Chatani, Akira 211	Ioukhnovets, Anton .... 98 (top)	Morris, Douglas 119	Thrasher, Christy 70, 71
Cheftel, Julia 100	IPSUM PLANET 108	Murphy, Brandon 217	Tu, Chung-Tao 206, 207
Cheng, Sy-Jenq 104, 105	Isaacs, John 221	Nakamura, Kazuto 90	Tubkam, Bird 207
Cheong, Kuokwai 51	Jackson, Kyle 197	Narges, Iran 43	Tutssel, Glenn 136
Cin, Sora 122, 123	Jacquinot, Jennifer 154, 155	Newham, Lee 164	Tutssel, Lauren 136
Clarke, Jo 198, 199	Jinkins, Curtis 192, 193	Onimaru, Toshihiro	Valter, Stephan 170
Clayton, Anthony 136	Ha, JJ 62, 63	.... 147 (fourth), 148 (bottom), 151 (third)	Varming, Søren 40, 41
Cox, Caroline 196	Johnson, Kathy 154, 155	Osada, Ai 154, 155	Ventress, Tom 149
Cozza, Marc 164	Jones, Dylan 178	Owens, Brian .... 152 (top, third), 153	Viana, Marcelo 43, 190
Creech, David 176	Jordan, Phil .... 224 (top)	Paganucci, Corey 110, 111, 128	Vidakovic, Sasha 100, 145
Davis-Birkenbeuel, JinJa 78	Kampa, David .... 146, 151 (second)	Park, David 122, 123	Vucic, Ivana 48, 49, 80, 81
Dawson, Claire 102	Katsuno, Akemi 112, 113	Pena, Fidel 102	Wagner, Eric 187
DeWilde, Chad 230	Kellerhouse, Neil 94	Peteet, Rex .... 151 (second)	Waldron, Skot 140, 141
Domoney, Gary 86	Kim, Moonsun 119	Pineda, Pablo (CD/Industrial Design) 201	Walters, Spencer .... 114, 115, 142, 148 (top)
Dotson, Tammy 156	King, Joseph 110, 111, 128	Pogers, Dory 213	Waluk, Iwona 162
Durkin, Martin 228	Kinzer, Benjamin .... 168 (bottom)	Post, Soe Lin 156	Ward, Charlie 232, 233
Elliott, Simon 64, 65	Kito, Luka 120, 121	Poulin, Richard 116	Watson, Dave 214, 215
Eplawy, Jason 92, 93	Klim, Marcus 169	Press, Sara 177	Westwood, James 184
Erhart, Marty 138	Klim, Matt 169	Price, Gini 142	Wheeler, Yvette .... 152 (fourth), 160
Ernstberger, Matthias 32, 33, 186	Klimkiewicz, Peter 169	Raquel-Santos, Arvi 181	Wintrob, Jande 120, 121
Fahrig, Daniela 223	Koch, Karen 139	Rawlins, Rick 216	Yagi, Takashi 112, 113
Feldmann, André 74	Komai, Mao 163	Reed, Paul .... 42 (top left)	Yagmourian, Gaston 198, 199
Ferreira, Lionel 130	Kraemer, Peter 124	Rocha, Michael 202	Yamada, Tomokazu 90
Ferrino, Marc 138	Kramer, Travis 154, 155	Root, Laura 217	Yamanaka, Midori 132
Fleming, Matt 95	Krebs, Hans 110, 111, 128	Rosales, Marco .... 106 (bottom)	Yee-Haw Industries 166, 167
Fox, Mark .... 147 (bottom)	Krol, Mike 194	Ross, Charlie 137	Yi, Jeseok 158, 159, 220
Francés, Tirso 30, 31	Kusbiantoro, Henricus 62, 63	Šabach, Jan .... 151 (bottom)	Yoo, Chung 122, 123
Frankovic, Orsat 48, 49, 80, 81	Kwok, Vera 70, 71	Sabin, Tracy 165	Young, Nathan 110, 111, 128
Frederick, Ken 198, 199	Kyu, Han 79	Sack, Ron 150, 172	Yuan, Tina 68

Artists

Amron, Scott 203, 204, 205
Brummelman, Dirkjan 30, 31
Cehovin, Eduard 101
Francs, Tirso 30, 31
Gronvold, Jan 72
Hodson, Peter / Mac Artist 214, 215
Kellerhouse, Neil 94
Kraemer, Peter 124
Lam, Linda T. .... 147 (top)
Lorenc, Jan 117
Machado, João 225
Phalle, Niki de Sainte 78
Sagmeister, Stefan 32, 33
Salcedo, Doris 91
Schoene, Cornelia Glanzmann 82, 83
Sifuentez, Anne Rix 138
Young, David 118

Illustrators

Adams, Gayle 150, 172
Amron, Scott 203
Anselmo, Frank 158, 159, 228
Arvizu, Jon .... 147 (third)
Berry, Dana 70, 71
Caron, Mona .... 168 (top)
Dorn, Barbara 143
Fernandez, Luis 143
Ferrino, Marc 138
Fox, Mark .... 147 (bottom)
Golson, Howell 164
Gruger, Lindy .... 168 (bottom)
Hardy, Tara 195
Hargreaves, Martin 164
Hasek, Mary Jane 143
Helms, Christian 188
Hersey, John 28, 29
Ilic, Mirko 127
Inglls, Kevin 143
Kit, Or Hoi 85
Klim, Matt 169
Klimkiewicz, Peter 169
Kozul, Kristian 48, 49
Kraemer, Peter 124
Kramer, Peter 28, 29
Lam, Linda T. .... 147 (top)
Langner, Cory 143
Lee, Tim 230
Ljubicic, Boris 234
Ljubicic, Igor 234
Machado, João 225
Madill, Warren 164
Muramatsu, Yuki 32, 33, 186
Nakamura, Joel 70, 71
Newham, Lee 164
Ogline, Tim E. 125
Owens, Brian .... 152 (top, third)
Rogers, Jon 164
Sabin, Tracy 165
Sahunalu, Sutti 143
Schoene, Cornelia Glanzmann 82, 83
Sharpe, Anne 164
Strange, James 173
Struzan, Drew .... 224 (top)
Tarbay, Sharif 164
Walter, Stephan 32, 33, 186
Walters, Spencer .... 142, 148 (top)
Wearing, Paul 28, 29
Wheeler, Yvette .... 152 (fourth), 160
Williams, Rexanne .... 42 (top left)
Ying, Chui Ka 85

Photographers

Alaverdian, Vahe 88, 89, 96, 97
Amron, Scott 203, 204, 205
Atkinson, Andy 171
Bettles, Andrew 104, 105
Bock, Elke 103
Borgas, Fernando Manoso 211
Broden, Fredrik 107
Bucklow, Christopher 104, 105
Buettner, Angelika 108
Calvert, Elizabeth .... 224 (bottom)
Cant, James 109
Capobianco, Jason 196
Chau, Jennifer 85
Cheil Communications 117
Clavijo, Sergio 91
Coinbergh, Christian 104, 105
Corwin, Jeff 70, 71
Creative Sources Photography 122, 123
Davis, Doug 217
Dobry, Scott 172
Doi, Koichiro 104, 105
Donovan, Drew 134
Dorrance, Scott 133
du Preez, Warren 104, 105
Dunkley, Andrew 91
Emmite, David 70, 71
Flood, Don 107
Friedman, Sarah A. .... 106 (middle)
Goldberg, Nathaniel .... 98 (top)
Gregoire, Peter 28, 29
Grimshaw, Andy 164, 179
Hansen, Lars 218
Heller, Steven A. 88, 89, 96, 97
Helmer-Petersen, Keld 34
Hill, Joel .... 42 (top left)
Huber, William 216
Johan, Simen 104, 105
Kacunic, Tomislav J. 48, 49
Keeley, Dennis 96, 97
Kent, Tim 66, 67
Knight, Nick 104, 105
Krasner, Carin 202
Kunkel, Albrecht 104, 105
Kushma, Deborah 116, 119
Lamarche, Michel .... 224 (bottom)
Lancefield, Steve 211
Lee, Lester 85
Leith, Marcus 91
Leutwyler, Henry 32, 33, 186
Marlow, Thomas 78
Messina, Patrick 70, 71
Miller, Don 76, 77
Miller, Harold Lee 166, 167
Moors, Steve .... 106 (top)
Nease, Robert (still life) 56, 57, 58, 59
Oku, Toshi 66, 67
Pearson, Trevor 70, 71
Peterson, Bruce 75, 197
Raskoff, Kevin .... 224 (bottom)
Redgrove, Benedict 104, 105
Richardson, Tim .... 98 (bottom)
Rizzo, Rion 122, 123
Robert, Francios 180
Rodriguez, Arturo 107
Sandro 69
Sato, Shinichi 112, 113
Siegrist, Billy 158, 159, 228
Smalling, Mark 180, 212
Staudenmaier, Eric 28, 29
Sures, Hans Heinrich 103
Tague, Steve 230
Tankersley, Todd 68
Thornton-Jones, Nick 104, 105
Tomlinson, Marcus 104, 105
Tule, Marc 178
Varda, Agnes 94
Various from Getty and Corbis 181
Vucic, Ivana 48, 49
Wagner, Eric 187
Weymouth, Michael (judge photography) 181
White, Stephen 91
Wiking, Andreas 40, 41
Wills, Bret 72
Wolff, André 104, 105
Wong, John 160, 161

Typographers

3 Deep Design 44, 45
Amron, Scott 203, 204, 205
Booth, Darren 107
Davis-Birkenbeuel, JinJa 78
Domoney, Gary 226
Ernstberger, Matthias 32, 33, 186
Foundry Types 40, 41
Kellerhouse, Neil 94
Lam, Linda T. .... 147 (top)
Leavitt, Kulhmann Inc. 133
Ljubicic, Boris 234
Sagmeister, Stefan 32, 33
Savage 134
Sowersby, Kris 232, 233
Westwood, James 184

PrintProducers

Amron, Scott 203, 204, 205
Baur, Chrisina 52, 53, 54, 55
Bohls, Kelly 164
Davis-Birkenbeuel, JinJa 78
Fleet, Tony 76, 77
Foote, Paul 103
Hornberger Druck 82, 83
ID3 .... 122, 123
Moe, Christine 218
Narayana Press, Denmark 40, 41
Patrick, Diane 138
Schulenberg, Shelley 154, 155
Siebdruck, Bösch (AG Stans) 189
Sirna-Brude, Anet 32, 33
Spilchuk, Gillian (Production) 213
Studio Sungshin Fabrication (Seoul) 117
Svebor (Croatia) 234
Tisk, Gorenjski (Slovenia) 101
Wide Ocean Printing Company Ltd. 85

ProjectManagers

Amron, Scott 203, 204, 205
Beth Cochran Journey Communications Inc. 122, 123
Blackwell, Liza 176
Bohls, Kelly 164
Box&Cox, Seoul 117
Bradley, Ellie 109
Carlson, Steve 218
Chasey, Alice 91
Cir, Jaroslav .... 151 (bottom)
Cooper, Malissa 118
Cury, Kate 120, 121
Davis-Birkenbeuel, JinJa 78
Gold, Jered 96, 97
Goldsmith, Erica 128
Hebert, Doug 134
Houk, Holly 178
Jagielski, Jen 200
Jensen, Nola 176
Kerr, Russell 39
Kiyohara, Toshiyuki 112, 113
Kontetski, Alex 171
Loader, Joanne .... 151 (bottom)
Martinussen, Lasse 213
Monberg, Chris 110, 111
Project Management, Korea 117
Regon, Christina 216
Suchor, Jennifer 198, 199
Truskoloski, Mara 138
Vannais, Judy 120, 121

Programmers

Amron, Scott 203, 204, 205
Frickelton, Matt 128
Gamradt, Neil / inovaone.com 130
Hickner, Ryan 110, 111
Johnson, Brian 132
Lee, Jordan 110, 111
MacGregor, Chris 134
Mann, Craig 135
Mueller, Gordon 128
Peck, Callie 135
Shao, Jessica 132
Taylor, Jason 132
Thompson, Jonathan 134
Tooms, Craig 134

Authors/Writers/Copywriters

Amron, Scott 203, 204, 205
Anselmo, Frank 158, 159, 220, 228
Apple, Heather 135
Atienza, Jayson 220
Bal, Mieke 91
Benda, Penny 133
Bolton, Andrew 36, 37
Borchardt-Hume, Achim 91
Boyer, Dave 125
Burton, Trent / Copywriter 195
Carter, Paul 44, 45
Cehovin, Eduard 101
Chicago Office of Tourism and Niki de Saint
Phalle Foundation 78
Cooke, Russell 125
Cox, Allan .... 42 (top right)
Cunningham, Paul 40, 41
Durkin, Martin 228
Errington, Charlie / Aquarium Writer 30, 31
Ferrick Jr., Tom 125

Fitzgerald, Laura 162
Gardner, Bob 209
Gilroy, Paul 91
Gjata, Frank .... 168 (top)
Gogolin, Jean 181
Gorelic, Michael 75, 197
Gray, Leslie 75
Greenhood, Adam 219
Hall, Gina 164
Harman, Ben 222
Harmon, Daniel 212
Healy, Lisa 209
Hide, Louise / Aquarium Writer 30, 31
Honneger, Kevin 228
Horton, Gwendolyn 68
Hutson, Andrew 44, 45
Ivall, Gerald 211
Jackson, Davina 44, 45
Jaksic, Jasna 48, 49
Judkins, Bryan 166, 167

King, Jon 66, 67
Koda, Harold 36, 37
Kovac, Leonida 48, 49
La Brecque, Donna 72
Machado, João 225
McAuliffe, Christopher 44, 45
McCann, Jason 214, 215
McClure, Tim 138
mono 46, 47, 131
Nevsimal, Charles 95
Newham, Lee 164
Prograis Jr., Lawrence .... 42 (bottom)
Rawlins, Rick / WORK 216
Redepenning, Scott 134
Rowe, Michael 171
Rudolf, Mia 40, 41
Rudolph, Laura 135
Sagmeister, Stefan 32, 33
Satullo, Chris 125
Schulman, Robert 60, 61

Seagrave, Andrew 158, 159
Seyle, Bill / Writer 69
Shaik, Leon van 44, 45
Shapiro, Mary 120, 121
Shears, Jenny 218
Sheridan, Michael 34
Stanard, Michael / Copywriter 184
Stefancic, Klaudio 48, 49
Thesing, .Kurt 84
Trinidad, Megan / Copywriter 201
Turitz, Jonathon 180, 212
Van Zandt, Jeff / Copywriter 197
Vukic, Fedja 101
Waggoner, Mark 164
Webster, Dave 209
Weizman, Eyal 91
Williams, Rexanne .... 42 (top left)
Wordwright 181
Yi, Jeseok 158, 159, 220
Zimmerman, Mike 95

Editors

Aaronson, Deborah 32, 33, 186
Amdur, Nikki 120, 121
Amron, Scott 203, 204, 205
Borchardt-Hume, Achim 91
Borrell, Amy 38

Cehovin, Eduard 101
Chicago Office of Tourism and Niki de Saint
Phalle Foundation 78
Hansen, Majbrit 40, 41
Holt, Joan 36, 37

Jaksic, Jasna 48, 49
Jeon, Jae-Kyung 79
JP/Politikens Forlag 40, 41
Kraemer, Peter 124
Satullo, Chris 125

Timpane, John 125
Valentine, Christine 120, 121
Vukic, Fedja 101
Wilkins, Amy 34

AdditionalContributors

3D Max / Special Process 234
5C + Flood varnish / Special Process 198, 199
Ace Graphics / Printer 184
A.J. Rosenberg / Special Process 197
Amron, Scott / Set Designer & Props, Web Developer 203, 204, 205
Assignments UK / Printer 103
Aston Martin, DB5 / Model 40, 41
California Lithographers / Printer 198, 199
Camilla / Model 40, 41

CSM Media / Printer 195
Daniella / Model 40, 41
EP Industries / Fabricator 231
Hand silk-screened / Special Process 187
Hernandez, Bob / User Experience Architect 56, 57, 58, 59
James, Reuben / Retouching and Artwork 164, 179
Kay, Matt / Retoucher 179
KC Tagliareni / Motion Grpahics 29

MacKinnon, Don / Model 120, 121
Your Majesty / Web Developer 131
Marek, Bruno / Web Developer 52, 53, 54, 55
Melissa / Model 40, 41
Ogier, Vivian / Stylist 133
One Zero Charlie / Production Company 184
Oneil Printing / Printer 142
Otto D'Ambrosio / Fabricator 197
Paul, Eddie / Set Designer & Props 231
Pietruska, Jan / Model 120, 121

Propaganda 3 / Web Developer 133
Robertson, George / Model 120, 121
Savage / Web Developer 134
Shepard, Scott / Model 120, 121
Stanard, Michael / Content Strategist 184
Tran, Minh / Photographer's Assistant 40, 41
True story / Printer 187
Zhu, Hugo / Web Developer 132

DesignFirms

3 Deep Design 44, 45
A3 Design 148 (fourth)
Ahn Sang-Soo Studio intro
American Airlines Publishing 106 (bottom)
American Way 106 (top, middle), 107
Amron Experimental 203, 204, 205
Art Center College of Design 88, 89, 96, 97
Bailey Lauerman 150, 172, 173
Barkley 154, 155
BBDO New York 220
Big Magazine 104, 105
Birkdesign Inc. 78
BlackDog 147 (bottom)
Brand Envy 148 (second)
Catapult Strategic Design ... 114, 115, 142, 147 (third), 148 (top), 151 (fourth)
Centerpoint Design 72
CIA 84
Concrete Design Communications Inc. 73
Desgrippes Gobé 162
Design Center Ltd. 101
Design Within Reach 68
Dietwee ontwerp en communicatie 30, 31
DNA Design 232, 233
Duffy & Partners LLC 200, 229
Esparza Advertising 219
feldmann+schultchen design studios GmbH 74
Ferreira Design Company 130
Finished Art, Inc. 143
Frost Design 109, 196
G2 Branding and Design 129, 177, 201
Glanzmann Schoene Design 82, 83
GQ magazine / Conde Nast 98, 99
Graphic Design, Apple Computer 174, 175
Graphics & Designing Inc. 147 (fourth), 148 (bottom), 151 (third)
GS Design, Inc. 95
GSD&M's Idea City 138
Hans Heinrich Sures 103
Hello Design 132
Hershey|Cause 151 (top)
Heye Group 227
Hornall Anderson Design Works 110, 111, 128
IA Collaborative 92 (top, bottom), 93
ico Design Consultancy 211
IPSUM PLANET 108
Jan Šabach 151 (bottom)
João Machado 225
John Isaacs 221
Ken-Tsai Lee design studio 208
Klim Design, Inc. 169
KMS TEAM GmbH 52, 53, 54, 55
KNARF 158, 159, 228
Kuhlmann Leavitt, Inc. 133
Kuokwai Cheong 51
Laboratorium 48, 49, 80, 81
Lam Design Group 147 (top)
Landor Associates 62, 63, 198, 199
Lorenc + Yoo Design 117, 122, 123
love the life 112, 113
mass 170
Matsumoto Incorporated 34, 36, 37
McGarrah/Jessee, CHAOS 146, 222
Melchior Imboden 189
MiresBall 178
Mirko Ilic Corp. 50, 127
mono 46, 47, 131
Neil Kellerhouse 94
Nike Golf Image Design 176
Nokia 35
Nordstrom 87, 126
Ogilvy 75, 135, 148 (third), 197
Ogline Design 125
Opto Design 28, 29
Parachute design 137
Pat Sloan Design 210
Paul Lam Design Associates 85
Pemberton & Whitefoord Design Consultants 164
Penguin Graphics 90
Pennebaker 147 (second)
Pentagram Design intro, 157, 182, 183, 191
Peter Kraemer 124
Peterson Milla Hooks 218
Phil Jordan and Associates, Inc. 224 (top)
Planet Propaganda 192, 193, 194
Poulin + Morris Inc. 116, 119
punktum design 40, 41
q30design inc. 224 (bottom)
Ralph Appelbaum Associates 120, 121
RBMM 152, 153, 161
Reed Hill 42 (top left)
Regina Rubino / IMAGE: Global Vision 223
Robert Louey Design 70, 71
Rose 64, 65, 91
Rubin Postaer & Associates 66, 67
Sabatino/Day 76, 77
SADI (Samsung Art & Design Institute) 79
Sagmeister Inc. intro, 32, 33, 186
SamataMason 69, 140, 141
Sandra Burch 56, 57, 58, 59
Sandstrom Design 164
Savage 134
Shin Matsunaga Design Inc. 163
Sibley/Peteet Design 151 (second)
Spark Studio 86, 226
Squires & Company 217
Stoltze Design 156
Stuart Karten Design 202
Studio @ One Zero Charlie 184
STUDIO INTERNATIONAL 234
SVIDesign 100, 145
TAXI Canada Inc 214, 215
tbdadvertising 168 (top, bottom), 230, 231
The Brand Union 136
the decoder ring design concern 188
The DesignWorks Group 42 (top right, bottom)
The Works 38, 39
TODA 213
Tracy Sabin 165
True story. 187
Turner Duckworth 164, 179
TW2 60, 61
Underline Studio 102
Ventress Design Group 149
Volt Positive 185
Volume Inc. 43, 190
VSA Partners 180, 212
WAJS 144
Wallace Church, Inc. 206, 207
WAX partnership 195
Webster Design Associates 139, 209
Weymouth Design 181
William Huber Productions, Inc. 216
Wren and Rowe Ltd 171
Young and Laramore 118, 166, 167

Clients

Abrams Inc. 32, 33, 186
Akasha Restaurant 148 (second)
Alan Kaplan 213
Alexandria Real Estate Equities, Inc. 28, 29
ALS Association (Lou Gehrig's Disease) 220
American Airlines Publishing 106 (bottom)
American Airlines 106 (top, middle), 107
Antler Ranch 152 (third)
Apple 174, 175
Art Center College of Design 88, 89, 96, 97
Austin Film Society 138
Australia Post 226
Banana Republic 162
Bank Insinger de Beaufort NV 30, 31
BlackDog 147 (bottom)
Berkshares, Inc. 221
Brad Radke 137
Bryant & Duffey Optometrist 148 (fourth)
Buell Motorcycle Company 95
Cafy's Roast House Café 149
Canada Post Corp. 224 (bottom)
Career Press 42 (top right)
CCA: California College of the Arts 43
Central Market 222
Chicago Office of Tourism 78
Christian Finnegan 188
City of Phoenix 148 (top)
Color Dynamics 217
Creative Intelligence Agency (C.I.A) 84
The Criterion Collection 94
CTT Correios de Portugal 225
Cultural Affairs Bureau of the Macao S.A.R. Government 51
D&AD 64, 65, 158, 159
Dallas Legal Foundation 152 (second)
D'Ambrosio 148 (third)
DERBY ENERGY DRINK 228
Deschutes Brewery 168 (bottom), 230, 231
Design Center Ltd. 101
Design Within Reach 68
Devon 198, 199
DLC Management Corp. Tarrytown, NY 122, 123
Domistyle 160, 161
Drum Room 152 (top)
Duffy & Partners 229
Dunhill 177
EFD 114, 115
El Pato Fresh Mexican Food 151 (second)
Ellipsis Arts 156
EVE GROUP CO., LTD. 90
Extreme Information 100
feldmann+schultchen design studios 74
Ferreira Design Company 130
The FLICK OFF Movement 204, 205
First Graduate 62, 63
Formica Corporation 133
Frasers Property 109
Gang Ri Development Company Ltd. 85
Geoff Scovil 219
George Simhoni 214, 215
Georgetown University Press 42 (bottom)
GQ magazine 99
Gregory R. Miller & Co., Inc. 34
Handled w/ Care 203
Helvetica 208
Henry and Elizabeth Segerstrom 56, 57, 58, 59
Hershey|Cause 151 (top)
High Noon Saloon 192, 193, 194
Hill Station 164
Hi-Speed Magazine 103
Hokotehi Moriori Trust Board 232, 233
Homebase Ltd 179
Honda 66, 67
Honens International Piano Competition 195
Hyatt Regency O'Hare 223
ico Design Consultancy 211
International Quilt Study Center 150
Jane Tutssel 136
JH Andresen 171
Jones Lang LaSalle 119
Jose Cuervo International 169
JP/Politiken Publishing 40, 41
Kannex Fung 143
KMS TEAM 52, 53, 54, 55
Kyriakos and Megan Pagonis 147 (top)
Laboratorium 80, 81
Lakewood Child Development Center 152 (fourth)
Lars Muller with the Museum of Zurich 189
LEVEL Vodka 129
Liberty Memorial Association 120, 121
Lida Baday 73
Lincoln Childrens Zoo 173
Lithographix, Inc. 70, 71
Lobo Tortilla Factory 152 (bottom)
LVMH 170
Make A Wish Foundation of Nebraska 139
The Metropolitan Museum of Art 36, 37
Michael Smith 154, 155
Miletta Vista 172
Museum of Contemporary Art Zagreb 48, 49
Myndology 200
NEO2 108
New Talent Conservatory 185
Nike Golf Inc 176
Nokia Design 35
Nordstrom 87, 126
Odell Brewing, Co. 168 (top)
Olynthia 145
One Zero Charlie 184
Pantone 201
Pat Sloan 210
Pentagram 182
Peter Kraemer 124
The Philadelphia Inquirer 125
Pioneer Mobile 76, 77
Playboy 127
Polshek Partnership Architects 116
Prefix Institute of Contemporary Art 102
PrismaGraphic Corp. 151 (fourth)
Rexanne Williams 42 (top left)
Riva Yachts 60, 61
RMIT University - The Works 39
RMIT University 38
Rockport 50
Ronald McDonald House of Chapel Hill 197
Ronald McDonald House 75, 135
Roy Harper 157
SADI 79
Samsung, Seoul, Korea 72, 117
Sandro 69
Sappi Fine Paper 181
Sappi Fine Papers of North America 180, 212
Science Channel 46, 47
Seafarer Baking Company 165
Seeds of Change 164
Sesame Workshop 140, 141
SFMOMA 190
Shattered Globe Theatre 187
Shiseido Co., Ltd. 163
Shure Microphone 178
Southern California Institute of Architecture 132
Space Needle 110, 111
Spoetzl Brewery 146
STUDIO INTERNATIONAL 234
Swarovski 104, 105
Sydney Dance Company 196
The Tagman Press 191
Target 218
Tate Publishing 91
Thames & Hudson 44, 45
Theater Mainfranken 227
Time Travelers 147 (second)
Tokyo Good Idea Development Institute Co., Ltd. 147 (fourth), 151 (third)
Tommy Bahama 128
TurboChef 131
Ugly Mug Coffee 166, 167
Unilever 151 (bottom)
Unison 92 (top, bottom), 93
United States Postal Service 224 (top)
VDMA-Verband Deutscher Maschinen-und Anlagenbau e.V. 144
Waitrose 164
Wallace Church, Inc. 206, 207
Watches of Swizerland 86
Webster Design Associates 209
WHR Architects 134
William Huber Productions 216
Williamson Printing Corporation 153
Witness 183
World Co., Ltd. 148 (bottom)
World Edventures 142
Yoshinori Watanabe 112, 113
Young and Laramore Advertising 118
Zwick Construction Company 147 (third)
Zyliss 202

Directory

3 Deep Design www.3deep.com.au
148a Barkly Street, St Kilda, VIC 3182, Australia
Tel +61 395 93 804 | Fax +61 353 42 414

A3 Design www.athreedesign.com
7902 Cadmium Court, Charlotte, NC 28215, United States | Tel 704 568 5351

Ahn Sang-Soo www.ssahn.com
Hong-Ik University, SangHwalGuan, 4th Floor, SsangWuMul-gil 37-ho,
SangSu-dong, Mapu-ku, Seoul, Korea | Tel +82 2 323 0593

American Airlines Publishing www.americanwaymag.com
4333 Amon Carter Boulevard, MD 5374, Fort Worth, TX 76155, United States
Tel 817 963 5378

American Way www.americanwaymag.com
4333 Amon Carter Boulevard, MD 5374, Fort Worth, TX 76155, United States
Tel 817 967 1793

Amron Experimental www.AmronExperimental.com
1299 Corporate Drive, Suite 220, Westbury, NY 11590, United States
Tel 516 835 5373 | Fax 501 665 1760

Art Center College of Design www.artcenter.edu
1700 Lida Street, Pasadena, CA 91103, United States
Tel 626 396 2338 | Fax 626 683 9233

Bailey Lauerman www.baileylauerman.com
1248 O Street, Suite 900, Lincoln, NE 68508, United States
Tel 402 479 0235 | Fax 402 475 0428

Barkley www.barkleyus.com
1740 Main Street, Kansas City, MO 64108, United States
Tel 816 423 6221 | Fax 816 423 7221

BBDO New York www.bbdo.com
10 West 15th Street, #204, New York, NY 10011, United States | Tel 516 413 3825

Big Magazine www.bigmagazine.com
393 Broadway, 4th Floor, New York, NY 10013, United States | Tel 646 837 0086

Birkdesign Inc. www.birkdesign.com
1415 W. Chicago Avenue, Storefront Ground, Chicago, IL 60622, United States
Tel 312 733 9200 | Fax 312 733 9670

BlackDog www.blackdog.com
855 Folsom Street, No. 931, San Francisco, CA 94107, United States
Tel 415 990 6112

Brand Envy www.brandenvy.com
306 Dexter Avenue North, Seattle, WA 98109, United States
Tel 206 728 6044 | Fax 206 441 7196

Catapult Strategic Design www.catapultu.com
4251 E. Thomas Road, Phoenix, AZ 85018, United States
Tel 602 381 0304 | Fax 602 381 0323

Centerpoint Design www.centerpointdesign.com
1 West 34th Street, 11th Floor, New York, NY 10001, United States
Tel 212 904 1620

CIA www.ciastudio.com
3600 Clipper Mill Road, Suite 115, Baltimore, MD 21211, United States
Tel 410 235 8332 | Fax 410 235 8335

Concrete Design Communications Inc. www.concrete.ca
2 Silver Avenue, Toronto, ON M6R 3A2, Canada
Tel 416 534 9960 | Fax 416 534 2184

Desgrippes Gobé www.dga.com
411 Lafayette Street, 2nd Floor, New York, NY 10003 USA
Tel 212 979 8900 | Fax 212 979 1401

Design Center Ltd. www.cehovin.com
Knezova 30, Ljubljana, SI-1000, Slovenia
Tel +386 1 5195072 | Fax +386 1 5195072

Design Within Reach www.dwr.com
225 Bush Street, 20th Floor, San Francisco, CA 94104, United States
Tel 415 676 6586

Dietwee ontwerp en communicatie www.dietwee.nl
Kruiswarstraat 2, Utrecht, 3581 GL, Netherlands
Tel +31 30 245 5089 | Fax +31 30 233 3611

DNA Design www.dna.co.nz
PO Box 3056 Wellington 6140, Level 2, 262 Thorndon Quay, Thorndon,
Wellington, New Zealand | Tel +64 4 499 0828 | Fax +64 4 499 0888

Duffy & Partners LLC www.duffy.com
710 South Second Street, Suite 602, Minneapolis, MN 55401, United States
Tel 612 548 2304 | Fax 612 548 2334

Esparza Advertising www.esparzaadvertising.com
423 Cooper Avenue NW, Albuquerque, NM 87102, United States
Tel 505 264 1039 | Fax 505 765 1518

feldmann+schultchen design studios GmbH www.fsdesign.de
Himmelstrasse 10-16, Hamburg 22299, Germany
Tel +49 40 51 0000 | Fax +49 40 51 7000

Ferreira Design Company www.ferreiradesign.com
335 Stevens Creek Court, Alpharetta, GA 30005, United States | Tel 678 297 1903

Finished Art, Inc. www.finishedart.com
708 Antone Street, Atlanta, GA 30318, United States
Tel 404 355 7902 | Fax 404 352 3846

Frost Design www.frostdesign.com.au
Level 1, 15 Foster Street, Surry Hills, NSW 2010, Australia
Tel +61 29 280 42 33 | Fax +61 29 280 4233

G2 Branding and Design www.g2ny.com
747 3rd Avenue, Floor 2, New York, NY 10017, United States
Tel 212 616 9007 | Fax 212 616 9095

Glanzmann Schoene Design www.glanzmann-schoene.com
Schlossgasse 9, Loerrach 79540, Germany
Tel +49 7621 4220461 | Fax +49 7621 4220469

GQ magazine/Conde Nast www.gq.com
4 Times Square, 9th Floor, New York, NY 10036, United States | Tel 212 286 7523

Graphic Design, Apple Computer www.apple.com
1 Infinite Loop, MS 83-PPS, Cupertino, CA 95014, United States
Tel 408 974 5286 | Fax 408 974 9649

Graphics & Designing Inc. www.gandd.co.jp
3-3-1 Shirokanedai, Minato-ku, Tokyo, 108-0071, Japan
Tel +81 3 3449 0651 | Fax +81 3 3449 0653

GS Design, Inc. www.gsdesign.com
6665 North Sidney Place, Milwaukee, WI 53209, United States
Tel 414 228 9666

GSD&M's Idea City www.ideacity.com
828 West 6th Street, Austin, TX 78703, United States
Tel 512 242 4622 | Fax 512 242 7622

Hans Heinrich Sures
23 Barrington Road, Crouch End, London N8 8QT, United Kingdom
Tel/Fax +44 0 208 348 0995

Hello Design www.hellodesign.com
8684 Washington Boulevard, Culver City, CA 90232, United States
Tel 310 839 4885 Fax 310 839 4886

Hershey|Cause www.hersheycause.com
1336 Fifth Street, Santa Monica, CA 90410, United States | Tel 310 656 1001

Heye Group www.heye.de
Ottobrunner Street 28, Unterhaching, Bavaria 82008, Germany
Tel +49 89 665 321 340 | Fax +49 89 665 321 380

Hornall Anderson Design Works www.hadw.com
1008 Western Avenue, Suite 600, Seattle, WA 98104, United States
Tel 206 826 2329 | Fax 206 467 6411

IA Collaborative www.iacollaborative.com
120 S. State Street, 7th Floor, Chicago, IL 60603, United States
Tel 312 727 0027 | Fax 312 727 0028

ico Design Consultancy www.icodesign.co.uk
75-77 Great Portland Street, London W1W 7LR, United Kingdom
Tel +44 020 7631 2427 | Fax +44 020 7323 1245

IPSUM PLANET www.neo2.es
San Bernardo, 63. 2F – 28015 Madrid, Spain | Tel /Fax+34 9 1 522 90 96

Jan Šabach http://web.mac.com/jansabach
Corneliusstrasse 7, Munich 80469, Germany
Tel/Fax +49 173 580 6590

João Machado www.joaomachado.com
Rua Padre Xavier Coutinho, 125, 4150-751, Porto, Porto 4150-751, Portugal
Tel +35 1 22 610 3772 | Fax +35 1 22 610 3773

John Isaacs www.johnisaacsdesign.com
12 Willowdale Farm, Claverack, NY 12513, United States
Tel 518 851 5905 | Fax 518 851 5905

Ken-Tsai Lee Design Studio www.kentsailee.com
17# 31 Lane 49 Alley Chung Cheng, St. Peitou, Taipei, 112, Taiwan, Province of China
Tel +88 62 28935236

Klim Design, Inc.
P.O. Box Y, Avon Park North Building 21, Avon, CT 06001, United States
Tel 860 678 1222

KMS TEAM GmbH www.kms-team.de
Tolzer Street 2c Munich, Bavaria 81379, Germany | Tel +49 89 490 4110

KNARF www.knarfny.com
10 West 15th Street #204, New York, NY 10011, United States
Tel 516 413 3825

Kuhlmann Leavitt, Inc. www.kuhlmannleavitt.com
7810 Forsyth Boulevard, 2W, St. Louis, MO 63105, United States
Tel 314 725 6616 | Fax 314 725 6618

Kuokwai Cheong
Rua Evora S/N, Edf. Lei Hau 37 Andar, Tapai-Macau, Macau | Tel +853 288 35908

Laboratorium www.laboratorium.hr
Zeleni trg 1, Zagreb 10000, Croatia (local name Hrvatska)
Tel +385 1 606 15 16 | Fax +385 1 606 15 15

Lam Design Group
4812 South 30th Street, Apt B2, Arlington, VA 22206, United States | Tel 703 625 7319

Landor Associates www.landor.com
1001 Front Street, San Francisco, CA 94111, United States
Tel 415 365 3737 | Fax 415 365 3190

Lorenc + Yoo Design www.lorencyoodesign.com
109 Vickery Street, Roswell, GA 30075, United States
Tel 770 645 2828 | Fax 770 998 2452

love the life www.lovethelife.org
3-12-10-803, Moto-Asakusa, Taito-Ku, Tokyo 111-0041, Japan
Tel +81 3 5806 3888 | Fax +81 3 5806 3889

mass www.mass.com
180 Varick Street, #1334, New York, NY 10014, United States
Tel/Fax 212 989 6999

Matsumoto Incorporated www.matsumotoinc.com
127 West 26th Street, 9th Floor, New York, NY 10001, United States
Tel 212 807 0248 | Fax 212 807 1527

McGarrah/Jessee, CHAOS www.mc-j.com
205 Brazos, Austin, TX 78701, United States
Tel 512 225 2557 | Fax 512 225 2020

Melchior Imboden
Eggertsbuhi Buochs, Nidwalden 6374, Switzerland
Tel +4179 4023892 | Fax +4141 6200904

MiresBall www.miresball.com
2345 Kettner Boulevard, San Diego, CA 92101, United States
Tel 619 234 6631 | Fax 619 234 1807

Mirko Ilic Corp. www.mirkoilic.com
207 East 32nd Street, New York, NY 10016, United States
Tel 212 481 9737

mono www.mono-1.com
2902 Garfield Avenue S., Minneapolis, MN 55408, United States
Tel 612 822 4135 | Fax 612 822 4136

Neil Kellerhouse www.kellerhouse.com
3781 Greenwood Avenue, Mar Vista, CA 90066, United States
Tel 310 915 0191 | Fax 310 915 0212

Nike Golf Image Design www.nike.com
One Bowermand Dr.-RG2, Beaverton, OR 97005, United States
Tel 503 671 6453 | Fax 503 532 8794

Nokia Design
Nokia Design, 10 Great Pultney Street, London W1F 9NB, United Kingdom
Tel +44 7824815202

Nordstrom www.nordstrom.com
1700 7th Avenue, Suite 400, Seattle, WA 98101, United States | Tel 206 303 4162

Ogilvy www.ogilvy.com/durham
115 N Duke Street, Durham, NC 27701, United States
Tel 919 281 0612 | Fax 919 281 0605

Ogline Design www.oglinedesign.com
1801 Delancey Way, Marlton, NJ 08053, United States
Tel 215 431 3086 | Fax 856 424 4228

Opto Design www.optodesign.com
214 Sullivan Street, 6C, New York, NY 10012, United States
Tel/Fax 212 254 4470

Parachute design www.parachutedesign.com
120 South 6th Street, Suite 1200, One Financial Plaza, Minneapolis, MN 55402, United States
Tel 612 359 4332

Pat Sloan Design
1933 Forest Park Boulevard, Fort Worth, TX 76110, United States
Tel 817 927 7247 | Fax 817 257 5814

Paul Lam Design Associates www.paullamdesign.com.hk
1/F, Centre Point, 181-185 Gloucester Road, Wanchai, Hong Kong
Tel +852 2836 3368 | Fax +852 25731992

Pemberton & Whiteford Design Consultants www.p-and-w.com
21 Ivor Place Marylebone, NW1 6EU, United Kingdom | Tel +44 020 7723 8899

Penguin Graphics
5-12-24-102 Ushitahonmachi, Higashi-ku, Hiroshima-City, Hiroshima, 732 0066, Japan
Tel +81 82 511 1371 | Fax +81 82 511 1372

Pennebaker www.pennebaker.com
1100 W. 23rd Street, Suite 200, Houston, TX 77008, United States
Tel 713 963 8607

Pentagram Design, London www.pentagram.com
11 Needham Road, London, London W11 2RP, United Kingdom
Tel+44 0 20 7316 8082 | Fax +44 0 20 7727 9932

Peter Kraemer
Lindermannstr. 31, Duesseldorf, NRW 40237, Germany
Tel +49 0211 2108087

Peterson Milla Hooks www.pmhadv.com
1315 Harmon Place, Minneapolis, MN 55403, United States
Tel 612 349 9116 | Fax 612 349 9141

Phil Jordan and Associates, Inc.
3420 Surrey Lane, Falls Church, VA 22042, United States
Tel 703 560 3567

Planet Propaganda www.planetpropaganda.com
605 Williamson Street, Madison, WI 53703, United States
Tel 608 256 0000

Poulin + Morris Inc. www.poulinmorris.com
286 Spring Street, 6th Floor, New York, NY 10013, United States
Tel 212 675 1332 | Fax 212 675 3027

punktum design www.punktumdesign.dk
Dampfaergevej 8, 5th floor Suite 513, Copenhagen, 2100, Denmark
Tel 45 203 200 063

q30design inc. www.q30design.com
366 Adelaide Street W. Suite 207, Toronto, ON M5V 1R9, Canada
Tel 416 596 6500

Ralph Appelbaum Associates www.raany.com
88 Pine Street, 29th Floor, New York, NY 10005, United States
Tel 212 334 8200 | Fax 212 334 6214

RBMM www.rbmm.com
7007 Twin Hills, Suite 200, Dallas, TX 75231, United States
Tel 214 987 6500 | Fax 214 987 3662

Reed Hill www.reed-hill.com
7056 Winthrop Circle, Castle Rock, CO 80104, United States
Tel 720 221 4451

Regina Rubino/IMAGE: Global Vision www.imageglobalvision.com
2525 Main Street, Suite 204, Santa Monica, CA 90405, United States
Tel 310 998 8898

Robert Louey Design www.loueyrubino.com
2525 Main Street, Suite 204, Santa Monica, CA 90405, United States
Tel 310 396 7724

Rose www.rosedesign.co.uk
The Old School, 70 St Mary Church Street, London SE16 4HZ, United Kingdom
Tel 020 0 7394 2800

Rubin Postaer & Associates www.rpa.com
2525 Colorado Avenue, Santa Monica, CA 90404, United States
Tel 310 633 6224 | Fax 310 633 6917

Sabatino/Day www.sabatinoday.com
9049 Springboro Pike, Miamisburg, OH 45342, United States
Tel 937 859 0599

SADI (Samsung Art & Design Institute) www.sadi.net
9th Floor East Wing, Bojun Building, 70-13 Nonhyun-dong, Kangnam-gu, Seoul, Korea
Tel +82 2 3438 0334 | Fax +82 2 3438 0319

Sagmeister Inc. www.sagmeister.com
222 West 14th Street, New York, NY 10011, United States
Tel 212 647 1789 | Fax 212 647 1788

SamataMason www.samatamason.com
101 S. First Street, Dundee, IL 60118, United States
Tel 847 428 8600 Fax 847 428 6564

Sandra Burch www.sothebys.com
Sotheby's 1334 York Avenue, New York, NY 10021, United States
Tel 212 735 5966 | Fax 212 894 1231

Sandstrom Design www.sandstromdesign.com
808 SW 3rd Avenue, Suite 610, Portland, OR 97204, United States
Tel 503 248 9466 | Fax 503 227 5035

Savage www.savagebrands.com
4203 Yoakum Boulevard, 4th Floor, Houston, TX 77006, United States
Tel 713 522 1555 | Fax 713 522 1582

Shin Matsunaga Design Inc.
98-4 Yarai-cho, Shinjuku-ku, Tokyo, 162-0805, Japan
Tel +81 6 6943 9077 | Fax +81 6 6943 9078

Sibley/Peteet Design, Austin www.spdaustin.com
522 East 6th Street, Austin, TX 78701, United States | Tel 512 473 2333

Spark Studio www.sparkstudio.com.au
19 Chessell Street, Southbank, Melbourne, VIC 3006, Australia
Tel +61 03 9686 4703 | Fax +61 03 9686 4704

Squires & Company www.squirescompany.com
2913 Canton Street, Dallas, TX 75226, United States
Tel 214 939 9194 | Fax 214 939 3464

Stoltze Design www.stoltze.com
15 Channel Center Street #603, Boston, MA 02210, United States
Tel 617 350 7109 | Fax 617 482 1171

Stuart Karten Design www.kartendesign.com
4204 Glencoe Avenue, Marina Del Rey, CA 90292, United States
Tel 310 827 8722 | Fax 310 821 4492

Studio @ One Zero Charlie www.onezerocharlie.com
5112 Greenwood Road, Greenwood, IL 60097, United States
Tel 815 648 4591 | Fax 815 648 4482

STUDIO INTERNATIONAL www.studio-international.com
Buconjiceva 43, Zegreb 10000, Croatia (local name: Hrvatska)
Tel +385 1 376 0171 | Fax +385 1 3760172

SVIDesign www.svidesign.com
Westbourne Studio 126, 242 Acklam Road, London W10 5JJ, United Kingdom
Tel +44 793 213 6333

TAXI Canada Inc. www.taxi.ca
495 Wellington Street West, Suite 102, Toronto, ON M5V 1E9, Canada
Tel 416 979 7001 | Fax 416 979 7626

tbdadvertising www.tbdadvertising.com
856 NW Bond Street #2, Bend, OR 97701, United States
Tel 541 388 7558 | Fax 541.388.7532

The Brand Union www.thebrandunion.com
11-33 St John Street, London EC1M 4PJ, United Kingdom
Tel +44 0 207 559 7047 | Fax +44 0 207 559 7001

the decoder ring design concern www.thedecoderring.com
410 Congress Avenue, Suite 200, Austin, TX 78701, United States
Tel 512 236 1610

The DesignWorks Group www.thedesignworksgroup.com
PO Box 1773, Sisters, OR 97759, United States
Tel 541 549 1096 | Fax 541 549 1097

The Works www.theworksdesign.com.au
Communication Design, RMIT University, GPO Box 2476V, Melbourne, Victoria 3001, Australia
Tel +61 3 9925 1243 | Fax +61 3 9925 5338

TODA www.toda.com
250 West Broadway, 6th Floor, New York, NY 10013, United States
Tel 212 343 1474 | Fax 212 343 1474

Tracy Sabin www.tracy.sabin.com
7333 Seafarer Place, Carlsbad, CA 92011-4673, United States
Tel 760 431 0439 | Fax 760 431 0439

True story www.truestoryinc.com
1801 W. Larchmont Avenue, Unit 201, Chicago, IL 60613, United States
Tel 773 244 8148

Turner Duckworth www.turnerduckwoth.com
831 Montgomery Street, San Francisco, CA 94133, United States
Tel 415 675 7777 | Fax 415 675 7778

TW2 www.tw2adv.com
Via dei Fontanili, 13, Via G. Sacchi, 7 Milano, 20121, Italy
Tel +39 (0)2 365 80792

Underline Studio www.underlinestudio.com
401 Richmond Street West, Suite 356, Toronto, ON M5V 3A8, Canada
Tel 416 341 0475 | Fax 416 341 0945

Ventress Design Group www.ventress.com
3310 Aspen Grove Drive, Suite 303, Franklin, TN 37067, United States
Tel 615 727 0155 | Fax 615 727 0159

Volt Positive www.voltpositive.com
400 Slater Unit 1505, Ottawa, ON KLR 7S7, Canada
Tel 613 262 7161

Volume Inc. www.volumesf.com
2130-B Harrison Street, San Francisco, CA 94110, United States
Tel/Fax 415 503 0800

VSA Partners www.vsapartners.com
1347 S. State Street, Chicago, IL 60605, United States
Tel 312 427 6413 | Fax 312 427 3246

WAJS www.wajs.de
Otto-Hahn Street 13, Hoechberg, Bavaria 97204, Germany
Tel +49 0 931 304990

Wallace Church, Inc. www.wallacechurch.com
330 East 48th Street, New York, NY 10017, United States
Tel 212 755 2903 | Fax 212 355 6872

WAX partnership www.waxpartnership.com
320 333 24 Avenue SW, Calgary, AB T2S 3E6, Canada
Tel 403 262 9323

Webster Design Associates www.websterdesign.com
5060 Dodge Street, Suite 2000, Omaha, NE 68132, United States
Tel 402 551 0503

Weymouth Design www.weymouthdesign.com
600 Townsend Street, Suite 320 East, San Francisco, CA 94103, United States
Tel 617 259 1442 | Fax 617 451 6233

William Huber Productions, Inc. www.williamhuber.com
355 Congress Street, Floor 2, Boston, MA 02210, United States
Tel 617 426 8205

Wren and Rowe Ltd www.wrenrowe.co.uk
4-6 Denbigh Mews Near Pimlico, London SW1V 2HQ, United Kingdom
Tel +44 207 828 5333

Young and Laramore www.yandl.com
407 North Fulton Street, Indianapolis, IN 46202, United States
Tel 317 264 8000 | Fax 317 264 8001

Two ways to dramatically save on our books!

1. Standing Orders:

50% off (You pay $35+Shipping)

Get our new books at our best deal, before they arrive in bookstores!

A Standing Order is a continued subscription to the Graphis Books of your choice.

2. Pre-Publication Sales:

35% off (You pay $45+Shipping)

Sign-up today at graphis.com to receive our pre-publication sale invitations!

Order early and save!

Graphis Titles

DesignAnnual2009

Summer 2008
Hardcover: 256 pages
200-plus color illustrations

Trim: 8.5 x 11.75"
ISBN: 1-932026-13-4
US $70

GraphisDesignAnnual2009 assembles an international trio of Designers as New York's **Stefan Sagmeister**, South Korea's **Ahn Sang-Soo**, and Pentagram London's **Harry Pearce** present their sagacious views on Design under the theme of "What's Personal Is Universal." Features over 300 award-winning designs in 30-plus categories by industry standouts like **Ogilvy, TAXI Canada, Frost Design, BBDO, Melchior Imboden, Turner Duckworth**, and **RBMM**, among many others.

NewTalentAnnual'07/'08

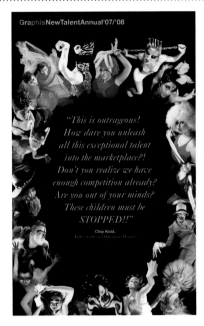

Fall 2007
Hardcover: 256 pages
300-plus color images

Trim:7 x 11 3/4"
ISBN: 1-932026-42-8
US $70

GraphisNewTalentAnnual'07/'08 is a forum for the year's best internationally produced student work. It provides young talent a rare opportunity for exposure and recognition, and serves as an invaluable resource for firms seeking the best and brightest new professionals. This year, we honor two highly respected organizations and their chairs: Designer **Chris Hill** of the Creative Summit student design show and the School of Visual Arts' Department Chair, **Richard Wilde**.

AdvertisingAnnual2009

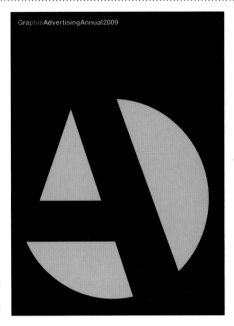

Fall 2008
Hardcover: 256 pages
300-plus color images

Trim: 8.5 x 11.75"
ISBN: 1-932026-52-5
US $70

GraphisAdvertisingAnnual2009 is a must-have for anyone in the Advertising industry, showcasing over 300 ads, created by the world's most respected agencies. Representing the top 10% of the print ad industry, all winners have earned a new Graphis Gold and/or Platinum Award for excellence. This year's edition includes case studies of winning artists and their work. Categories include *automotive, fashion, public service* and *software*. A detailed index completes the book.

PhotographyAnnual2008

Fall 2007
Hardcover: 256 pages
200-plus color illustrations

Trim: 8.5 x 11.75"
ISBN:1-932026-45-2
US $70

GraphisPhotographyAnnual2008 honors the year's best photographs and includes interviews with renown Photographers **Parish Kohanim**, **Henry Leutwyler** and **Hugh Kretschmer**. This year's Annual also marks the introduction of the new Graphis Awards, and all featured photographs have earned a new Graphis Gold Award for excellence. Winning Photographers include **Joel-Peter Witkin**, **Ron Haviv**, **Norman Jean Roy**, **Ilan Rubin**, **Vic Huber**, and **Phil Marco**, among many others.

Logo7

February 2008
Hardcover: 256 pages
500 plus color images

Trim: 8.5 x 11.75"
ISBN: 1-932026-03-7
US $70

LogoDesign7 features profiles and interviews with some of the world's most respected designers: **Steve Sandstrom** of Sandstrom Design, Pentagram's **Michael Bierut**, G+D's **Toshihiro Onimaru**, **Joe Duffy** of Duffy & Partners, **Don Sibley** and **Rex Peteet** of Sibley / Peteet Design, Catapult's **Art Lofgreen**, RBMM's **Brian Boyd**, and the creator of the Recycling logo, **Gary Anderson**. The solutions presented in this collection are the world's best.

PosterAnnual'08/'09

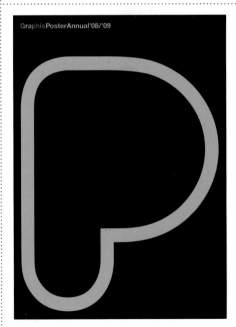

Summer 2008
Hardcover:256 pages
300-plus color images

Trim: 8.5 x 11.75"
ISBN: 1-932026-12-6
US $70

GraphisPosterAnnual'08/'09 features a symposium of poster curators and collectors from MoMA, the German Poster Museum, Hong Kong Heritage Museum, Switzerland's Basler Afrika Bibliographien, Lahti Poster Museum, Cuba's Casa de las Américas, and Rene Wanner's Poster Page. Topics include selection criteria and current trends. Presenting over 200 of the year's best posters by Designers like **Milton Glaser**, **Niklaus Troxler**, and **Takashi Akiyama,** this is a must-have!

Available at www.graphis.com

www.graphis.com